Table of Contents

Reproducible pages are in italics.

Chapter 3

Chapter 4

The Handbook for

Collaborative
Common Assessments

Tools for Design, Delivery,
and Data Analysis

CASSANDRA ERKENS

Solution Tree | Press

a division of
Solution Tree

the Solution Tree
Assessment Center

555 North Morton Street
Bloomington, IN 47404
800.733.6786 (toll free) / 812.336.7700
FAX: 812.336.7790

email: info@SolutionTree.com
SolutionTree.com

Visit **go.SolutionTree.com/assessment** to download the free reproducibles in this book.

Printed in the United States of America

Library of Congress Cataloging-in-Publication Data

Names: Erkens, Cassandra, author.
Title: The handbook for collaborative common assessments : tools for design,
    delivery, and data analysis / Cassandra Erkens.
Description: Bloomington, IN : Solution Tree Press, [2019] | Includes
    bibliographical references and index.
Identifiers: LCCN 2018050782 | ISBN 9781942496861 (perfect bound)
Subjects: LCSH: Teachers--Rating of. | Teacher effectiveness. | Professional
    learning communities. | Group work in education.
Classification: LCC LB2838 .E749 2019 | DDC 371.14/4--dc23 LC record available at https://lccn.loc.gov/2018050782

Solution Tree

Jeffrey C. Jones, CEO
Edmund M. Ackerman, President

Solution Tree Press

President and Publisher: Douglas M. Rife
Associate Publisher: Sarah Payne-Mills
Art Director: Rian Anderson
Managing Production Editor: Kendra Slayton
Senior Production Editor: Tara Perkins
Senior Editor: Amy Rubenstein
Copy Editor: Jessi Finn
Proofreader: Evie Madsen
Text Designer: Abigail Bowen
Cover Designer: Laura Cox
Editorial Assistant and Proofreader: Sarah Ludwig

Acknowledgments

This handbook is filled with the invaluable tools, templates, and strategies that I have created with and for incredible teachers, leaders, schools, and districts committed to doing the work of collaborative common assessments. Educators from large teams to small ones and from urban districts to rural districts have iteratively used and refined the materials herein. There is no possible way I could name the hundreds of educators, to whom I am so grateful, who have had a hand in making these tools practical. Still, I must acknowledge a few amazing educators for their ongoing commitment, their willingness to share their results, and their investment in improving the work of collaborative common assessments.

Mario Andrade	Catherine Holmes	Linda Savastano
Happy Carrico	Ken Mattingly	Tom Schimmer
Susan Cole	Alyssa McCanne	Sarah Schuhl
Michelle DeMers	Jadi Miller	Rea Smith
Paula Dillon	Susannah O'Bara	Eric Twadell
Amanda Ellis	William Olsen	Nicole Dimich Vagle
Angela Freese	Marnie Pauly	Kim Zeidler Watters
Lynn Fuller	Diane Sanna	
Chris Hansen	Melissa Sarasty	

I invite you to do as these amazing educators did: make the tools found herein your own. Try them, modify them, improve them, and share them. Together, let's create collaborative common assessment systems that enrich professional development opportunities and improve learning for all.

Chapter 5

Chapter 6

Chapter 7

About the Author

Cassandra Erkens is a presenter, facilitator, coach, trainer of trainers, keynote speaker, author, and above all, a teacher. She presents nationally and internationally on assessment, instruction, school improvement, and professional learning communities.

Cassandra serves as one of the architects, along with Tom Schimmer and Nicole Dimich Vagle, of the Solution Tree Assessment Center. Their research-based assessment framework guides educators in deepening their own assessment literacy. The framework serves as the core of all writing and training work Cassandra continues to do.

The author of several books, Cassandra has also authored and coauthored a wide array of published trainings, and she has designed and delivered the training of trainers programs for both the private and public sectors.

As an educator and recognized leader, Cassandra has served as a senior high school English teacher, a director of staff development at the district level, a regional school-improvement facilitator at the state level, and a director of staff and organization development in the private sector.

To learn more about Cassandra's work, visit http://allthingsassessment.info or follow @cerkens on Twitter.

To book Cassandra Erkens for professional development, contact pd@SolutionTree.com.

Introduction

Teamwork. Instruction. Results.

Anyone engaged in the true work of professional learning communities (PLCs) understands that common assessments are the engine of a PLC (DuFour, DuFour, Eaker, Many, and Mattos, 2016). Each of the four critical questions of a PLC that a collaborative team must answer is linked to the work of common assessments.

When teams address the first question—What knowledge, skills, and dispositions should every student acquire as a result of this unit, this course, or this grade level?—they are clarifying where they need common assessments. When they answer the second question—How will we know when each student has acquired the essential knowledge and skills?—they are using common assessment data to study the effectiveness of their instructional efforts. Using those common assessment results, teams can then successfully address both questions three and four: How will we respond when some students do not learn? and How will we extend the learning for students who are already proficient? Done well, the entire collaborative common assessment process provides educators with the necessary, timely, and relevant information to make informed, real-time instructional maneuvers. Teams that focus on learning must use their common assessment data to determine the effectiveness of their efforts and improve their overall results.

Phases of the Collaborative Common Assessment Process

The book *Collaborative Common Assessments: Teamwork. Instruction. Results.* (Erkens, 2016) outlines the common assessment process in five different phases, highlighting the need for collaboration in each phase: (1) preparation, (2) design, (3) delivery, (4) data, and (5) re-engagement.

In the preparation phase, team members form the agreements necessary to guide their work (for example, team norms, essential standards, SMART goals, and assessment road maps indicating when and where common assessments will be used). Though much of this foundational work happens before the common assessment process launches, it is never done. Teams are constantly revisiting their norms and essential standards.

In the second phase, the design phase, teachers work together to unpack and repack standards. The conversation is critical to the team's success in understanding what the standards mean and what student proficiency will ultimately need to look like. Simply reading documents outlining what is expected of each teacher does not guarantee common understanding or interpretation. Once a team has reached key agreements, it can begin designing the summative assessments and then plan backward for formative assessments that will ultimately lead to student success on the summative assessments.

During the delivery phase, phase 3, teachers provide instruction in their individual classrooms and the team of teachers gathers periodically during collaborative time to monitor the progress of the students in their room. During this phase, teachers use common formative assessments (CFAs), as well as some of their own assessments, to identify errors and strategize regarding the instructional interventions they can use to prepare students for the summative assessments.

In phase 4, the data phase, teachers examine the results of their instructional impact during a previous lesson (formative) or a completed unit of study (summative) by mining the data and artifacts they generated from assessments. In this phase, teachers isolate which students need what type of support and for what reasons; then, together they strategize ways they can further the learning for all of their students through interventions or extensions.

In the final phase, the re-engagement phase, teachers activate the plans they made during the data phase. If they used an intervention, teams reassess to ensure the intervention closed the learning gaps so that all students can continue moving forward. If they used an extension, teams celebrate the learning and help students find ways to share the resulting products or processes that deepened their learning.

Use of This Book

Clearly, each phase of the collaborative common assessment process involves many steps and many decisions. Teams need resources and tools to help them be effective and efficient through collaborative preparation, design, delivery, data, and re-engagement. This handbook serves as a companion to *Collaborative Common Assessments* (Erkens, 2016). It is intended to assist any team—from the classroom level to the central office level—in implementing the collaborative common assessment process. The handbook offers resources in the form of protocols, templates, tools, and even quality criteria for decision making. While no tool is perfect because it cannot address every context in which a team operates, every tool in this book is offered in the hopes that teams will customize and integrate it to support their own context and effort.

A quick visit to AllThingsPLC (www.allthingsplc.info) will provide readers with compelling evidence of just how powerful schools can be when they embrace the common assessment process. Time and again, K–12 schools of varying sizes, locations, demographics, and cultures prove that schools that embrace common assessments can make staggering academic gains, often in short periods of time. This book offers a multitude of reproducible resources to support your work in this arena. Visit **go.SolutionTree.com/assessment** to download the free reproducibles featured throughout this book.

Overview of Chapters

Chapter 1 offers foundational information to support readers' understanding of collaborative common assessments. Chapter 2 introduces readers to research and evidence that show the benefits of collaborative common assessment systems, and sets the tone for the work that teams must do. Chapters 3–7 support teams in implementing and analyzing the collaborative common assessment process. Chapter 3 gives readers tools to navigate the preparation phase of collaborative common assessment work by attending to teamwork, unpacking standards, determining learning targets, and creating assessment road maps. Chapter 4 guides readers through design protocols for planning and writing collaborative common assessments. Chapter 5 focuses on the role of teachers' instructional agility as they deliver common assessments in the classroom. Chapter 6 shows readers how to review data gleaned from assessments so they ensure all students continue learning. Chapter 7 explores how teams can plan re-engagement opportunities after identifying student needs based on common assessment data. Finally, the epilogue offers a fictional story—based on the collaborative common assessment work from many different schools—illustrating how a cross-curricular team can engage in the work of using common assessments with critical competencies. While the story does not provide specifics of each phase, it is meant to provide creative approaches and plausible options regarding the challenges that most often stop a team from engaging in the work at all. It is also meant to reveal how fulfilling and exciting the work can be.

The chapters in this book offer protocols and tools identified as reproducibles so that teams can put them to immediate use. In most cases, the author developed the tools herein alongside teams to support their efforts; in a few cases, teams created the tools and shared them with the author in order to help others embarking in the work. Each chapter also ends with reflection questions that individuals, collaborative teams, and leadership teams can discuss as a means to gauge progress or reflect on general understandings. These questions focus teamwork and guide leadership teams in exploring key areas for decision making as they develop a schoolwide support system for their individual teachers and teams. Looking at the past or the present can always help to guide next steps. Ultimately, the questions are intended to help teams ponder key ideas from the chapter to help them move forward in their own collaborative common assessment efforts. Please accept the challenge to join the ranks of highly effective PLC schools and employ or customize the reproducible resources herein to support your collaborative efforts.

1

Understanding Collaborative Common Assessment

It's critical that educators ensure every learner graduates prepared to thrive in the complex world that awaits. Toward that end, educators must vigilantly monitor the arc of learning over time. Checklists and tools for designing and monitoring standards, assessment, curriculum, and instruction are key. How do schools and districts equip teachers to harness the power of assessment while bringing joy and passion back to teaching? The answer lies in the collaborative common assessment process. When teacher teams properly design, deliver, and analyze collaborative common assessments, it helps teachers build *instructional agility*, the ability to quickly adjust instruction so it responds to learners' needs. Done well, collaborative common assessments are the educators' formative assessments; the resulting information from common assessments gives educators, like students, additional opportunities to improve their results over time.

As a summary to his meta-analysis of over eight hundred research studies in education, John Hattie (2012) provides a ringing endorsement of the power of common assessments to generate excellence in education when he concludes:

> a major theme is when teachers meet to discuss, evaluate, and plan their teaching in light of the feedback evidence about the success or otherwise of their teaching strategies and conceptions about progress and appropriate challenge. This is not critical reflection, but *critical reflection in light of evidence* about their teaching. (p. 19)

Using such evidence can increase precision, flexibility, and responsiveness among teachers, making common assessments the vehicle for creating teachers who are instructionally agile and teams that are collectively efficacious.

As teams begin the journey of implementing the collaborative common assessment process, they will find it helpful to understand certain foundational concepts of the process. To begin, it's important teams have a clear, working definition and established criteria for collaborative common assessments. Fortunately, there are many protocols and tools that can help teams determine whether they are meeting quality indicators for their work.

Defining Collaborative Common Assessments

Experts agree that common assessments yield data that educators can use to improve learning (Ainsworth & Viegut, 2006; Bailey & Jakicic, 2012; DuFour et al., 2016; Hattie, 2009; Reeves, 2006). Every author on this subject offers a slightly different definition of *common assessments*, but all authors—even those who do not classify themselves as professional learning community (PLC) experts—stick with the same theme; namely, common assessments provide the real-time evidence required for educators to reflect critically on their impact so they can then design targeted responses to move learning forward for their students (Ainsworth & Viegut, 2006; Bailey & Jakicic, 2012; DuFour et al., 2016; Hattie, 2009; Reeves, 2006).

The collaborative common assessment process puts educators in the driver's seat and provides teachers with the necessary opportunity to assess according to their learners' needs. The process needs to remain as close as possible to the classroom for teachers and their learners. When teachers reference their *local classroom assessment results* with their observations, experience, and curricular expertise, they tend to have a higher degree of clarity regarding what comes next in the learning for the students they serve. Likewise, *schoolwide interventions* can miss the mark if the classroom teacher's concerns and insights are ignored. Teachers must drive the assessment and intervention decisions at the classroom level first.

A *collaborative common assessment* is any assessment that meets all five of the following criteria.

1. Formative or summative
2. Team created or team endorsed
3. Designed or approved in advance of instruction
4. Administered in close proximity by all instructors
5. Dependent on teamwork

Each of these criteria is integral to the collaborative common assessment process.

Formative or Summative

The goal of using formative assessments is to provide information that *improves* a learner's ability to be successful, whereas the goal of using summative assessments is to *prove* a learner's level of proficiency at the conclusion of the learning journey (Chappuis, Stiggins, Chappuis, & Arter, 2012; Erkens, Schimmer & Vagle, 2017, Wiliam 2011, 2018). Because both are necessary to support learning, common assessments should be both formative and summative in nature (Erkens, 2016). A team requires a common summative assessment (CSA) in order to ultimately certify mastery on a predetermined priority standard. If teams do not start by framing a collaborative summative assessment, then their CFAs serve as loose pebbles on a meandering pathway, rather than sequential rungs on a ladder with a clear trajectory and targeted destination. A team requires common formative assessments to discover and address areas needing improvement before the summative assessment is given. It is far better to intervene during the unit of instruction than it is to re-engage students in learning after the summative has been given. Teams that develop and effectively employ CFAs typically find that they need to conduct fewer and fewer re-engagement strategies following a CSA.

Team Created or Team Endorsed

The entire team must either write the assessment together or co-review and endorse the assessment that it has selected for use. This detail matters greatly. Asking teachers to give an assessment over which they have little ownership is like asking them to ride a city bus and care deeply about the road signs the bus encounters along the way. They will care deeply about the many road signs only if they are *driving* the bus. Moreover, if one person writes the assessment for the team and something goes wrong with the assessment process, the team generally blames the author. The entire team must take an active role in determining the assessments that it will use to monitor its instruction.

Designed or Approved in Advance of Instruction

Everyone loses when teachers retrofit assessments to the instruction that preceded the testing experience. Since instruction is the visible and immediate actionable step in the teaching and learning process, it feels natural to plan it first. However, a closer look reveals how that practice costs teachers and students time and learning opportunities. Teachers lose because they have to try to remember all the things they said during instruction and then begin the time-consuming process of prioritizing what's important to test. Many times, this leads to inaccurate assessments, primarily because they don't align to the standards. Instruction that wanders without a known, specific target has no chance of hitting its desired mark for teachers or their learners (Erkens et al., 2017; Hattie, 2009; Heritage, 2010, 2013; Wiliam, 2011, 2018). When teachers don't frame the assessment road map or architecture in advance of the instruction, the instructional designs can misfire, and learners then miss critical components and interconnected concepts.

The greatest concern when teachers retrofit assessment to instruction, however, is that inaccurate assessments yield inaccurate results. In such a case, both the teacher and the learner draw conclusions based on dirty data. *Dirty data* contain inaccuracies, hide truths with oversimplifications, or mislead with false positives or false negatives. Such data can only lead to inaccurate feedback. When that happens, learners cannot receive the appropriate support they need to master not only *what* they learn but also *how* they learn. Conversely, when teams clarify summative assessments in advance of instruction, teams are often able to *find* instructional time, instead of waste it, because they can strategically determine what it will take for each learner to be successful on the assessment, they can ensure alignment of their assessment and curricular resources, and they can respond more accurately and with a laser focus in their intervention efforts. While the educational literature has recognized this model—backward design—since the 1990s (Jacobs, 1997; McTighe & Ferrara, 2000; Wiggins & McTighe, 2005), it is still not a prevalent practice.

Administered in Close Proximity by All Instructors

While most teams succeed in having all students take a common assessment on the same day, that isn't always doable, as many things (school cancellations, emergency drills, and so on) can easily interrupt the school day. If teams are to respond to learners who have not yet achieved mastery and learners who need extension, then individual teachers must give the assessment in a relatively short time frame so that they can collaboratively respond in a timely fashion.

Imagine that a team has designed an assessment task that requires students to use the school's only computer lab, so the team members' students take turns using it (for example, teacher A's students use the lab and complete the task in September, teacher B's in October, and teacher C's in November). This is the *same* assessment, but it does not function as a common assessment should. The team members provide the exact same task with the same criteria and grade-level content. However, the team members are on their own for strategizing how to intervene or extend the learning for their individual classrooms. They miss the power of the collective wisdom and creativity of their peers in addressing the challenges that emerge from their individual results. In a case where teachers do not give the same assessment in the same time frame, teams can only look at the data in hindsight and then produce program-level improvements that answer the following questions.

- "Was the assessment appropriate and engaging?"
- "Were the scoring criteria accurate, consistently applied, and sufficient?"

- "Did the curriculum support the learners in accomplishing the task?"

- "Were the instructional strategies successful overall? Do we need to make any changes moving forward?"

The pace of data collection in this case cannot support instructional agility. The learners in September will not benefit from the team's findings in November, when all the learners have finished the task.

Dependent on Teamwork

The collaborative common assessment process requires teamwork to help ensure accurate data; timely re-engagement; consistent scoring; and alignment between standards, instruction, and assessment so all students learn. Collaboration is central to the process as teams examine results, plan instructionally agile responses, analyze errors, and explore areas for program improvement.

Collaboratively Examined Results

When teachers use a common assessment, that does not guarantee it will generate common results. The notion of common data implies a high degree of *inter-rater reliability*, meaning the data generated are scored similarly from one rater to the next. Even when using test questions that have clear right and wrong answers, teachers can generate uncommon results. For example, teachers may interpret student responses differently, or some teachers may offer partial credit for reasoning while others only offer credit for right answers. Many variables impact the scoring process, and many perceptions lead teachers to different conclusions, which can create data inconsistency from classroom to classroom. No matter the test method, teachers must practice scoring together on a consistent basis so that they can build confidence that they have inter-rater reliability and accurate data.

Instructionally Agile Responses

The purpose of using collaborative common assessments is to impact learning in positive, responsive, and immediate ways, for both students as learners and teachers as learners. When teachers analyze assessment data to inform real-time modifications within the context of the expected learning, they improve their instructional agility and maximize the assessment's impact on learning. It seems logical that teams of high-quality instructors will have more instructional agility than an individual teacher for the following reasons.

- **More accurate inferences:** Teams have more reviewers to examine the results, conduct an error analysis regarding misconceptions, and collaboratively validate their inferences.

- **Better targeted instructional responses:** Teams have more instructors to problem solve and plan high-quality extension opportunities for those who have established mastery, as well as appropriate corrective instruction for those who have various misconceptions, errors, or gaps in their knowledge and skills.

- **Increased opportunities for learners:** Teams simply have more classroom teachers surrounding the learner who can provide informed interventions and skilled monitoring for continued follow-up.

This is not to suggest that teams will always develop better solutions than individual teachers might, especially if an individual teacher has reached mastery in his or her craft, knowledge, and skill. Rather, it is to suggest that educators can increase the likelihood of accuracy, consistency, and responsiveness over time if they collaboratively solve complex problems with the intention to increase their shared expertise and efficacy.

Error Analysis

There is no such thing as a perfect test; all tests will have some margin of error. So typically, before teachers employ a measurement tool (such as a scale, rubric, or scoring guide) or an assessment (such as a test, an essay, or a performance task), the designers must attempt to find, label, and address the potential errors in the measurement tool, the assessment, or the administration process itself, noting that a margin of error could exist in the findings. This practice helps trained test designers review the results for any potential dangers in students' resulting inferences. By using a similar error-analysis process, classroom teachers—not trained as assessment experts—can identify potential mistakes and misconceptions in their classroom assessments. *Error analysis* involves examining various students' responses to an individual task, prompt, or test item and then identifying and classifying the types of errors found. Identifying the learners' errors is critical to generating instructionally agile responses that guide the learners' next steps, as the type of error dictates the appropriate instructional response.

Program Improvements

A benefit of engaging in collaborative common assessments involves gathering local program improvement data. When teachers do not create, use, and analyze assessments collaboratively and commonly, they have only isolated data to offer. Such data are filled with more questions than answers: What happened in that classroom? Was it an anomaly? Or, did the instruction, the chosen curricular resources, the pacing, the use of formative assessments, or the student engagement practices cause it? The data from one classroom to the next will have too many variables to provide valid and reliable schoolwide improvement data. When data are common and teams assemble them in comparative ways, however, patterns, themes, and compelling questions emerge. These allow teams to make more informed, strategic decisions and establish inquiry-based efforts to answer complex problems. Using common data, teams may focus their program improvements in the following areas.

- **Curriculum alignment and modifications:** Teams make certain that they have selected a rigorous curriculum that aligns with the standards. For example, using collaborative common assessment data, team members might discover they need to increase their focus on nonfiction texts, which alters their future curricular choices.

- **Instructional strategies and models:** Having teams analyze instructional strategies and models or programs does *not* mean teachers must teach in the exact same ways. It does mean, however, that teachers must isolate the strategies (which they can deliver with their own creative style) that work best with rigorous content, complex processes, or types of challenges that learners may be experiencing.

- **Assessment modifications:** When assessment results go awry, teams will often engage in improving the assessment before they examine curriculum or instructional implications. But by doing so, teams can accidentally lower the assessment's rigor to help learners meet the target when the assessment may not have caused the issue. For this reason, teams should explore needed assessment modifications *after* they explore curriculum alignment and instructional implications. But it is always important that teams examine the assessment itself. Sometimes, weak directions or confusing questions or prompts are the variables that cause common student errors.

The more valid, reliable, and frequent local improvement data become, the more likely teams and schools can manage program improvements in significant and timely ways without relying so heavily on external testing data.

Overall, the collaborative common assessment process requires a far greater commitment to teamwork, instruction, and results than the simplistic, popular notion that teams give benchmark assessments and look at the results together.

Ensuring Safety and Shared Commitments

Without a doubt, learning in a public setting by exposing personal successes and failures is risky business. Because of this, the mere suggestion of common assessments may terrify teachers. Without clarity of purpose and commitments of support from administrators, teachers may fear that a negative motivation underpins the organization's intent.

In truth, common assessments were always only meant to serve as a promising practice to increase teacher success and student achievement. But if teams, schools, and districts don't handle the common assessment process with thought and great care, concerns regarding uniformity, competition, compliance, or overtesting could become a reality. Think of the common assessment process like any other tool; for example, a hammer could help build a house, but it could also help tear a house down.

When all levels of the organization—teams, schools, and even districts—manage common assessments in collaborative ways, and when teachers receive clear expectations and participate in generating and endorsing shared commitments, then teachers can feel safe to take intellectual risks and explore what deep learning looks like in their content area and grade level. This, then, makes collaborative common assessments the most promising practice teachers can use to support job-embedded, real-time learning regarding the complex issues they face daily in the classroom.

To support the right work happening, leaders must have transparency. Transparency, however, must exceed simply clarifying purpose, as that rarely removes suspicion of motivation. It's extremely helpful when leaders engage teachers in generating shared commitments to allow for an ego-free zone. Shared expectations provide clarity of purpose, but *truly* shared commitments provide teachers with the language and tools to keep each other safe and hold each other mutually responsible for the work at hand. It is only when teams feel safe on the journey that they will launch into the risk taking necessary to learn from their experiences.

Shared commitments establish clear understanding and develop parameters to guide the work at all levels of the organization. Such commitment statements offer the organizational promises necessary to create the culture of safety required for intellectual risk taking among professionals.

The following examples of shared commitment statements highlight the kinds of agreements teams might create in order to guide their future decision making and hold each other mutually accountable to the work of common assessments.

- Team commitments statements:
  - We will strive to set preferences aside and come together collaboratively to examine best practices and appropriately adapt in data-based ways to address individual student learning needs. Ultimately, we will increase student achievement.
  - We will use the collaborative common assessment process to become more reflective and to improve our core instruction, our assessment practices and tools, and our curricular resources.

- We commit to provide extensions and interventions for all of our learners, ensuring they receive the targeted support required to move them forward. We will continue to work with them to ensure mastery on our prioritized learning expectations.

- School commitment statements:

    - We will use collaborative common assessments within our teams and across this school to generate evidence of learning. We will use the evidence to reveal successes, learn about improvements, and create supporting learning structures for our students.

    - We will build a system of interventions to target the instructional needs that emerge from common assessments. We will monitor the effectiveness of our intervention system and commit to improve it when and where necessary.

    - We will improve and refocus instruction based on emerging evidence from common assessments so we can better prepare our learners to succeed beyond our school walls and ultimately to contribute to a global and competitive society.

- District commitment statements:

    - We commit to employ rigorous and relevant benchmark assessments with stakeholder input and to monitor the consistency of opportunity from school to school and classroom to classroom.

    - We will empower PLCs to elicit, analyze, and act on evidence of student learning for the purpose of continuous improvement in teaching and learning. A shared ownership of learning is critical to the success of both teachers and students.

    - We will work with schools to identify areas of concern so that we can support teachers in understanding and implementing the work.

Collective commitments, developed by all who have a hand in doing the work, provide the safety net teachers require to feel safe during the common assessment process. Figure 1.1 (page 14) outlines a general process that organizations can use to develop commitment statements.

While developing commitment statements can take time, the work allows all stakeholders to become clear and comfortable with the changes the statements ask them to make. Commitment statements increase buy-in and provide the assurances needed to encourage intellectual risk taking. Shared agreements naturally form the parameters for all future decision making.

Step 1	Share the collective statements with the broader stakeholder group in a deliberate and systematic way. Make sure everyone knows the following. • Where, when, and with whom you developed the collective statements • The timeline and process for turning them into commitment statements • The purpose and use of commitment statements
Step 2	Invite feedback and input on the statements.
Step 3	Refine the statements by editing their content and including the input that you have gathered along the way.
Step 4	Publish the commitment statements, and seek endorsement from stakeholders.

Figure 1.1: Transforming collective statements into commitment statements.

*Visit **go.SolutionTree.com/assessment** for a free reproducible version of this figure.*

Navigating the Process

Seeing the big picture of the process of collaborative common assessments does for teams what the global positioning system (GPS) does for drivers: it helps teams see the path ahead so they can anticipate next steps. And, just as most maps offer no straight line or single option to get from point A to point B, the road map for collaborative common assessments is recursive and iterative. Teams may find themselves moving from the foundation to monitor learning and going back to the foundation for clarification, and so on. Figure 1.2 offers a pictorial representation of the collaborative common assessment process. This figure maintains the same elements of the collaborative common assessment process defined in *Collaborative Common Assessments* (Erkens, 2016); however, inside arrows have been added to show the relationships among different parts of the process, and some terminology is different within the individual boxes because, as with any quality process, improvements must occur.

Teams find it helpful to keep figure 1.2 on hand during their work, especially as they initially learn the process. In addition, it helps when teams consider the criteria for quality during the design, delivery, and data phases.

Using Quality Indicators

Because the quality of the common assessment system can vary based on how teams implement it, it's helpful to have a set of quality indicators to guide teams as they develop and continuously monitor their common assessment system. Figure 1.3 (pages 16–17) offers a tool for discussing, planning, and monitoring quality indicators during the design, delivery,

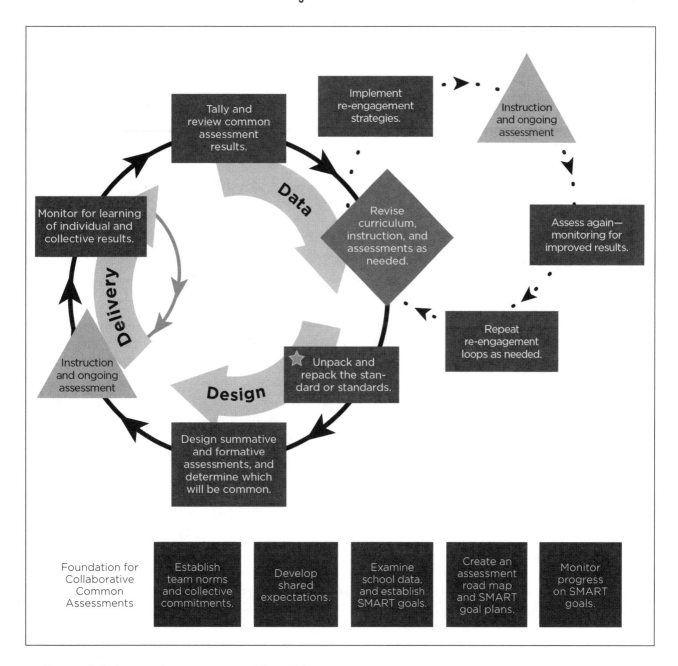

Figure 1.2: A pictorial representation of the collaborative common assessment process.

*Visit **go.SolutionTree.com/assessment** for a free reproducible version of this figure.*

and data phases of the collaborative common assessment process. Teams can use the listed indicators to guide decision making during the planning phases or to evaluate their current efforts. The tool includes a rating scale for teams that prefer to use it as a discussion tool about quality levels for each criterion.

Directions: Work as individuals or as a team to score each of the quality indicators using the following scale.

1: I understand the concept but would have difficulty engaging with it in our team.

2: Our team has just begun to try this practice, but it is not *natural* or embedded in our routines yet.

3: Our team routinely engages in this practice.

4: Our team has refined this practice, and we could easily share our protocols, processes, and results to teach the process to others.

Design				
1. The assessment is collaboratively developed.	1	2	3	4
2. The assessment aligns with the priority standards (the most important learning expectations).	1	2	3	4
3. The assessment is tied tightly to clearly identified learning targets within the priority standards.	1	2	3	4
4. The assessment is designed to meet challenging expectations (for example, identified levels of rigor or depths of knowledge) as outlined by the district, school, or team itself.	1	2	3	4
5. The assessment is designed for accuracy, and the selected method is appropriate for the target requirements.	1	2	3	4
6. Any supporting assessment tools (rubrics, exemplars, and so on) align with any quality-focused indicators of learning as established in the standards or outlined in team-identified expectations.	1	2	3	4
7. The assessment is designed to avoid sources of bias that distort results.	1	2	3	4
8. The assessment itself, or the overall assessment plan for the intended learning, gathers sufficient evidence to indicate mastery of student learning.	1	2	3	4
Delivery				
9. All staff members are aware of and supportive of the assessment plan.	1	2	3	4
10. Team members deliver the common assessments in the same time frame.	1	2	3	4
11. The team's focus is results oriented by learning target to measure whether students are learning, and the results empower learners in addressing their own gaps through the intervention strategies.	1	2	3	4
12. The team bases all its efforts—before, during, and after it gives the assessment—on determining ways that teachers and staff can identify students needing interventions or enrichments.	1	2	3	4

13. The team employs tools, processes, and policies that allow for student involvement in responding to the results (data interpretation).	1	2	3	4
14. The team's assessment plan promotes continued learning with formative opportunities and additional assessments to monitor achievement.	1	2	3	4
15. Staff and procedures are in place to monitor the plan's execution.	1	2	3	4
Data				
16. The data are gathered and analyzed in a timely fashion for immediate responses.	1	2	3	4
17. The data shared with learners are presented as meaningful feedback and information designed to engage the learners in motivated responses to support continued learning.	1	2	3	4
18. All decisions regarding the data are aligned with proficiency levels that have been predetermined by district, school, or team itself.	1	2	3	4
19. Practices and protocols are utilized to guarantee common data result from the use of common assessments (collaborative scoring is used to calibrate all scores to be consistent with team expectations).	1	2	3	4
20. The data are arranged in a manner that enables teacher teams to target appropriate interventions for specific classrooms and students.	1	2	3	4
21. The data are arranged in a manner that enables teacher teams to identify appropriate program (curriculum, instruction, and assessment) modifications.	1	2	3	4
22. The data report requires a display of the data, a reflection of team learning, and a response plan to address the results with clearly determined ways for teachers and staff to respond to learners needing interventions.	1	2	3	4
23. The data are used to monitor progress toward achieving SMART goals.	1	2	3	4
24. The data are shared for schoolwide involvement to support learning as necessary.	1	2	3	4
25. The data are monitored for celebrations of student and teacher learning (and are not used to judge teacher performance).	1	2	3	4

Figure 1.3: Quality indicators for collaborative common assessments.

*Visit **go.SolutionTree.com/assessment** for a free reproducible version of this figure.*

Teams can use such a tool in many ways. At the school level, teachers could submit their individual responses anonymously to designated leaders (teacher leaders or administrators) so those designated key leaders have a sense of how the collaborative common assessment process is going across the building. Or, a team with high levels of trust and rapport could simply conduct a round-robin to share what teachers individually scored each item and then discuss their final results. If they do not use this as a survey tool, teams could use each indicator as a discussion point as they strive to revise and continuously improve their design, delivery, and data systems. Healthy and productive teams consistently self-evaluate their processes and then make the necessary modifications or refinements to guarantee their ultimate success (Erkens & Twadell, 2012).

Conclusion

Confusion and mistrust reign when the common assessment process is approached as a series of disparate activities rather than a cohesive and integrated system. Staff need to see the big picture of the common assessment process. Members need to understand the rationale, co-create commitments to one another, and then, with a high degree of comfort in place, make themselves vulnerable and available to learning. The teaching and learning process should never be something educators reserve exclusively for the classroom. When collaborative team meetings involve exploring the team's impact from a place of openness, inviting intellectual risk taking for creative problem solving, and sharing responsibility for challenges that loom ahead, then teachers engage the teaching and learning process within their team meetings.

Team Reflections

Take a few moments to reflect on the following questions.

- What benefits do we anticipate having, or what benefits have we already experienced, from the process of engaging in collaborative common assessment?

- Do the staff (or does our team) clearly understand the work of collaborative common assessment? If so, what evidence do we have to support our belief? If not, what evidence do we have to support our belief, and how can we help them understand it?

- Do staff (or does our team) feel safe? How do we know? Are there promises we need to provide to create a safety net? If so, what might those be? What process or processes would we have to use to create and share those promises?

- How will our current teamwork help us fully utilize the collaborative common assessment process? Are there things we might need to improve on? If so, what, and how?

- Is our team, school, or district system ready for the collaborative common assessment process? Have we identified the elements that we will need to add, modify, or delete as we embark on the collaborative common assessment process? If so, what are they?

2

Evidence and Research Supporting the Collaborative Common Assessment Process

As noted in *Collaborative Common Assessments* (Erkens, 2016), in a culture of assessment fatigue:

> Collaborative common assessments provide a powerful mode of inquiry-based professional development that seeks to improve student achievement *and* professional practice. For teams to develop the shared knowledge and skills of assessment literacy and instructional agility, they must work together to ask the right questions, explore their own results, and create solutions to complex challenges. (p. 5)

Collaborative common assessments require teachers' involvement in the entire process—from accurate design to effective use of classroom assessment information. Research and evidence show that, when teachers do this well, the full process benefits learners, teachers, and schools and systems.

A Win for Learners

When everyone fully participates in the consistent and systematic process of collaborative common assessment, no question, the learners win. Educational researchers and experts (Chenoweth, 2008, 2009a; Gallimore, Ermeling, Saunders, & Goldenberg, 2009; Hattie, 2009; Levin, 2008; Odden & Archibald, 2009) as well as practitioners consistently find that when teams use collaborative common assessment strategies, their schools experience remarkable change. See, for example, www.allthingsplc.info/evidence, which showcases the tremendous results K–12 schools of all sizes and socioeconomic circumstances, from all parts of the United States, and other countries as well, can achieve when they fully embrace the common assessment process as PLCs. The examples featured on this site highlight how schools' student achievement dramatically increases when teams have consistent and clear work patterns and maintain a laser focus on using the practices necessary for collaborative common assessment. These achievement results have driven experts to unpack and analyze the strategies that teams use in these schools, which include collaborating, narrowing the curriculum and aligning it to standards, employing formative assessments for frequent results monitoring, and using data to inform instruction. Two such schools, Hawk Elementary in Texas and Rutland High School in Vermont, made great gains using the common assessment process in unique ways. While their stories began some time ago, the conditions under which they launched the work are worth noting.

In 2012, all grade-level teams at Mildred M. Hawk Elementary School (affectionately known as Hawk Elementary), a K–5 building in Texas's Denton Independent School District, set about raising student achievement in mathematics through the use of collaborative common assessments. While Hawk Elementary didn't have terrible aggregate scores compared with the state, they weren't at 100 percent success, and they clearly had groups of learners who were struggling. The staff wanted to make certain that they did not simply focus on the results of the State of Texas Assessments of Academic Readiness (STAAR) test but instead prepared their learners to be career and college ready. They developed a schoolwide goal to increase the learners' proficiency levels in the areas of problem solving and critical thinking, as they firmly believed that if their learners could do that level of rigorous work, they would perform well on any state test they encountered. That year, the third-grade team received its 2012 STAAR test results for mathematics, which table 2.1 shows.

Based on these state data, each team from kindergarten to grade 5 established improvement goals, commonly identified as *SMART goals*, that aligned to the building-level goal to improve mathematics scores (see chapter 3, page 41, for an in-depth explanation of SMART goals). All the teams then monitored learners' growth, using their ongoing and grade level–appropriate classroom mathematics assessments. The entire building used common formative and summative mathematics assessments. Together, the teams created rubrics for three mathematical areas—(1) computational accuracy, (2) mathematical language, and (3) problem solving—that they would consistently use across all the grade levels.

Table 2.1: Hawk Elementary School's Third-Grade STAAR Mathematics Results, 2012

Students	Total Number of Students	Percentage of Students Passing
All	122	73
Economically Disadvantaged	7	29
Asian	8	100
Black or African American	7	57
Hispanic	22	68
Biracial or Multiracial	3	67
White	82	73
Female	57	74
Male	65	72
Students Receiving Special Education	14	36

Source: © 2016 by Susannah O'Bara. Used with permission.

As vertical K–5 teams, teachers practiced scoring student work together to monitor student learning, calibrate scoring for common data, align their expectations across all the grade levels, and ultimately improve their targeted instructional decision making. Each teacher was randomly assigned a learner, whose work he or she always brought to the monthly staffwide data team meetings for vertical scoring (for example, kindergarten teacher A always brought student 3's work to the team meetings). Simultaneously, all teachers monitored learners in all classrooms (not just the student whose work they brought to every team meeting) and engaged all their learners in the various common assessments, using the exact same measurement tools for all their learners in their grade levels. Vertical teams reviewed work samples during monthly meetings, and they posted the results as evidence to monitor progress toward their overall student achievement goal.

Gradually, teams increased the rigor of their expectations. For instance, once the kindergarten teachers realized the caliber of work their learners would face in third grade, they were able to better align their expectations for their kindergarten learners. Over time, teams noticed a significant improvement in the quality of all their learners' work in mathematics. All the teams posted significant gains (S. O'Bara, personal communication, July 2016). As an example, table 2.2 (page 24) features the third-grade team's results.

Table 2.2: Hawk Elementary School's Third-Grade State STAAR Mathematics Results, 2012–2014

Students	2012	2013	2014
All	122 students 73 percent of students passing	115 students 83 percent of students passing	101 students 91 percent of students passing
Economically Disadvantaged	7 students 29 percent of students passing	10 students 60 percent of students passing	7 students 100 percent of students passing
Asian	8 students 100 percent of students passing	4 students 75 percent of students passing	6 students 100 percent of students passing
Black or African American	7 students 57 percent of students passing	7 students 43 percent of students passing	2 students 100 percent of students passing
Hispanic	22 students 68 percent of students passing	12 students 83 percent of students passing	7 students 100 percent of students passing
Biracial or Multiracial	3 students 67 percent of students passing	1 student 100 percent of students passing	3 students 100 percent of students passing
White	82 students 73 percent of students passing	90 students 87 percent of students passing	81 students 90 percent of students passing
Female	57 students 74 percent of students passing	62 students 79 percent of students passing	44 students 93 percent of students passing
Male	65 students 72 percent of students passing	53 students 87 percent of students passing	57 students 89 percent of students passing
Students Receiving Special Education	14 students 36 percent of students passing	7 students 29 percent of students passing	5 students 60 percent of students passing

Source: © 2016 by Susannah O'Bara. Used with permission.

The qualitative data were equally rewarding. In Hawk Elementary, teachers commonly voice appreciation for their peers' work. For example, in the spring of 2014, fifth-grade mathematics teachers noted their surprise and delight at the deep problem solving and rigorous work the kindergarten students generated in mathematics (S. O'Bara, personal communication, July 2016). Moreover, the principal was able to stop in any classroom and have conversations with random students that revealed rigorous thinking in their mathematics work. Even though the teachers had experienced great results, they knew their work was not yet done. All the teams had similar SMART goals, and all teams continued their energies in mathematics while adding in other focused areas (such as reading) with equal commitment and diligence.

Another school, Rutland High School in Rutland, Vermont, established itself as a PLC and started using collaborative common assessments after it learned the school needed improvement (B. Olsen, personal communication, July 2016). The staff could have found it challenging to develop collaborative common assessments when the teams were so small (just one or two people per course), but the staff members worked together to develop a consistent set of rubrics that they could use schoolwide, while still assessing their individual departments' content standard expectations. Rutland High found innovative ways to organize small teams at the secondary level, such as the following.

- Ninth-grade mathematics and earth science teachers meet as an interdisciplinary team that focuses on science, technology, engineering, and mathematics (STEM).

- English 1 and World History 1 teachers meet as an interdisciplinary team that focuses on global studies.

- English 2 and World History 2 teachers meet as an interdisciplinary team that focuses on global studies.

- Special educators and paraeducators are integrated into the core-subject teams.

- Singletons who don't have colleagues to collaborate with on-site instead collaborate off-site with colleagues in other schools.

The teams also found innovative ways to use common assessments with interdisciplinary subjects. They began with rubrics in technical reading and writing and, over time, added rubrics in cross-cutting skills and processes, like public speaking, analytical thinking, creative thinking, and researching. Teams meet for an hour every Wednesday, and they regularly use the schoolwide rubrics to monitor student achievement through the common assessment process within their individual curricula. New England Common Assessment Program (NECAP) data indicate that their hard work has improved their students' learning in *all* tested areas. In addition, they continue to make significant gains in learning for *all* students, including the economically disadvantaged students who qualify for free and reduced-price lunch (FRPL). Students have demonstrated significant gains in reading, the area where teams began their focal work with common assessments across the content areas (as shown in table 2.3, page 26).

Table 2.3: Percentage of Students Meeting the NECAP Reading Standard

	All Rutland High School Students	All Students in the State	All Rutland High School FRPL Students	All FRPL Students in the State
2007–2008	63 percent	68 percent	45 percent	47 percent
2013–2014	79 percent	74 percent	67 percent	60 percent

Source: © 2016 by Bill Olsen. Used with permission.

In 2015, Rutland High moved from lagging behind the state average in reading, writing, mathematics, and science to matching or—more often—exceeding the state average with consistency, even as the state average had increased in all but one area. While the gaps between Rutland High's students and the state's students have narrowed since 2013, Rutland High's overall trajectory continues to go in an upward direction for all students, especially the economically disadvantaged—a group that continues to increase in size each year.

These two brief case studies—(1) Hawk Elementary, from a large urban district of approximately 25,000 students at the time, and (2) Rutland High, from a small rural district of approximately 2,200 students at that time—offer student achievement gain stories, and they are only a sampling of the repeated success stories educators can find in the literature and on websites like AllThingsPLC (www.allthingsplc.info). It makes sense that when educators work together to solve a complex problem, such as addressing gaps in student achievement, amazing things can happen. Learners win when teachers collaborate on their behalf.

A Win for Teachers

Richard DuFour, Rebecca DuFour, and Robert Eaker (2008) believe that the practice of using common assessments is critical in the work of PLCs. In fact, it is the engine that drives success. They highlight how the practice ultimately impacts student achievement but also offers teachers and their teams additional advantages; it increases their efficiency, promotes equity, improves monitoring, informs and refines teacher practice, and develops teacher capacity (DuFour et al., 2008). Collaborative common assessment helps teachers work smarter, not harder. The early stages of any new process can feel laborious and time consuming, but as with any process that becomes a standard operating procedure, time and experience can increase a team's level of comfort, knowledge, and skills in a manner that increases efficiency and effectiveness.

Undoubtedly, teachers make a difference. "Educational researchers have proposed that teachers themselves are one of the most important determinants of their teaching practices and students' achievement" (Guo, Connor, Yang, Roehrig, & Morrison, 2012, p. 4). But schools face the challenge of finding ways they can develop all teachers' abilities to have the same powerful and positive impact on student learning. Through the collaborative common assessment process, teachers work smarter, highlight and share early successes and performance satisfaction, and develop a collective strength in navigating challenging situations. One of the greatest benefits, then, of the collaborative common assessment process is seemingly intangible and long term: it increases collective teacher efficacy.

When teachers have *efficacy*, belief in one's ability to reach desired outcomes, it has a tremendous impact on student learning. In fact, as Anita Woolfolk points out in a 2004 interview:

> Teachers who set high goals, who persist, who try another strategy when one approach is found wanting—in other words, teachers who have a high sense of efficacy and act on it—are more likely to have students who learn. (as cited in Shaughnessy, 2004, pp. 156–157)

In her research on teacher efficacy, Nancy Protheroe (2008) notes that:

> Teachers with a stronger sense of efficacy—
>
> - Tend to exhibit greater levels of planning and organization;
> - Are more open to new ideas and more willing to experiment with new methods . . . ;
> - Are more persistent and resilient when things do not go smoothly;
> - Are less critical of students when they make [mistakes]; and
> - Are less inclined to refer a [challenging] student for special education. (p. 43)

Imagine, then, the power of a team of teachers exhibiting collective efficacy. Researchers who have studied the phenomenon note that some schools demonstrate a collective sense of efficacy (Goddard & Skrla, 2006; Hoy, Sweetland, & Smith, 2002; Ross & Gray, 2006; Supovitz & Christman, 2003). In such schools, teachers are less likely to shift blame for poor student performance to the students themselves or outside contributing factors (such as economic limitations, limited English proficiency, and lack of parent involvement) and are more likely to instead take responsibility with a positive attitude, willingly accept challenging student achievement goals, and persist in accomplishing those goals (Goddard, Hoy, & Hoy, 2000). Collaborative common assessments create the constructs that support the development of collective efficacy. Dana Brinson and Lucy Steiner (2007) indicate that although the research is in its early stages, the following constructs for leadership and teacher teams improve collective efficacy:

- Build instructional knowledge and skills [such as plan the common formative and summative assessments needed to guide instruction].

- Create opportunities for teachers to collaboratively share skills and experience [for example, map and execute instruction, intervention, and enrichment strategies to monitor and address results].

- Interpret results and provide actionable feedback on teachers' performance [such as review data and student evidence to find opportunities for continued learning and action steps for closing achievement gaps].

- Involve teachers in school decision making [for example, use results to design, modify, and improve response to intervention strategies for behavioral and academic needs]. (p. 3)

Teaching is challenging work, and when teachers operate in collaborative teams, individual teachers can move away from confronting seemingly insurmountable challenges with individual learners and instead collaboratively monitor student needs, strategize, and ultimately problem solve and find solutions.

Albert Bandura (1977), an early theorist and researcher of teacher efficacy, defines *efficacy* as "the conviction that one can successfully execute the behavior required to produce the outcome" (p. 193). He also identifies beliefs that efficacious teachers hold regarding their impact on student learning (Bandura, 1997), the following four of which can be directly linked to and impacted by collaborative common assessment. Efficacious teachers believe they can:

1. Influence decisions made in school

2. Overcome the influence of adverse community conditions on student learning

3. Create pathways that make students enjoy coming to school

4. Help students believe they can do well on schoolwork

Through the collaborative common assessment process, teachers influence decisions made in school. They gather data to answer complex questions such as the following.

- "What SMART goals will we write to address our areas for growth?"

- "What priority standards will we need to have in order to address our areas of concern?"

- "How will we need to modify the curriculum so it better aligns with our standards?"
- "What assessments must we modify or create to track progress toward our SMART goals?"

At the very core of their work, collaborative teams must make critical decisions with students in order to guarantee learning, and they anchor those decisions in data they gather from common assessment processes. Moreover, such decisions at the classroom and grade or department levels have a schoolwide impact.

Efficacious teachers understand that their task to help all learners succeed in their school requires them to think outside the box so they can work around hurdles over which they have no control. In their collaborative efforts as a team, and often as an entire school community, teachers address and find answers to demanding questions such as, "How can we re-engage intentional nonlearners?" "How can we support the learners who struggle to keep track of their homework, who have difficulty focusing during class time, or who have limited access to resources like parent support once they leave the school?" and "How can we improve the effectiveness of our pyramid of interventions?" Many of these concerns extend beyond the teachers' direct contact with learners during class time, yet the answers to these concerns directly impact the learning that happens in class.

Researchers Ronald Gallimore, Bradley A. Ermeling, William M. Saunders, and Claude Goldenberg (2009) find that teachers can better attribute student success to their teaching, especially in situations where students do not initially learn, when they engage in "(1) focusing on concrete learning goals, (2) tracking progress indicators, and, most critically, (3) getting tangible results in student learning" (p. 542). When collaborative teams look at their data with an eye toward ensuring student learning, they engage in a form of instructional inquiry that draws teachers' attention to and helps them discover "causal connections between their teaching and student performance" (Gallimore et al., 2009, p. 542). Teachers engaged in the collaborative common assessment process often extend their assessment practices to inquiry-based strategies that help them gather additional information to better understand their learners' needs. They become, as DuFour et al. (2008) assert, action researchers while they seek the best ways to ensure all students learn at high levels. Empowered, efficacious, and collaborative teacher teams do the work that Hattie (2009) finds best influences student outcomes: they establish challenging student achievement goals, engage in conversations that contest the status quo of achievement, seek current and new ways to address emerging concerns, design and implement strategies intended to enhance achievement, and monitor progress and effectiveness of teaching.

When teams experience success in their current work, including their assessment work, they are more apt to stretch themselves and their goals for students. Success with early assessment experiences provide teams with insight and motivation to challenge the quality of their own assessments. Teams can challenge and stretch their assessments' quality by asking themselves questions such as, "What will engage the learners in meaningful ways? What will a true representation of learning look like? If the demonstration of learning must be performance oriented, how could we make that happen? What assessment strategies best promote true learning and retention?"

Interestingly, the more excited teachers feel about preparing their learners for the planned assessments, the more exciting they make the assessments for their learners. It becomes self-fulfilling. When teachers strive to design and employ accurate, meaningful, and interesting collaborative common assessments, they are better able to enjoy the assessment process.

Growth in achievement data helps teachers engage individual learners in believing they can do well in their schoolwork. Success breeds success; a positive momentum in collective achievement results fosters a collective belief that the work is doable and *all* learners can have success. In many cases, the entire class pitches in to encourage mastery on everyone's behalf; learning becomes collaborative and creates an environment of success and social celebration. When teams use the right data in the right ways, they can empower them.

A Win for Schools and Systems

If collaborative common assessment increases student achievement, involves working smarter rather than harder when ensuring learning happens, and positively impacts teachers' collective efficacy, then the process must benefit schools too. When schools employ collaborative common assessments with consistency across all buildings and programs within the organization, every grade level and department experiences the same process, and student achievement increases at the building level. Allan R. Odden and Sarah J. Archibald (2009) conducted research at effective schools that have doubled their student achievement. Odden and Archibald (2009) note that teachers at these schools consistently team up at critical junctures and use the common assessment process to isolate and collaboratively respond to what their learners do and do not understand. These teachers intentionally focus their professional dialogue on what matters most: student learning.

The collaborative common assessment process leads to systemic change within a school. It impacts critical systems, like curriculum and assessment, in positive and profound ways. The following sections will show how using collaborative common assessments supports a guaranteed and viable curriculum, assessment literacy, accurate assessment design, and effective data use.

Guaranteed and Viable Curriculum

Discrepancies have long existed between the intended curriculum, the implemented curriculum, and the attained curriculum (DuFour & Marzano, 2011; Marzano, 2003). A curriculum becomes *guaranteed* when teachers prove that they have delivered the intended curriculum through the results of the attained curriculum. Unfortunately, there are many opportunities for inaccuracy or error in this work.

- The *intended curriculum*, often articulated through curriculum maps, may not be viable if it gives teachers too many things to teach. In addition, the selected curricular materials the teachers use may not even connect to the standards' requirements.

- Even though specific pacing guides and agreed-on standards spell out the *implemented curriculum*, interpretations can still differ from teacher to teacher. Left to their own professional judgment, classroom teachers may choose to emphasize, add, or remove key features in their daily instruction (DuFour & Marzano, 2011).

- The *attained curriculum*, as measured through evidence of student learning on the assessments, may show either inconsistencies in content (questions asked do not adequately match expectations from the intended curriculum) or insufficiencies in mastery (too many learners do not achieve mastery for each target expectation).

In essence, what teachers assess and how they assess it are as important as what interventions they employ when students do not attain the desired learning. Grant Wiggins and Jay McTighe (2007) advise:

> The job is not to hope and assume that optimal learning will occur, based on our curriculum and initial teaching. The job is to *ensure* that learning occurs, and when it doesn't, to intervene in altering the syllabus and instruction decisively, quickly, and often. (p. 55; emphasis added)

When the educational system accepts all scores that learners receive—including failing scores—without providing interventions that support all learners in reaching proficiency, it is fair to say that the system is not concerned about guaranteeing the curriculum becomes attained.

Teachers face an essentially insurmountable amount of curriculum. In a 2000 keynote address, curriculum design expert Heidi Hayes Jacobs states:

> Given the limited time you have with your students, curriculum design has become more and more an issue of deciding what you

won't teach as well as what you will teach. You cannot do it all. As a designer, you must choose the essential. (as cited in Ainsworth, 2003a, p. 12)

But when this is left to individual teachers, schools cannot get to a guaranteed and viable curriculum. According to Richard DuFour and Robert J. Marzano (2011):

> If schools are to establish a truly guaranteed and viable curriculum, those who are called upon to deliver it must have both a common understanding of the curriculum and a commitment to teach it. PLCs monitor this clarity and commitment through the second critical question that teachers in a PLC consider, "How will we know if students are learning?" That question is specifically intended to ensure that the guaranteed curriculum is not only being *taught to* students but, more importantly, is being *learned by* students. (p. 91)

The collaborative common assessment process requires that collaborative teams come together to determine their priority standards, the learning targets within those standards, the assessments required to measure the intended learning, the pacing of their work, and their re-engagement plans for learners who've yet to attain the expectations. Schools that engage teams in the work of collaborative common assessment are far more likely to attain a guaranteed and viable curriculum than those that choose to follow premade curriculum programs (Hattie, 2009).

Assessment Literacy

Most teachers in North America have had insufficient formal training, practice, feedback, and ongoing support regarding the principles of sound assessment. As Rick Stiggins (2008) notes, education has primarily relied on textbook and testing companies to design high-quality assessments. Both undergraduate and graduate teacher-preparation programs have an obvious and alarming absence of courses regarding effective assessment design and use (Stiggins & Herrick, 2007). When teachers do not understand the theory and practice of valid and reliable assessments, teachers have no option but to use predesigned assessments from their textbooks or make up assessments. Often, they replicate the poor assessment practices that they themselves experienced as K–12 students.

Unless a teacher uses sound assessments, the teacher has no way to ensure that the teaching has actually transferred into learning. Assessment is a core teaching process. Teaching in the absence of constant sound assessment practices is really just coverage of content. The only way teachers can guarantee learning is if they all use sound assessment practices effectively.

If that's the case, wouldn't it suffice if teachers just used already provided assessments in the way the assessment materials advise? Absolutely not. Time and again, when teachers use existing assessments, it accidentally creates gaps in teaching and learning because teachers rarely analyze a prewritten assessment carefully before they administer it, and then, they accept the resulting data at face value. Table 2.4 includes some of the inaccuracies and insufficiencies that result from this lack of analysis.

Table 2.4: Possible Inaccuracies and Insufficiencies Resulting From Assessment Errors

Assessment Error	Inaccuracy	Insufficiency
Item or Task Quality	The items or tasks are often set up to gather data in the quickest possible manner. When that happens, the assessment falls short of truly measuring the full intent of the standards it is designed to assess (for example, many performance-oriented standards are assessed with the more easily scored pencil-and-paper test).	The items or tasks fall short of deep application or higher-order reasoning. Many assessments stop at ensuring students possess content information and in some cases can execute the algorithms that accompany the knowledge. Few assessments move to the level of requiring students to integrate knowledge or construct new solutions and insights in real-world applications.
Sampling	An assessment might include standards that are *not* within the expectations of the teachers engaged in that curricular material.	An assessment might include too many standards and not have enough samples of each standard to ensure any reliability.
Results	All items have equal weighting—even items that the curricular resource itself might have deemed *nonsecure goals*. Teachers tally and report the full data for decision making even though the final results should not include some of the generated data. The data may result in learners unnecessarily receiving interventions.	Error analysis of what went wrong in an individual student response (reading error, concept error, or reasoning error) frequently stops at the point of the resulting percentage or score. Item analysis is limited to whether the item or prompt was of high quality based on the responses it generated. The data do not offer insight into student thinking or inform next instructional steps.

According to Helen Timperley (2009), "Knowledge of the curriculum and how to teach it effectively must accompany greater knowledge of the interpretation and use of assessment information" (p. 23). Teachers must experience assessment development and deployment in order to understand it. Designing assessments in advance of teaching creates a laser-like focus on and comprehensive understanding of the instruction required to attain mastery. This does not mean that teachers should *only* use assessments they themselves create; instead, it means that they can no longer depend solely on the assessments that come premade from outside testing vendors with their curricular materials and software item banks.

When teacher teams design and employ assessments and interpret their results, they build shared knowledge regarding assessment accuracy and effectiveness. Teachers who engage in the collaborative common assessment process learn both how to design assessments accurately and use assessment data effectively.

Accurate Assessment Design

Teams are better able to create more accurate assessments when they agree to design their assessments so that they align to standards; have clear, uniform targets; feature accurate prompts and measurement tools; include varied assessment methods and data points; and foster increased rigor and relevance. The adage *Many hands make light work*, is as relevant here as the notion that many eyes can bring multiple perspectives into clear focus.

Alignment to Standards

From the late 1980s until the early 2000s, schools and districts told teachers to follow the pacing guide and implement the curriculum with fidelity. In some schools and districts, mandates and monitoring made it dangerous for teachers to deviate from the prescribed curriculum plan. As of 2019, no single curriculum has fully aligned with any state's standards. While textbook companies can demonstrate that their curricular materials address a state or province's standards, they cannot prove that the materials address *every* standard, that they do so at the depth that the state or province's testing system requires, or that their curriculum-based assessments match the types of questions the state or province might ask. When teachers develop collaborative common assessments, they begin with the standards, not the curriculum, to make their instruction and assessment decisions. That early alignment process can better support accurate design.

Clear, Uniform Targets

When teachers unpack standards together, they develop a shared understanding of the target expectations that the standards require. It is imperative that teachers agree to the specific learning expectations outlined in the standards. It is equally imperative that they agree on the meaning of key verbs. For example, they might ask, "What exactly does *summarize* mean? Is *summarize* similar to or different from *generalize*? What type of task would best engage learners in the process of summarizing, and what quality criteria would guarantee high-quality summaries in *every* classroom?" If teams are clear on the individual terms and the specific demands of the standards, they can provide more consistent and accurate instruction leading into the assessments. They can also make individual decisions that allow for variances in the assessments but that remain contingent on clear, agreed-on lists of learning targets unit by unit.

Accurate Prompts and Measurement Tools

It is impossible to write a perfect assessment task, item, or rubric; it is sometimes hard to even write a good one. However, when teams work collaboratively, they generally develop such prompts and measurement tools in a more thoughtful way. They often seek clarifying examples, challenge each other's personal schemas, refine their work based on the evidence it generates over time, and, most importantly, calibrate their expectations so they have consistency from classroom to classroom.

Varied Assessment Methods and Data Points

A deep exploration into standards and target language engages teams in exploring the proper questions, prompts, or tasks that will truly assess students' expected attainment and mastery of the content. This exploration makes it apparent that one assessment, or even one type of assessment, will not suffice to accurately certify a learner's degree of mastery of a standard. For example, it is important to assess the small, specific tasks (such as identifying text-specific details) of a large concept or skill (for example, drawing conclusions or making predictions) to verify that learners are ready to engage in the larger concept or skill, but it is equally important to engage learners in a comprehensive assessment that certifies that they can put all the parts together. Multiple assessment methods and multiple data points provide a more comprehensive and accurate picture of student learning.

Increased Rigor and Relevance

Teachers can find it hard to write a high-quality assessment, much less a high-quality, rigorous, and relevant assessment. Too often, an assessment—which seeks to assess what teachers taught—misses the importance of the learning's larger context. For example, the Common Core State Standards (CCSS; National Governors Association Center for Best Practices [NGA] & Council of Chief State School Officers [CCSSO], 2010a) require students to understand text features. But after teaching text features, how should teachers assess students' understanding of text features? Should teachers just assess that students can point to features, identify them with appropriate labels, and explain how those features make a text easier to comprehend? Many summative assessments stop at the level of knowledge and skill instead of getting to strategic or extended thinking. While it is necessary to ensure such basics are in place, a check on the basics can take place in formative stages. Ultimately, however, such assessments at the summative level miss the mark of having students create meaning within a complex text *because* of their ready access to and interpretation of the document's text features. When teacher teams collaborate to write assessments, they question the relevance of the learning and the rigor of the potential tasks or items. They challenge their assumptions, materials, and practices as they explore rigor and relevance while writing the assessment.

Effective Data Use

While assessment literacy requires that teams design assessments accurately, it is equally imperative that teams use the data effectively. For example, an adult could take a child's temperature over and over with a thermometer and generate an accurate reading of 103 degrees. But the data generated won't suffice to effectively address the findings. The adult would need to administer an aspirin in response to the data that the child has a fever. Teachers need to understand how to effectively address their classroom assessment findings. To do this, teams must agree on the best ways to respond to their assessment results; possible responses include identified error analysis, targeted instructional responses, effective feedback, dynamic student involvement, systemic reflection, and positive cultural change.

Identified Error Analysis

Teachers could easily look at assessment data by the resulting percentages and then sort learners based on their percentage scores into groupings for re-engagement and extension opportunities. Percentage-based scores, however, never suffice. They should serve only as an indicator requiring deeper exploration, not as an exact conclusion requiring on-the-spot decision making. When teachers deeply own the results of their team-created assessments, they look at percentages as indicator data, which drives them more deeply into the actual student work so they can gain insights into what went wrong. Did students make reading errors? Concept errors? Reasoning errors? Collaborative teams use data to launch deeper investigations through error analysis.

Targeted Instructional Responses

A deeper exploration into data points and student work can offer significant insights into the appropriate instructional responses. For example, a student might have scored 65 percent on the learning target of "drawing conclusions," but what went wrong? Teams using the collaborative common assessment process engage in error analysis to find critical answers to questions like, Did the student identify explicit evidence but neglect to identify implicit evidence before drawing a conclusion? Did the student have insufficient evidence before drawing a conclusion? Did the student have sufficient implicit and explicit evidence but employ faulty reasoning when drawing the conclusion? Clearly, it would be a mistake to reteach all of this learning target to a student who scored 65 percent. Teams would find it far better to analyze the type of error the learner has made and then identify a targeted instructional response. With such information in their hands, teacher teams can close learning gaps in short order because they directly match their interventions to the type of error the learner made.

Effective Feedback

When collaborative teams share unified commitments to consistent learning targets, employ uniform criteria for evaluating quality, and collectively explore the specific types of errors students make in the learning process, they can better provide the necessary feedback that supports learners in reducing the discrepancy between where they currently are and where they need to be. In the absence of such work, individual teachers provide feedback of varying degrees of quality. John Hattie and Helen Timperley (2007) argue that feedback "is most powerful when it addresses faulty interpretations, not a total lack of understanding" (p. 82). In order to identify the right feedback to offer, teachers should work together to find and analyze learners' faulty interpretations of concepts. According to Hattie (2009), feedback is one of the most powerful instructional strategies a teacher can employ. Yet assessment experts continue to cite research that indicates teachers often misunderstand this strategy and seldom employ it with a high degree of effectiveness (Chappuis, 2009; Hattie, 2009; Hattie & Timperley, 2007; Ruiz-Primo & Li, 2011, 2013; Wiliam, 2013).

Feedback is a two-way street—teacher to students and students to teacher. Both directions require tremendous clarity and energy. Hattie (2009) reminds teachers that:

> Feedback to students involves providing information and understanding about the tasks that make the difference in light of what the *student* already understands, misunderstands, and constructs. Feedback from students to teachers involves information and understanding about the tasks that make the difference in light of what the *teacher* already understands, misunderstands, and constructs about the learning of his or her students. It matters when teachers see learning through the lens of the student grappling to construct beliefs and knowledge about whatever is the goal of the lesson. This is never linear, not always easy, requires learning and over learning, needs dollops of feedback, involves much deliberative practice, leads to lots of errors and mis-directions, requires both accommodating and assimilating prior knowledge and conceptions, and demands a sense of excitement and mission to know, understand, and make a difference. (p. 238)

A deep analysis of common assessment data leads collaborative teams to better understand the errors their learners are making so they can help their learners autocorrect. Likewise, the process enables teams to stand behind their proffered feedback with focused instruction and ongoing monitoring.

Dynamic Student Involvement

Assessment should never be something that teachers do *to* learners; rather, they must do it *with* and *for* learners. This requires that they utilize even common assessments with the ultimate end user—the learner—in mind. Jan Chappuis (2009) asserts:

> Formative assessment *is* a powerful tool in the hands of both teachers and students and the closer to everyday instruction, the stronger it is. Classroom assessment, sensitive to what teachers and students are doing daily, is most capable of providing the basis for understandable and accurate feedback about the learning, while there is still time to act on it. And it has the greatest capacity to develop students' ability to monitor and adjust their own learning. (p. 9)

Teams that develop assessment literacy through common understandings and practice embrace the conversation of engaging learners in analyzing and responding to their own results. In this way, an instructional re-engagement strategy exponentially increases in power as teachers target their responses to specific gaps in understanding while students rally their attention and energy around mastering their own gaps.

Systemic Reflection

The work of collaborative common assessments is ultimately about professional inquiry and learning. In teams, teachers gather the necessary data to explore their instructional impact, identify and deliver strategic responses, and reflect on their practices and beliefs. Timperley (2009) observes:

> When teachers . . . interpret assessment data in order to become more responsive to their students' learning needs, the impact is substantive. Teachers, however, cannot do this alone. . . . Creating the kinds of conditions in schools in which teachers systematically use data to inform their practice . . . requires that they teach in contexts in which such practice becomes part of the organisational routines. (p. 24)

The entire system engages in reflective practice; the findings of a few inform the work of many. Collaborative common assessment engages the entire system as a professional *learning* community.

Positive Cultural Change

Strategies and initiatives may come and go, whereas a school's culture can seem steadfast—almost to the point that it serves as an insurmountable wall of resistance when the school requires change. Educational literature has clearly and forthrightly shown that any school-improvement effort that does not positively impact culture is doomed to failure (DuFour & Fullan, 2013; Muhammad, 2018). The work of collaborative common assessments embeds itself in teacher teams' routines, practices, and even beliefs—that is, it can impact culture in significant ways. The resulting gains in student achievement lead to changes in belief and practice. Richard F. Elmore (2003) says:

> Teachers have to believe there is some compelling reason for them to change practice, with the best direct evidence being that students learn better. The key to enduring change in teacher practice is demonstrable results in terms of student achievement. (p. 38)

The moral authority of the right work coupled with the public celebration of learning creates a sense of both shared responsibility and momentum. The positive peer pressure that emerges from shared responsibility steadies the individuals on a team and propels the entire organization on a confident course (Blanchard, 2007; DuFour et al., 2008; Erkens & Twadell, 2012; Fullan, 2008, 2011; Gallimore et al., 2009; Lencioni, 2005; Patterson, Grenny, Maxfield, McMillan, & Switzler, 2008). The success of any professional development enterprise requires teachers to engage in informed practices that ultimately shape their collective beliefs and instructional responses to complex situations and positively influence the normative environment of the school. Any effort that does not reach that level of impact will almost certainly fail.

Conclusion

Conversations during the collaborative common assessment process should touch on curriculum, standards, instructional strategies, and assessment design, use, and results. These conversations, which are found at the core of teacher practice, engage staff in developing a deeply rooted shared commitment, a powerful and collective sense of efficacy, and a drive to raise expectations for all.

Assessment literacy development is also a core component of high-quality teaching. This work challenges teachers, but they can accomplish it, and it has numerous and profoundly rewarding benefits. However, the work doesn't happen when schools dictate the assessments to use—including test-item banks, testing company materials, district benchmarks, or curricular materials. Instead, schools must put the work directly into the hands of educators and allow them the freedom to collaboratively design and employ common assessments and then strategize ways to respond appropriately to their learners' needs. If educators are ever to change the predominant paradigm that only high-stakes testing situations guarantee increased student achievement, then they must dedicate effort to doing this work at the building and classroom levels. Such work improves assessment literacy, builds collective efficacy, and develops schools' organizational capacity to become instructionally sensitive places for learners of all ages.

Team Reflections

Take a few moments to reflect on the following questions.

- Do we have any evidence of effectiveness already? If not, why not?

- How could we use evidence to build our compelling *why* and our collective commitments to this work?

- If our team or school requires evidence of effectiveness in order to get started in this work, where could we get it? How or when might we share it?

- How can we monitor our progress so we always have local evidence at the ready?

The Preparation Phase

3

Putting teachers into teams is a great beginning for collaboratively designing and employing common assessments, but the work ahead will challenge teams, and they will require a firm foundation in order to successfully engage in the work. A firm foundation, whether it's a concrete structure, such as the base to a skyscraper, or the intangible emotional base of a healthy childhood, always bolsters the probability of success and will underpin all future endeavors. Successful teams begin by establishing the parameters that will guide future decisions; exploring current realities; co-creating a new, preferred reality; and designing a visible and shared pathway. Specifically, preparing the foundation for collaborative common assessments involves the following five steps.

1. Establishing team norms and collective commitments
2. Developing shared expectations
3. Examining school data and establishing SMART goals
4. Creating an assessment road map and SMART goals plans
5. Monitoring progress on SMART goals

Figure 3.1 (page 42) outlines this work.

Teams launch the foundational work in advance as a means to support themselves in the design phase, but they revisit it repeatedly as they move forward; in other words, early agreements are necessary but insufficient to sustain the work. Once teams launch the work, they must constantly review and refine those agreements throughout the year.

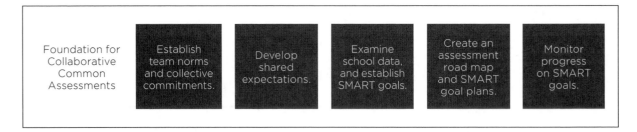

Source: Adapted from Erkens, 2016.

Figure 3.1: Steps of the preparation phase.

Moreover, teams can have more success with each phase when they have protocols and tools to guide their processes. The work can be challenging enough when teams enter the process without the necessary support procedures and strategies to smooth out anticipated hurdles. For each of the five steps of the preparation phase, there are tools and protocols to support teams as they prepare to implement the collaborative common assessment process.

Establishing Team Norms and Collective Commitments

The collective commitments outlined in chapter 2 are not the same as team norms. Collective commitments are part of the preparation phase. However, when it comes to clarifying the work and building commitments to create safety, the work of collective commitments on the organizational level precede individual team preparation. Teams need collective commitments because those are the agreements members make to each other regarding the work they need to do together. The language of collective commitments allows team members to hold each other mutually accountable to the work at hand, and it keeps the team focused.

It could be easy to confuse collective commitments with team norms, but the two are not interchangeable, so one cannot substitute for the other. Although norms and collective commitments both provide options for holding each other accountable, they serve very different purposes. Table 3.1 outlines the differences between team norms and collective commitments. Norms and commitments are both used to create clarity, parameters, and even permission for team members to be empowered, but they serve different purposes.

Early on, all teams must identify team norms. All team members—even late additions to an existing team—need a clear and agreed-on set of commitments to guide their individual and collective interactions. Members need team norms to help them navigate emotion during the very human endeavor of collaborating.

Table 3.1: Team Norms and Collective Commitments

	Team Norms	Collective Commitments
What	Team-specific agreements to outline productive meeting conduct	Statements of organizational values that permeate the entire organization and create promises for the agreed-on work
Why	To create safety in a meeting, outlining how team members will communicate with one another	To clarify shared values that outline the work and to provide the framework with which educators are empowered to lead change
When	During team meetings	All the time—in team meetings, staff meetings, passing in the hallway meetings, and so on
Examples	• Remain fully present. • Seek first to understand before striving to be understood. • Paraphrase before speaking. • Share what you are thinking.	• We will identify our priority standards and pace alike. • We will use collaborative common assessments to monitor student learning. • We will intervene to support struggling learners.

Cassandra Erkens and Eric Twadell (2012) offer a working definition of *team norms*:

> Norms are most commonly defined as a group's agreements—implied and explicit—for meeting conduct. . . . We suggest a different definition: *norms* are our collective, public promises to keep one another safe while working collaboratively. Leaders need to employ team norms both in and out of meetings, as collaboration is the way the team or organization does business and *business* requires navigating through tumultuous situations and complex problem solving at all times—not just during team meetings. (pp. 31–32)

The more proactively and transparently a team behaves in the norm-setting process, the quicker it can build trust and interdependence. Further, teams should follow a formal norm-setting process. Figure 3.2 (page 44) outlines the guidelines that teams must use when they create norms.

When team leaders keep the guidelines in place during the norm-setting process, they can safely lead their teams into developing high-quality norms. Teams can use the protocol in figure 3.3 (page 45) to navigate the norm-setting process.

The protocol for developing norms that figure 3.3 outlines provides teams with easy steps to create their norms.

Use the following guidelines to frame productive team norms.

- Create substantive agreements (above and beyond the expected professional courtesies, like, "We will show up on time," "We will all contribute," and "We commit to turning our cell phones off") that will keep individuals safe while they collaborate. Create norms such as, "We will use data rather than opinion or personal experience to frame team decisions. If we don't have existing data, we commit to gather them" (Erkens, 2016, p. 57).

- Avoid norms that preserve the status quo or are counterproductive to collectively ensuring quality and systematically co-creating shared understanding of the best-practice strategies for teaching and learning (for example, "We agree to disagree").

- Create consistency and clarity regarding the meaning of nebulous or *soft* terms (such as *respect*). For example, some cultures consider it a sign of respect to make eye contact when talking while other cultures consider that a sign of disrespect. Make sure the team has the opportunity to express what such terms both do and don't mean.

- Secure individual public statements of commitment to the norms. Person by person, norm by norm, ask, "Is there any norm on this page with which you cannot live?" Resolve each issue as it arises.

- Develop agreements that outline one or more strategies that team members can use to hold one another accountable to the norms. Without such agreements, written norms simply become nice words that the team rarely employs.

- Generate collective understanding of what participation looks like when the will of the team is clear, but an individual does not agree, and the team is moving forward.

Figure 3.2: Guidelines for creating team norms.

*Visit **go.SolutionTree.com/assessment** for a free reproducible version of this figure.*

Developing Shared Expectations

Understanding *what* to teach can pose as much of a challenge as deciding *how* to teach. Collaborative teams share common knowledge of their essential learning expectations. Sometimes teams (for example, grade-level or discipline-specific teams) share the exact same standards, but sometimes, when teams don't share standards, they seek to find similar skills or literacies. In either case, it's critical that teams come to a shared understanding of what complex standards or reasoning skills or processes mean.

When teams share common standards, they need protocols to help them prioritize standards. The process helps teams develop shared understanding of and commitment to their work.

Priority Standards

Not all standards are created equal. Some standards represent the core of a discipline and will require far more time and energy to teach. Teams must determine what those standards will be. Teachers call standards that have top priority a variety of names, including *essential learnings, power standards, key learnings,* and *priority standards.* In the end, it doesn't matter

Step 1	Ask team members to take a few moments to individually record their concerns about collaborating, especially when it comes to sharing individual results about student performance in the classroom.
Step 2	Have team members share their individual concerns while someone records the responses so all members can see the list. Honor responses by noting them in the list and acknowledging the experiences and feelings of the members without debating the reality of those contributions.
Step 3	Have team members brainstorm ideas for team norms, writing each norm on its own sticky note, taking care to address the following. • Necessary agreements for examining data (for example, preventing judgment or maintaining confidentiality) • Guidelines for learning together (for example, presuming positive intent before responding, or probing when something needs further clarification) • Processes for decision making
Step 4	Begin to gather and cluster sticky notes in like categories, giving each cluster a label that defines it.
Step 5	Have team members generate a norm for each cluster in the brainstormed list by looking at the cluster's sticky notes and framing the norm that best represents the ideas on them.
Step 6	Create a final list of norms. Strive to keep the list manageable in number (approximately eight norms or fewer). Review the list to make sure it has addressed all key points.
Step 7	With the list posted in front of the team, clarify any *soft* terms (for example, *respect*, *trustworthiness*, or *integrity*). Provide examples and nonexamples until all members clearly understand the terms' meaning.
Step 8	With the list posted at the front, move about the team in a round-robin fashion, asking each team member, "Is there any norm on this list with which you cannot live?" For each norm that generates conversation, the team must rectify the difference. For example, if a team member confesses to struggling with a proposed norm that would not allow sidebar conversations, the team must then decide if it will keep the norm and require its members to modify behavior, or modify the norm to allow for the behavior. Without this step, the team will not have actionable agreements.
Step 9	Develop a strategy that will ensure the team holds itself accountable to its norms (for example, answering the question, "What will we do when someone is off norm?"). In the absence of a strategy to address this question, the team has generated a list of *nice to knows* that it may or may not fully implement.
Step 10	Document agreements, and share them with all team members. The team should regularly or, at a minimum, periodically monitor the norms.

Figure 3.3: Protocol for developing team norms.

*Visit **go.SolutionTree.com/assessment** for a free reproducible version of this figure.*

if teams call these critical agreements, as long as all team members have shared knowledge of the what, why, and how surrounding them. This book will refer to them as *priority standards*.

To begin the process of determining priority standards, teams must clarify their decision-making criteria as they prioritize their standards. The following list offers a common set of five criteria for determining priority using clarifying questions that teams can ask to decide whether a standard meets the criteria.

1. **Endurance:** "Will this standard provide students with knowledge and skills that will have value beyond a single test date?" (Reeves, 2002).

2. **Leverage:** "Will this standard provide knowledge and skills that will have value in multiple disciplines?" (Reeves, 2002).

3. **Readiness for the next level of learning:** "Will this standard provide students with the essential knowledge and skills that they need to have success in the next grade or the next level of instruction?" (Reeves, 2002).

4. **Testing requirements:** "Will an accountability feature, such as a state, provincial, or national test or a district benchmark, test this standard? If so, *how*? What are the cognitive demands involved?" (Ainsworth, 2013).

5. **Student needs:** "What do external data suggest our learners most need in the area of study that this standard outlines? How much knowledge or skill do our students have in this standard's area? Will it require sustained instructional attention, or do our students already have a relatively firm foundation with the necessary knowledge or skills in this area?" In the case of having no external data upon which to draw, the first question becomes "What do our previous years' of classroom evidence and our professional experience suggest our learners need in the area of study that this standard outlines?" The questions that follow remain the same.

Decision-making criteria 4 and 5 (testing requirements and student needs) require that teams have access to the relevant information during the decision-making process. They should ensure they have test specifications (from testing agencies, state departments, and even in-house guidelines) and student data from previous and recent external exams, internal exams, or classroom assessments. When teams have ready access to this information, the prioritization process will go more smoothly, and they can make better decisions.

Once teams have agreed on their decision-making criteria, they can begin the prioritization process. Figure 3.4 provides a protocol for identifying priority standards, and the reproducible "Template for Prioritizing Standards" (page 68) offers a template that teams can use to complete the work.

Step 1	Identify the area of focus and the related standards for review.
Step 2	Define the following decision-making criteria (which Reeves [2002] and Ainsworth [2013] identify) to ensure team clarity: endurance, leverage, readiness for the next level of learning, testing requirements, and student needs. Modify, add, and define additional criteria as needed. Agree to the final list before proceeding.
Step 3	Provide each team member with a list of the standards. Establish a guideline for the maximum number of standards that individual members should select (generally in the ballpark of eight to ten standards per area of study) to determine the final list. Have individual team members use highlighters to denote the standards they consider most important.
Step 4	Create a collective set of the resulting choices of standards for consideration and final selection. Display a clean set of the standards to walk through as a team, and determine how decisions regarding which standards to select as priority standards will be made at this point. *Note: If the team is in agreement, and the number of selected standards falls within the team guideline, skip to step 6.*

Step 5	Narrow or enhance the list in a team discussion.
	
	Review the list standard by standard, discussing each decision-making criterion per standard and noting which criteria fit most with each standard. Code the standards to denote appropriate criteria by using terms, symbols, or colors. There are several options for coding.
	
	• Discuss, come to agreements, and then code on a single list that is projected for all to see.
	• List the identified standards on poster paper, and have individual team members code each standard with designated colors or symbols to represent each of the five criteria. For example—
	  • Use yellow or a star to identify standards that address endurance.
	  • Use pink or a check mark to identify standards that address leverage.
	  • Use green or a circle to identify standards that address readiness for the next level of learning.
	  • Use blue or an underline to identify standards that address testing requirements.
	  • Use orange or a box to identify standards that address identified student areas of need.
	• Have team members code standards on their own (see the reproducible "Template for Prioritizing Standards," page 68) and then aggregate those results by listing the codes each standard was awarded and the number of times that same code was offered to that standard (for example, three team members thought this standard had endurance, two coded it for leverage).
	
	As a team, select the standards that meet the greatest number of the most significant criteria.
	
	Note: During the discussion, review test specifications and student achievement data as necessary to resolve questions regarding the testing requirements and student needs criteria.

Figure 3.4: Protocol for prioritizing standards.

continued →

Step 6	Identify the priority standards.
	Review the resulting list.
	Seek team approval of and commitment to the resulting list.
Step 7	Document final decisions so you can share them with other teams for future discussions on vertical alignment.
	Alternate option: Create a graphic organizer or visual map of the prioritized list as a way to demonstrate relationships between and among the prioritized standards. It sometimes helps to see the big picture of the individual standards in relation to the overarching category. Create a graphic organizer or visual map of the prioritized list as a way to demonstrate relationships between and among the prioritized standards. It sometimes helps to see the big picture of the individual standards in relation to an overarching category (for example, the reading standards for comprehension, fluency, vocabulary, text features, and other similar reading expectations might fit in the broad areas of fiction and nonfiction text, or they might fit within the single skill of reading comprehension). Drawing a graphic organizer helps teams discuss and agree upon hierarchy and priority when linking ideas. When teams put standards into the categories they deem most significant, they have a clearer picture of how many standards fit within a single category.

*Visit **go.SolutionTree.com/assessment** for a free reproducible version of this figure.*

The prioritized list that the team generates during this protocol is still preliminary. Once teams have completed the process and developed an agreed-on list of standards, they have what they need to share their list with other teams for review, vertical or horizontal alignment, and confirmation. Teams can revisit their lists to fill gaps or remove overlaps between grade-level or discipline-specific teams. Once teams make all of these decisions, they can move their prioritized list from preliminary to confirmed and begin to operationalize their agreements.

The protocol for prioritizing standards involves criteria-based decision making, a process that is necessary to guide decisions and ensure a degree of confidence in the results. In order to use criteria-based decision making successfully, teams must first clarify the what, why, and how of applying those criteria. The following list highlights things to consider before making criteria-based decisions.

- **The list of criteria to use**: Keep this list focused and few.

- **The definitions or clarifications of each criterion:** Be certain everyone agrees on terminology.

- **The range of quality for each criterion:** Consider if there is a range of proficiency (for example, determining how good is good enough, considering levels 1 through 4 or low, medium, and high).

- **The possible prioritization of the criterion:** Some criteria may be deemed more important than others. In that case, determine how much weight to give a criterion.

Weight can be determined by awarding some criteria more points than others during the evaluation phase.

- **The process used to apply the criteria:** Teams can be formal or informal in their discussions; they can create their own decision-making protocol or search for existing options; they can choose between reaching consensus or voting, or some combination of the two, to make their final selections.

There are no specific rules or guidelines for which of the criteria are most valuable or how many points to award a criterion. The team makes those internal decisions as members discuss what they value most. Teams can avoid frustrating discussions or even arguments when they are very clear about what criteria will be used and what their process for using the criteria will be *in advance* of decision making. Unless such agreements are made on a staffwide basis so every team is expected to use the same criteria and process, individual teams are always in control of the selection of criteria, the definitions, the values placed on their criterion, and the processes that will be used during decision making.

Imagine, for example that teams prefer to use a tool that helps individual members think or vote prior to discussing and coming to consensus. A team will miss the step of creating shared knowledge if it skips the critical discussions needed during decision making. Discussion remains the best way to secure collective understanding of and commitment to the work ahead. Team members may use the reproducible "Template for Prioritizing Standards" (page 68) to help them make weighted decisions with preliminary voting.

Teams should formally document or publish prioritized standards for ready access in future team meetings and schoolwide grade-level, discipline-specific, or interdisciplinary discussions. Eventually, teams will develop common assessments to support and monitor their work using the prioritized standards.

Shared Expectations Within Uncommon Content

Some teacher teams do not necessarily have the exact same standards or curriculum; they may instead share a set of generalizable skills or modern literacies, just as all mathematics courses share the same mathematical practices.

For example, career-based courses (family and consumer science, agriculture, woodworking, automotives, metals, computer assisted design [CAD], architecture, and so on) often share several core processes such as technical reading, diagnosing, problem solving, decision making, and communicating. When a team has different content standards, members first work to determine shared expectations around the things they have in common. It's nearly impossible to come to shared knowledge in the early stage as there are too many standards for everyone to understand from the various courses represented, and some standards are outside the areas of expertise for various team members. After the team develops shared expectations, it moves to create shared knowledge of what each of those expectations truly means. There are a few different team formations schools can use when trying to create collaborative common assessments in uncommon circumstances, including a whole-school effort such as writing across the curriculum, vertical or horizontal, cross building, and plus one, as described in the following list.

- **Whole-school effort such as writing across the curriculum:** The staff within a school create an agreed-on set of shared expectations like core competencies or modern literacies (defined on page 52) and then create measuring tools (rubrics or proficiency scales) for scoring those shared expectations with consistency. Then each individual teacher or team member (if there are more than two people teaching a similar course) uses the agreed-on tools many times throughout the year to measure student learning of those shared expectations in their various classrooms. Data are shared within a team on an ongoing basis (for example, throughout a unit of study) and at the schoolwide level during predetermined times (such as once per quarter or trimester).

- **Vertical or horizontal:** Teams that are vertical (the grade-level teams spanning two or more years) or horizontal (interdisciplinary teams spanning two or more disciplines) follow the same process used in whole-school collaborative common assessments. However, instead of working as a whole school, teams work within the confines of their horizontal (for example, sixth-, seventh-, and eighth-grade mathematics use the same mathematical practices) or vertical (for example, English, social studies, and science use the same criteria and protocols for nonfiction reading) configuration. Typically, members organized into vertical or horizontal teams meet regularly within those formations, so data are shared within the team on an ongoing basis.

- **Cross building:** Cross-building teams can be discipline specific (such as all art teachers from multiple elementary schools), vertical (all middle school sixth- through eighth-grade art teachers), or interdisciplinary (all creative disciplines like art, music, drama, photography, web design, and fashion design from multiple high schools). The combinations for teams across multiple schools are only limited by the imagination of what's possible. Using similar processes to the whole-school common assessment approach, cross-building teams must identify their shared expectations, create the tools for monitoring those expectations, and outline the process for when and how they will monitor those expectations. When team members cross multiple buildings it is hard for them to meet physically with any frequency, unless the buildings are in close proximity or the school schedules generously include travel time. So, cross-building teams often employ digital media. They might use web-conferencing mediums to meet virtually and then employ collaborative meeting tools like Google Docs to develop assessments and Google Sheets to record their results when they do not have the luxury of meeting face to face.

- **Plus one:** The plus-one common assessment option generally means that a grade-level or discipline-specific team (such as the first-grade team) adds a team member or members who work across all grade levels (like the physical education teacher or the science specialist) or disciplines (like a special education teacher or intervention specialist). In order to engage in common assessments, all members of the team must have shared expectations regarding what to assess and when. Plus-one teams can use the same processes for common assessments and the same criteria and protocols to identify their shared expectations.

Figure 3.5 highlights these team formations.

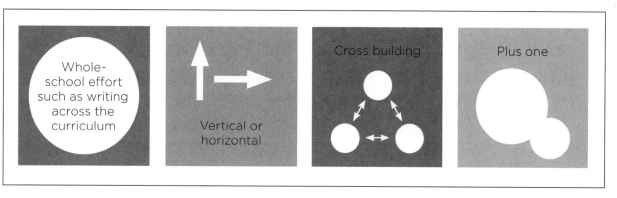

Source: Erkens, 2016, p. 36.

Figure 3.5: Design options for common assessments in uncommon circumstances.

Collaborative Common Assessments (Erkens, 2016), the companion book to this handbook, provides a host of ideas regarding how such teams can engage in the common assessment process, especially if they do not share the exact same content or resources.

When teams do not have the exact same curricular materials or standards, they still need shared expectations in order to engage in the work of common assessments—they just approach their work differently. They do not share standards to prioritize, so they must use alternative criteria and protocols to find common ground. *Common ground* means they have consistent elements or processes, like core competencies (technical reading, technical writing, decision making, and so on) or modern literacies (information literacy, implications literacy, and so on), that will generate like results, even though the content with which they apply the skills varies.

Education is rich with core competencies or modern literacies that cross all disciplines and grade levels. *Core competencies* are skills that transcend time and discipline. They are so prevalent and highly valued that students use them daily and they become indispensable. Seven core competencies are readily found in the local, state, provincial, and national educational standards of 2019: (1) self-regulation, (2) communication, (3) collaboration, (4) critical thinking, (5) creative thinking, (6) digital citizenship, and (7) social competence (Erkens, Schimmer, & Vagle, 2019). Generally, these skills are robust in that many consistent, time-honored, and universal steps are necessary to acquire the skills or accomplish the process, no matter the discipline (Erkens et al., 2019). The core competency of creative thinking, for example, is a process that includes five commonly understood steps (Erkens et al., 2019).

1. **Preparation:** Prepares by identifying an area of curiosity for further investigation

2. **Incubation:** Incubates ideas by synthesizing, imagining, and constructing possibilities

3. **Illumination:** Illuminates ideas with insights or epiphanies

4. **Verification:** Seeks feedback and validation during the formative phase to verify whether the potential solution or solutions are worth pursuing; self-assesses and makes personal decisions regarding concluding steps

5. **Implementation:** Implements idea, moving it from concept to reality

Each step can apply to multiple disciplines, and teachers can teach, observe, and assess each; therefore, teams can define and evaluate each step, no matter the content.

Modern literacies, which slightly differ from a specific process like problem solving, involve a collection of abilities and competencies that form cultural and transferable practices that can morph over time to accommodate modern requirements (National Council of Teachers of English, 2008; www.ncte.org/governance/literacies). For example, rapid changes in technology have altered what it means to have technological literacy, and expectations for technological literacy expand with each new iteration of computing options. In addition to understanding how to navigate emerging platforms, new hardware, and new software programs, technologically literate individuals must have core competencies like communication, collaboration, creativity, and digital citizenship as well as specific skills like researching, solving problems, making decisions, critically consuming information, and arguing from evidence. Modern literacies, generally deemed more robust than a single skill or process or even a core competency, adhere to current cultural demands and universally apply to many disciplines. Table 3.2

provides an initial list of plausible options for core competencies or specific skills and modern literacies that teams could use in common assessments with uncommon courses.

Table 3.2: List of Core Competencies and Modern Literacies

Core Competencies	Modern Literacies
• Technical reading • Technical writing • Decision making • Problem solving • Analyzing • Arguing from evidence • Communicating or justifying thinking • Speaking and listening • Collaborating	• Information literacy • Implications literacy • Civic literacy • Global literacy • Financial literacy • Data literacy • Multimedia literacy • Innovation literacy

Teams may find it a bit more challenging to assess with core competencies or modern literacies in uncommon situations, but it has its benefits. For example, it gives teams the opportunity to think anew about the ways to teach and assess, and it increases the likelihood that subject-matter content will become the vehicle through which students access critical skills and habits, rather than the more traditional alternative. Too often, teams base assessments on content in isolation, which they can more readily assess with a pencil-and-paper test that has students recall facts and details.

To begin assessing with core competencies or modern literacies, individual teachers will find it beneficial to scan their content standards and first determine whether they would best target skills or literacies in their field, and then determine which skills or literacies naturally fit best within their field. Because such skills and literacies are so robust (they contain many subskills), and they are so central to the discipline (teams revisit them multiple times throughout the year), teams can typically identify two to five target areas for their common assessment work.

Then, just like when teams prioritize with common standards, teams with uncommon standards must clarify their decision-making criteria as they prioritize their standards. The following list provides a common set of five criteria for identifying shared expectations within uncommon content.

1. **Centrality:** The identified literacy or skill is central and thus invaluable to the individual teachers' subject matter. They can readily employ it and assess it in many (if not most) of the units of study within the course. Teachers should never assess students for skills that are not a natural, valuable part of the learning experience.

2. **Universality:** The identified literacy or skill readily, easily, and consistently applies to the disciplines seeking common ground. The processes involved are consistent, even though the content or context in which learners employ them may vary. For example, the problem-solving process *always* involves isolating the problem, identifying the issues involved, creating alternative solutions, selecting a solution to apply, and verifying that the solution solved the problem, no matter the context in which the problem occurred.

3. **Endurance:** The learners' use of the identified literacy or skill is relevant and will transcend coursework and sustain in the field at large. Teams also use this criterion when they prioritize their standards.

4. **Robustness:** The identified literacy or skill includes many steps or a collection of skills and competencies that teams can isolate and assess in multiple media over many occasions and within different units of study for the same course. For example, in a family and consumer science foods course, problem solving can apply in all the following units: kitchen safety, basic food preparation, nutrition, healthy weight management, and foods and fitness; in an agriculture course, problem solving can apply in all the following units: machine safety, technology applications, soil science, plant science, forestry, animal science, pest management, and agribusiness leadership.

5. **Student needs:** Oftentimes, courses that are not directly responsible for reading, writing, or mathematics (such as in subjects like science or social studies or career-based courses) do not have external data from large-scale assessments to help teachers target areas for improvement. Student needs still exist even if there isn't a formal testing mechanism to isolate those needs, and a team's decision on where to focus additional time and energy in its instruction should always be needs based. However, skill-based needs can be identified from the preponderance of evidence teachers accumulate from classroom assessments over an extended period of time or from a broad base of learners. If a team wishes for more concrete evidence before identifying student needs, it can design an assessment for the skill it wishes to explore, the various members can pretest for that skill in their own content areas, and then the pretest data can be used to help identify student needs based on their results.

After teams have agreed on the criteria they will use, they can begin to identify core competencies or modern literacies. Figure 3.6 provides a protocol for identifying core competencies or modern literacies.

Step 1	Identify the courses and subjects that the cross-curricular or multiyear team represents. Create a list of these courses and subjects for all to see.
	Define core competencies and modern literacies, and clarify key terms, possibly including examples of each, so all team members have a shared understanding of the discussion at hand.
Step 2	Invite team members to consider their content areas and identify core competencies and modern literacies. They should brainstorm a list of core competencies, modern literacies, or both that could apply to the various courses represented on the team.
	Ask team members to write each core competency or modern literacy on its own sticky note.
	After a few minutes of individual brainstorming, ask team members to place their sticky notes in a given area (such as on a table or whiteboard).
	Begin to cluster like ideas into common categories.
	Label the common categories.
	Review the categories as a large group. If anything is missing, add it. If you find redundancies, merge them or remove them.
	Note: Identifying interdisciplinary competencies or literacies requires creative thinking. So, unlike the prioritizing standards protocol where the criteria for decision making are shared in advance of selections, teams might choose to brainstorm options first and identify criteria for final selections second. If they know the criteria in advance, it can block creative thinking. Criteria most often refine thinking, not inspire it.
Step 3	Create a comprehensive set of all team members' choices.
	Display a clean set of the identified core competencies and modern literacies to walk through as a team (there will be more than two or three).
Step 4	Establish a guideline regarding the ideal number of core competencies or modern literacies the team desires to employ. Because these are robust enough to include multiple skills, teams may not want to identify more than two or three core competencies and modern literacies.
	Note: It's helpful to have a longer list of options to discuss when searching for common ground in uncommon disciplines, so limiting the number to select happens after brainstorming. Otherwise, team members stop short when brainstorming options and limit the options too early in the process.
Step 5	Prioritize the criteria, and if the team will use a voting process, establish each criterion's value by assigning it a number of points for weighting decisions later. (This step will be helpful when using the reproducible "Template for Prioritizing Standards," page 68.)
Step 6	Narrow or enhance the list in a team discussion.
	Review each core competency or modern literacy), discussing each decision-making criterion per item and noting which criteria best align with each item. Code the items to denote appropriate criteria (see the reproducible "Template for Prioritizing Standards," page 68).
	As a team, select the items (core competencies or modern literacies) that meet the greatest number of the most significant criteria.

Figure 3.6: Protocol for identifying core competencies or modern literacies.

continued →

Step 7	Identify two to three shared core competencies or modern literacies, or a combination of the two.
	Review the resulting list.
	Seek team approval of and commitment to the resulting list.
Step 8	Define each of the identified core competencies or modern literacies (see the reproducible "Template for Identifying Core Competencies or Modern Literacies," page 69).
	Identify the individual skills, components, or steps for each core competency or modern literacy. Define the steps if needed.
	Explore examples of each step or component within the individual disciplines that the team represents. This step ensures that all team members can see how the specific skills fit and can be assessed within their individual content areas.
Step 9	Document final decisions so you can share them with other teams for future discussions on vertical alignment.

*Visit **go.SolutionTree.com/assessment** for a free reproducible version of this figure.*

Teams can use the reproducible "Template for Identifying Core Competencies or Modern Literacies" (page 69), a decision-making tool similar to the protocol in figure 3.4 (pages 47–48), to help them come to agreement on their shared competencies or literacies. The same processes are used to determine what criteria are included and how they are prioritized or weighted for these decisions as those for the decision-making tool in figure 3.4.

Unlike the protocol for prioritizing standards, teams identifying core competencies or modern literacies can skip the process of seeking vertical alignment. However, like the process of sharing agreements for prioritized standards, teams who have adopted core competencies or modern literacies should publish them for ready access in future team meetings and school-wide grade-level, discipline-specific, or interdisciplinary discussions. Eventually, teams will use common *attending tools*—tools that *go with* or *attend* the actual assessment to support the evaluation process (for example, scoring guides, rubrics, or proficiency scales)—and develop assessments to support and monitor their work addressing these skills and literacies. While all teams must eventually create shared measurement tools, interdisciplinary teams will want to begin from this place to ensure their skills and literacies apply to the many individual teachers involved.

So, once the team identifies approximately two to three core competencies or modern literacies, it must break them down into their specific process components, define those components to create consistency from subject to subject, and develop the attending tools that it will use with its assessments to monitor student proficiency. When competencies and literacies meet the criterion of robustness, they have many moving components. For example, a career and technical education (CTE) high school team consisting of automotive, agriculture, woodworking, architecture, and metals teachers in West Delaware Community High

School in Manchester, Iowa, created the four C (concern, cause, correction, and confirmation) problem-solving process (West Delaware CTE Department faculty, personal communication, July 2016) outlined in figure 3.7.

Problem solving = concern + cause + correction + confirmation	
Concern	What is the root of the problem? What makes the problem a concern?
Cause	What variables created or complicate the concern?
Correction	What are some plausible solutions, and which one will best solve the problem?
Confirmation	What evidence do we have or will we generate to ensure our solution accurately addresses the concern and solves the problem?

Source: © 2016 by CTE Department, West Delaware Community Schools, Manchester, Iowa. Adapted with permission.

Figure 3.7: Sample breakdown of the four C problem-solving process.

Their work in creating the four C model and offering clarifying questions for each C within the problem-solving model helped them make the process consistent across their disciplines and transparent for their students to see. It also outlined for them what specific skills they would be able to assess in their individual curricula when engaged in the common assessment process.

Like any robust competency, each of the four Cs in the problem-solving model has its own substeps that can be outlined as a progression to achieving mastery. For example, teams could break down each C in the four C problem-solving process even further. They might break down the skill of isolating a concern into six subskills, as figure 3.8 outlines. The items appear in descending order because the easiest skills are at the bottom of the figure, starting with number 1, and they increase with intensity as the progression increases, making number 6 the most challenging in the list.

> 6. Isolate the variables that the concern impacts, and name the potential impact a possible solution may have on each variable.
>
> 5. Identify the main concern in a complex problem.
>
> 4. Understand where and how concerns fit within the problem-solving process.
>
> 3. Identify concerns in given scenarios.
>
> 2. Determine what criteria will be used to identify something as a concern.
>
> 1. Define *concern.*

Figure 3.8: Breakdown of the subskills of concern in the four C problem-solving process.

The subskills build on one another, outlining the progression of learning required to get to proficiency in the overall problem-solving skill, a skill that all professionals use almost daily in CTE-related fields such as automotive repair, agriculture, woodworking, architecture, and metalsmithing. Teachers can assess each subskill, allowing many opportunities for individual teachers to use common assessments within their respective disciplines regarding problem solving.

Teams engaged in interdisciplinary work do not need to unpack standards together; individually, however, teachers will still need to unpack their particular course standards and expectations to make certain they properly align their curricula to their common core competencies and modern literacies.

Examining School Data and Establishing SMART Goals

PLCs are data driven. They pay attention to both internal and external data regarding their learners' successes and needs. When teams set goals, they do so in the context of student needs that their available assessment measures reveal. Activating common assessments without improvement goals is like moving a football around a field that lacks goalposts. Common assessments operate *in the service of* school-improvement goals.

So, any school wishing to make significant gains in student achievement, whether functioning as a PLC or not, must create SMART goals and then employ common assessments to monitor progress toward their SMART goals along the way; otherwise, they have no way of tracking improvement over time, and their impending success or failure will surprise everyone at the end of the year.

SMART is an acronym, and a simple internet search can reveal many variations of terms. The PLC architects define *SMART* as specific and strategic, measurable, attainable, results oriented, and time bound (Conzemius & O'Neill, 2014; DuFour et al., 2016). Each term serves an important role in creating a clear and purposeful goal. Table 3.3 provides the definition and rationale for each key term.

Each feature of the SMART acronym is significant to a team's overall performance along the way and ultimate success at the end. Goals that incorporate each letter of the acronym may look like the following examples.

- By the end of the 2019–2020 school year, we will increase fifth-grade mathematics scores from 68 percent proficient to 80 percent proficient on the state mathematics test.

- By the end of the 2020–2021 school year, 85 percent of all students will score proficient or higher on all reading assessments (both internal and external measures).

- By the end of the semester, all tenth-grade writing students will score a 3 or higher on the writing rubric for paragraph development.

Table 3.3: Defining the SMART Acronym

Acronym	Terms	Purpose in Creating a Clear and Purposeful Goal
S	Specific and strategic	Goals that are specific help teams clarify *exactly* what they are trying to accomplish. As a frontline feature of improvement, goals should cause stretch and challenge. Goals that target improvements are strategic.
M	Measurable	Quality goals are linked to features that can be measured. A trajectory of improvements in reading, for example, can be measured using assessment results over time. Academic measures are tied to clear and universally accepted criteria for quality. Academic assessments are field tested and approved using industry standards. Improving soft skills like nonverbal communication or attitudes would prove more challenging to measure because there are no definitive, common ways to measure such things.
A	Attainable	Though quality goals are strategic, they are also based in reality. A goal that offers too great a stretch will not be attainable. If the goal is perceived to be unattainable, little effort will be applied from the start.
R	Results oriented	When a goal is results oriented, it leads to the production of data (from the measures) that can be used comparatively to show growth or change over time.
T	Time bound	When a goal is time bound, it promotes increased focus and energy for a limited amount of time. Time-bound goals can generate motivation and commitment. In fact, a goal that is not time bound is more likely an aspiration.

SMART goals can be written at the building level, the team level, or both. In fact, goals are most powerful when they are aligned and they can harness the collective energy and commitment of all staff. When a staff sets a schoolwide goal to improve reading scores overall, each team then writes a SMART goal tied to increasing reading scores at their individual grade level or discipline. For example, if a high school had the SMART goal, *By the end of the 2020–2021 school year, 85 percent of all students will score proficient or higher on all reading assessments (both internal and external measures)*, then each department would set an aligned SMART goal related to their specific contribution for the success of the overall schoolwide goal. A few examples follow.

- **Social studies:** By the end of the 2020–2021 school year, 85 percent of all students will score proficient or higher on comprehension of all nonfiction reading assessments.

- **Science:** By the end of the 2020–2021 school year, 85 percent of all students will score proficient or higher on technical reading with charts and graphs of scientific materials.

In order to make SMART goals actionable, teams must identify the specific learning targets within the goals that they will need to monitor. Teams can only select a few key target areas to monitor, so they must prioritize what will most help them meet their overall goal (Conzemius & O'Neill, 2014). Generally, teams select targets based on the most challenging components of the standards involved within the goal area. Teams identify how challenging something might be by examining testing evidence that isolates areas of weakness or by referencing the teachers' awareness of weaknesses based on past classroom assessments and experiences.

For example, if a team had the SMART goal, *By the end of this semester, 85 percent of our students will have proficient grade-level writing skills*, many different learning targets could support it: topic sentence construction, concluding sentence construction, sentence fluency, organization, idea development, and so on. Imagine that the team selected the following targets to monitor regarding its SMART goal:

> **Precise focus:** States clear, precise focus (thesis, claim, or controlling idea) that demonstrates understanding of the topic or text, accurately represents the discipline, and maintains the focus clearly and consistently throughout the writing
>
> **Development:** Clarifies most relationships among claims, reasons, evidence, and counterclaims, and provides logical reasoning backed with sufficient and relevant data, evidence, or examples from the text (as relevant) to support the claim thoroughly and clearly
>
> **Language and style:** Uses grade-appropriate academic and discipline-specific vocabulary and maintains a consistent, proper tone and style for the field of expertise
>
> **Fluency:** Connects ideas using syntactic variety (varied sentence structures with smooth transitional words and phrases), generating a natural cadence that enhances reader comprehension and interest; minor errors do not interrupt message flow (Erkens et al., 2019, p. 205)

With identified target areas, team members now need to decide which common assessments they will use, when they will use them, and what they will monitor within each target area as they assess it. When it comes to monitoring target areas in the goal-setting process, teams commonly use *cut scores*, cut-off points for what will be deemed sufficient during decision making (for example, if a student scores 80 percent or higher on the assessment, he or she is deemed proficient on the learning targets involved). While that strategy *can* help teams monitor success over time, it also hides many truths or harsh realities. Percentages should not serve as decision-making tools; rather, they should serve as windows into areas that teams need to explore more deeply. A better approach includes establishing cut criteria for taking a deeper look at how the work is advancing. *Cut criteria* include any quality indicators that teams must consider, like levels of proficiency, levels of rigor, and number and types of items correct within a specific skill or target area. There are many different ways to evaluate proficiency, and many different frameworks for rigor and so on. As established previously, when engaged in the *collaborative* common assessment process, teams decide what criteria they deem most important and what levels of proficiency will suffice for each selected criterion.

When considering levels of rigor, for example, teams most frequently use Webb's Depth of Knowledge (DOK) framework (Webb, Alt, Ely, & Vesperman, 2005). This framework offers four different levels of rigor that measure the degree of cognitive complexity a task is requiring students to apply. The levels build in complexity, making level 4, extended thinking, the most rigorous level in the DOK framework, as follows.

1. **Recall and reproduction:** Task requires students to recall facts, details, or information or use the rote application of a simple procedure.

2. **Skills or concepts:** Task requires more than one cognitive step in skills or concepts such as estimating, summarizing, comparing, planning, or representing, to name a few. The multiple steps require students to use information or conceptual knowledge to make decisions along the way.

3. **Strategic thinking and reasoning:** Task involves multiple options to get to solutions, multiple solutions, and multiple rationale for validating thinking. Logic or reasoning is involved as students plan, execute, and defend their response. Students might be asked to solve complex, nonroutine problems, analyze errors within a provided solution, prove an answer right or wrong, or justify their own thinking.

4. **Extended thinking:** Task involves design, synthesis, integration, or exploration of multiple sources or bodies of knowledge across domains or over extensive periods of time. Extended thinking requires extended time. Students might be asked to design and conduct an experiment and then analyze and publish the results, collaborate with peers and coordinate efforts with members of the broader community to solve an authentic problem, or write a literary analysis on a given theme that crosses multiple genres, to name a few options.

So, for example, when a team uses cut criteria regarding rigor in its SMART goal planning, it might assert that a student must be able to complete DOK level 3 tasks with accuracy and a high degree of quality in order to qualify as proficient on the learning targets involved.

Creating an Assessment Road Map and SMART Goal Plans

A great SMART goal can instantly be rendered ineffective in the absence of a solid plan for the measurable and results-oriented features. A true SMART goal, then, is only as *smart* as the road map of assessments created to implement and monitor it. In *Collaborative Common Assessments* (Erkens, 2016), assessment road maps show the sequence of assessments per target that teams will use over time to ensure a high degree of readiness in the formative phases before they evaluate students' degree of proficiency at the summative level. Teams use the road map to help them create the progression of learning and determine where they will place their common assessment work along that progression. Figure 3.9 outlines what an assessment road map might look like for each of the individual targets involved. The *x* in each target indicates a point of assessment.

Common Core State Standards, Reading Informational Texts

Target 1: RI.3.1 Ask and answer questions to demonstrate understanding of a text, referring explicitly to the text as the basis for the answers.

Target 2: Determine the main idea of a text.

Target 3: RI.3.2 Recount the key details and explain how they support the main idea.

Target 4: RI.3.3 Describe the relationship between a series of historical events, scientific ideas or concepts, or steps in technical procedures in a text, using language that pertains to time, sequence, and cause/effect.

Assessments: (H) homework, (CP) checkpoint, (Project) projects, and (Final) final assessments

	H1	H2	H3	CP1	H4	H5	CP2	H6	H7	Project	Final
Target 1	X	X		X					X	X	X
Target 2		X	X	X		X	X			X	X
Target 3			X		X	X	X	X	X	X	X
Target 4					X		X	X	X	X	X

Source: Erkens, 2016, p. 66.

Source for standard: NGA & CCSSO, 2010a.

Figure 3.9: Elementary assessment road map example.

Once a team adds the other targets related to a prioritized standard to the tool in figure 3.9, it can see the big picture or blueprint of its overall assessment plan and can designate which of its assessments will be data gathering points in the common assessment process. In figure 3.9, a team might select only one formative assessment and one summative assessment to be their common assessments for that single target.

SMART goal plans use the agreed-on common assessments from an assessment road map and give them more details related to the SMART goal, outlining the specifics for what to assess (learning targets), when to assess (dates of common assessments), and how to assess (common assessment measures to be used) and then provide a breakdown of what to expect from the results incrementally in order to reach the goal based on cut criteria and acceptable levels of results at that particular stage of the learning process. Figure 3.10 (pages 64–65) offers an example of a completed SMART goal plan (adapted from Conzemius & O'Neill, 2014) for writing.

Note that in a SMART goal plan, teams can use a range of assessments for each target. For example, in figure 3.10 (pages 64–65), collaborative common assessment 1 includes three different assessments—(1) a quality-claims test, (2) a paragraph writing that will cover two targets, and (3) a sentence-fluency test. The reproducible "SMART Goal Plan Template" (pages 70–71) offers a blank version of the template, which teams can alter. A team can have fewer than four learning targets and more than three collaborative common assessments, for example.

Without a very clear assessment road map or plan to make a SMART goal actionable, SMART goals become happy wishes. As the adage says, *What gets monitored is what gets done.*

Monitoring Progress on SMART Goals

The SMART goal plan guides teams in what to monitor over time. Once they outline the specific assessments and establish the criteria, teams must actually track students' progress after using any of the assessments the SMART goal plan includes. Figure 3.11 (page 66) provides a completed example of a SMART goal data-tracking tool. In this example, a team tracks learning targets from its SMART goal plan over time, using CFAs and CSAs. Teams aim to see students' scores for each target area (column 3) increase as they gradually meet their goals over time. In column 4, teams document the decisions they make regarding desired improvements once they analyze scores from one CFA before attempting the next CFA.

The reproducible "SMART Goal Data-Tracking Tool" (page 72) offers a blank data-tracking tool template for ready use. Like with all the other templates in this handbook, the team can modify the number of columns and rows to meet its needs.

SMART goal: By June of 2020, 85 percent of our students will be proficient (level 3 or 4) writers at their grade level (determined by the grade-level rubric).

	Learning Target 1: Precise Focus	Learning Target 2: Development	Learning Target 3: Language and Style	Learning Target 4: Fluency
Collaborative common assessment 1	Quality-claims test	One-paragraph written-response assessment	One-paragraph written-response assessment	Sentence-fluency test
Date	9/30	10/15	10/15	9/20
Cut criteria				
DOK level	2	2	2	2
Proficiency level	2	3	3	2
Other cut criteria (if applicable)	N/A	N/A	N/A	No major errors or omissions in basic sentence structures
Incremental goal (Percentage of students meeting all cut criteria by date of assessment)	70 percent of students meeting all cut criteria by date of assessment	65 percent of students meeting all cut criteria by date of assessment	65 percent of students meeting all cut criteria by date of assessment	70 percent of students meeting all cut criteria by date of assessment
Collaborative common assessment 2	Thesis development in three-paragraph essay	Evidence and supporting details provided in three-paragraph essay	Discipline-specific style and language in three-paragraph essay	Syntactic variety in three-paragraph essay
Date	11/2	11/2	11/2	11/2
Cut criteria				
DOK level	2	3	3	2

Collaborative common assessment 3	Claim in five-paragraph essay	Evidence and supporting details provided in five-paragraph essay	Discipline-specific style and language in five-paragraph essay	Syntactic variety in five-paragraph essay
Proficiency level	3	3	3	3
Other cut criteria (if applicable)	N/A	No major reasoning errors	Discipline-specific terms all accurate	N/A
Incremental goal (Percentage of students meeting all cut criteria by date of assessment)	75 percent of students meeting all cut criteria by date of assessment	70 percent of students meeting all cut criteria by date of assessment	70 percent of students meeting all cut criteria by date of assessment	75 percent of students meeting all cut criteria by date of assessment
Date	12/5	12/5	12/5	12/5

Cut criteria			
DOK level	3	4	3
Proficiency level	3	3	3
Other cut criteria (if applicable)	N/A	N/A	N/A
Incremental goal (Percentage of students meeting all cut criteria by date of assessment)	80 percent of students meeting all cut criteria by date of assessment	75 percent of students meeting all cut criteria by date of assessment	80 percent of students meeting all cut criteria by date of assessment

Source: Adapted from Conzemius & O'Neill, 2014.

Figure 3.10: Sample completed SMART goal plan.

SMART goal: By the end of the school year, 90 percent of our third-grade students will read at grade level.

Target area: Comprehension; students will extract and construct meaning by using prior knowledge, applying text information, and monitoring comprehension while reading grade-level text.

Desired proficiency level for focus area: 90 percent

Learning Targets	Assessment Types and Dates	Team Assessment Results (Total Percentage of Students Passing)	Notes and Next Steps Based on Findings
1. **Summarize and analyze the main idea from informational text using supporting details.**	CFA: 9/15	67	Find the main idea when subtopics are present.
	CFA: 10/15	70	Separate the main idea from supporting details.
	CSA: 10/30	72	Provide more instruction and practice with analysis of details.
2. **Understand and apply knowledge of organizational patterns found in informational text (for example, sequence, description, cause and effect, compare and contrast, and fact and opinion).**	CFA: 9/21	55	Continue providing practice and examples of pattern options.
	CFA: 10/1	53	Separate fact from opinion and cause from effect.
	CFA: 10/16	62	Use graphics to demonstrate patterns.
	CSA: 10/26	67	Use a variety of text types. Keep practicing.
3. **Apply knowledge of text features (for example, indexes, maps, charts, tables, graphs, headings, and subheadings) to locate information and gain meaning from a text.**	CFA: 9/15	71	Create a separate test for text features (not linked to the summarizing test as that seemed to be too much on a single test).
	CSA: 10/5	75	Provide more instruction and practice with charts and graphs.
	CFA: 10/9	74	Provide additional instruction and practice with charts and graphs, and incorporate error analysis so students can identify common errors to avoid.
	CSA: 11/2	82	Revisit maps.

Figure 3.11: Example SMART goal data-tracking tool.

Conclusion

Tracking progress on SMART goals is a critical part of the collaborative common assessment process. Anything less would mean using hope as a strategy, and hope does not increase achievement. Thankfully, the foundational work of the collaborative common assessment process—establishing team norms and commitments for collaboration, identifying and developing shared knowledge of essential learning, examining school data and establishing SMART goals, creating a road map of collaborative assessments and targets, and monitoring progress on SMART goals—helps teams maintain focus and provides all of the parameters needed for future decision making.

When teams take the time to launch their collaborative common assessment process on a firm foundation, they make the critical commitments (through team norms, prioritized standards, and SMART goals) that will frame their future work together and help them more smoothly navigate the challenges they face more smoothly. Moreover, they develop shared understanding along the way and, hopefully, a degree of trust and rapport.

Team Reflections

Take a few moments to reflect on the following questions.

- Do our team norms serve as collective agreements to hold each other safe during challenging conversations? If so, how do we know that's true? How could we check for that reality without assuming it to be true? If not, how, when, or with whom would we create those collective agreements?

- Do we always launch our work from the place of shared commitments and shared responsibility? If not, what steps could we take in that direction?

- How can we be certain we have clarity about our priority standards? What do we need to do if we don't have such clarity?

- What skills or literacies could we assess on a schoolwide basis?

- How have we aligned our common assessment process to our priority standards and SMART goals?

Template for Prioritizing Standards

Directions: Identify your decision-making criteria, and place each criterion in the appropriate column. Consider using the Other column for write-in criteria when the process illuminates that criteria might have been missing from the original list. If desired, assign points to each predetermined criterion based on its value (for example, three points for endurance, two points for leverage, and three points for student needs) as determined by the team. Fill in the standards to discuss, and then work as a team on the document together or distribute it to each team member to fill out prior to the team conversation.

Standards	Team Criteria and Assigned Value					
	Endurance ____ points	Leverage ____ points	Readiness for the Next Level of Learning ____ points	Testing Requirements ____ points	Student Needs ____ points	Other ____ points	Total ____ points

Template for Identifying Core Competencies or Modern Literacies

Directions: Identify your decision-making criteria, and place each criterion in the appropriate column. Consider using the Other column for write-in criteria when the process illuminates criteria that might have been missing from the original list. If desired, assign points to each predetermined criterion based on its value (for example, three points for endurance, two points for leverage, and three points for student needs) as determined by the team. Fill in the core competencies or modern literacies to discuss, and then work as a team on the document together or distribute the document to each team member to fill out prior to the team conversation.

| Core Competencies or Modern Literacies | Team Criteria and Assigned Value | | | | | |
	Centrality ____ points	Universality ____ points	Endurance ____ points	Robustness ____ points	Student Needs ____ points	Other ____ points	Total ____ points

SMART Goal Plan Template

SMART goal:

	Learning Target 1:	Learning Target 2:	Learning Target 3:	Learning Target 4:
Collaborative common assessment 1				
Date				
Cut criteria				
DOK level				
Proficiency level				
Other cut criteria (if applicable)				
Incremental goal (Percentage of students meeting all cut criteria by date of assessment)				

Collaborative common assessment 2				
Date				
Cut criteria				
DOK level				
Proficiency level				
Other cut criteria (if applicable)				
Incremental goal (Percentage of students meeting all cut criteria by date of assessment)				
Collaborative common assessment 3				
Date				
Cut criteria				
DOK level				
Proficiency level				
Other cut criteria (if applicable)				
Incremental goal (Percentage of students meeting all cut criteria by date of assessment)				

Source: Adapted from Conzemius & O'Neill, 2014.

References

Conzemius, A. E., & O'Neill, J. (2014). *The handbook for SMART school teams: Revitalizing best practices for collaboration* (2nd ed.). Bloomington, IN: Solution Tree Press.

SMART Goal Data-Tracking Tool

SMART goal: _____

Focus area: _____

Desired proficiency level for focus area: _____

Learning Targets	Assessment Types and Dates	Team Assessment Results (Total Percentage of Students Passing)	Notes and Next Steps Based on Findings

4

The Design Phase

Designing assessments is serious business. Just as a builder would never attempt to construct a house without an architectural blueprint, so should a teacher or a teacher team never design assessments without serious preplanning and consideration of each assessment's role in the comprehensive determination of student mastery.

The work can seem tedious, maybe even laborious, for the inexperienced or untrained. But the benefits—direct and clear pathways to assessing standards, relevant evidence for ready decision making about next steps, valid and reliable data when reporting achievement against the standards, and increased student investment in the assessment process—significantly outweigh the costs. Fortunately, time, practice, experience, and multiple eyes attending to detail can make the process faster, easier, and more accurate with time and experience. The collaborative common assessment design process includes unpacking and repacking standards; creating summative assessments, attending tools, and formative pathways; and vetting and approving assessments for quality.

Reviewing the Assessment Design Process

The preparation phase serves as the foundation to all of the other phases in the collaborative common assessment process. It is absolutely central to the design phase. Once teams know their priority standards, their learning targets from within those standards, their criteria for quality on student performances, the methods of assessment design that will be needed, and the attending tools (like rubrics or proficiency scales) that will need to be developed to support their desired outcomes on their SMART goal plans, they are ready to consider designing their assessments.

Simply *knowing* the assessment road maps and SMART goal plans is helpful for individual teachers to make decisions on how best to approach their instruction, but it is insufficient for getting great results. A team's ability to increase student achievement levels depends on how well it designs the assessments named within its road maps in advance of providing the instruction.

So, the design phase has a preparatory nature to it, but it is where the work of unit design and instructional planning actually begin. Figure 1.2 (page 15), the pictorial representation of the collaborative common assessment process, shows the design phase as sitting on top of the preparation phase and involving the process of further clarifying standards before writing the actual assessments. Teachers and their learners are at a distinct disadvantage when the most significant assessments are developed during or near the conclusion of a unit of study.

Wiggins and McTighe (2005) recommend that teachers design backward, using their standards as guideposts and then designing the assessments that will accurately produce sufficient and acceptable evidence of the required learning, long before planning the curriculum or instructional strategies they will use to teach the standards. The design phase for common assessments always begins with the priority standards. In Wiggins and McTighe's (2005) backward design model, it is important to understand the standards first, from the small, unpacked parts that inform the learning targets to the essence of the comprehensive, repacked picture.

Modern standards (like Next Generation Science Standards, National Curriculum Standards for Social Studies, Common Core State Standards, updated state standards, or 21st century skill–oriented standards) incorporate critical competencies and literacies, making them sophisticated, multifaceted, and complex. The assessment road map, highlighting the formative or summative pathway and delineating the summative assessments, offers teachers one of the first steps to designing backward: clarity on the desired results and the types and timing of assessments needed to get there. With summative assessments in place, teachers can more accurately and easily shape and reshape small formative assessments as the unit unfolds if they have already determined the parameters delineating their purpose in advance. Figure 4.1 outlines ten steps to the assessment design process. Teams engage in more comprehensive assessment design when they create an assessment road map.

Step 1	Unpack the standards into the learning targets in order to isolate the instructional components, clarify key terms, and ultimately reveal the formative assessments pathway.
Step 2	Create the learning targets. Make sure they are manageable in number and clear in terminology. It helps to put the targets in student-friendly language.
Step 3	Repack the standards, and bundle them with like standards in order to create the summative assessments. Always plan to write the summative assessments before the formative assessments.
Step 4	Establish the required levels of rigor.
Step 5	Clarify criteria for quality assessment design.
Step 6	Develop an assessment road map delineating the formative or summative assessments pathway.
Step 7	Create summative assessments. Many standards require more than one summative assessment (for example, "participate in a range of conversations"). Teams always need to have sufficient summative assessment evidence (produced over time) so they can comfortably certify levels of proficiency.
Step 8	Create any required attending tools (such as rubrics, scales, checklists, or scoring guides). The attending tools clarify the quality criteria that the team will monitor during the assessment experience and the proficiency levels that it will determine throughout the assessment process.
Step 9	Create formative assessments. Modify or continue to create formative assessments once the unit has begun, but begin with an initial sense of where the unit will need the formative assessments and what they might need to look like.
Step 10	Design student engagement processes and tools. It is important to create all tools in advance of instruction.

Figure 4.1: Steps for the macro level of the assessment design process.

Unpacking Standards

Standards can be lengthy and challenging to interpret, so it is necessary to unpack them into the many smaller parts that comprise the entire standard or domain of standards. Protocols for unpacking standards often stop short of clarifying the assessment design, but it is the assessment design that will help teams *see* the standards in action. Figure 4.2 (pages 76–78) offers a protocol to unpack standards in a manner that begins to frame the assessment road map that will need to accompany the standards.

Begin with the big picture. Select a standard domain to target your work (for example, Reading: Informational Text). This could be a single standard, a standard complete with its subtext or bulleted components (the cluster of standards), or a set of standards within a category (for example, all standards related to nonfiction reading). Examine the requirements involved. In many cases, it is best to unpack a standard's or standards' content using processes such as those outlined in the following protocol. Note that in some cases, however, you'll select a standard that is heavily laden with content, and unpacking in those instances only creates additional confusion, as things start to seem redundant or disconnected. In that case, it's best to step back and look at the overall standard first and see if you can identify the essence of the standard in a single sentence or even a title of three words or fewer.

Step 1	Read the entire cluster of standards within the domain, and come to agreement on what it means when everything is put together. What evidence would students have to produce, and at what level of rigor would the assessment tasks need to be in order to meet the entirety of the standard? *Name* the desired level of complexity for the overall standard. If helpful, write the appropriate DOK level (or reference other models for labeling rigor) next to the main verbs, but determine the final level by looking at the entire standard's combined parts. *Note: A single verb—the starting words of standards like* engage, identify, explain, *and so on—can often be addressed at all four levels of rigor in the DOK framework.* *Hint: It's important to make certain that significant parts of the standard will require higher-level reasoning (DOK level 3 or 4).*
Step 2	**Highlight (or circle)** all the verbs. What will students need to do to complete this standard? *Note: Standards sometimes hide the verb, so you may need to write it in. For example, at almost every grade level in the Speaking and Listening standards, students must "engage effectively in a range of collaborative discussions" (NGA & CCSSO, 2010a). But* engage *is not the main verb. Teams must decide if the main verb is* discuss *or* collaborate *or something different and then write that main verb near the word* engage. *Hint: Use the verbs to determine the assessment method.*
Step 3	**Underline** any part of the standard that you believe will require direct instruction in order for students to be successful. This can include verbs you've already circled, new knowledge components, or reasoning processes. If the team disagrees on whether something will require direct instruction, place a *double underline* under that idea. *Note: Double underlines indicate where teams need to use small preassessments in order to gather evidence for decision making. Healthy teams use data, not opinions or prior experiences, to make important instructional decisions.* *Hint: Underlines denote the places that teams will likely want to place the formative assessments.*

Step 4	**Bold (or star)** any skills in the standard that require direct observation. You will specifically watch or listen for these items with each student during a performance task (for example, making eye contact during a speech, speaking in a foreign language with fluency, and so on). If you can evaluate a skill in the final product (for example, a completed product like a research report, a lab report, a model built to scale, and so on), do not put a star next to it. *Note: You may find standards that have no stars in them.* *Hint: Starred or bolded features require performance assessments and a set of quality criteria and clear proficiency levels incorporated into rubrics for evaluation purposes.*
Step 5	**Italicize (or box)** any items or quality indicators that need to be part of required products (if any) for standard completion (for example, a lab report with data displays). *Note: Many standards do not delineate the specific products that students must develop.* *Hint: These are performance assessments that result in products and will require a set of quality criteria and clear proficiency levels incorporated into rubrics for evaluation purposes.*
Step 6	**Identify** the context and the content that you will use to teach and assess the standard. • *Context:* Where does the standard fit in the sequence of instruction? What broader relationships does this standard have (for example, Does it have a connection to technology? Will it create a base for future learning? Or does it interconnect with other standards?)? • *Content:* Which subject or units will the standard involve? What content will students study with the skills at hand, or what skills must they practice with the content at hand?
Step 7	**Create** student-friendly learning targets for the content and process standards involved. *Note: Keep the number of targets to a manageable few. It's helpful to list and rank the targets from hardest at the top to easiest at the bottom and then use the top (hardest) targets for the overall student learning targets, as the lower-level targets are often already included within the harder ones.*
Step 8	**Develop** a brief description of a summative assessment needed to measure student learning on the standards selected. *Note: It is important to have more than one data point of reference when certifying proficiency levels.* *Hint: When teams revisit a standard through multiple assessment opportunities, learners have the option to improve over time. When students can demonstrate learning multiple times, it makes feedback more likely to feed forward.*

Figure 4.2: A protocol for unpacking standards.

continued →

Step 9	**Write** a brief description for the assessment road map of scaffolded assessments (summative, formative, and individual, and which of these will serve as the common assessments) that will both offer valuable insight into student readiness and provide a clear vision of additional instruction and assessment supports so learners will have success with the overall summative assessment. Add any sense of a timeline you need to make it all manageable.
	Note: Not all assessments need be common assessments. Team members can add more assessments than what they have identified in the map, or modify the existing assessments in the map to best meet their needs in supporting their students' ability to achieve mastery on the common summative. The assessment road map lays out the formative assessment scaffolding needed for student success. Team members can have more than one summative assessment (for example, a pencil-and-paper test, a performance task, and so on) as they seek sufficient evidence to certify mastery.
	Hint: Select the common formative assessments that will best help team members, at strategic moments, capture the most helpful information to support advancing student learning overall. Create the common summative assessment that will provide the most sufficient and accurate evidence to evaluate student proficiency in the standards being assessed.

*Visit **go.SolutionTree.com/assessment** for a free reproducible version of this figure.*

Teams must collaboratively complete the unpacking process when they strive to develop common assessments. They make many key decisions along the way that can lend both clarity and collective commitment to the task at hand. Figure 4.3 provides an example of what an unpacked standard might look like—in this case, Common Core English language arts (ELA) standard SL.8.1 (NGA & CCSSO, 2010a)—after a team follows steps 1–5 in the unpacking protocol.

It's important to note that many decisions made in the unpacking process will vary from one team to the next, and there is no one right answer. For example, one team might think the main verb of Common Core Speaking and Listening standard 8.1 is *discuss* while another team might think the main verb is *collaborate*. Clearly, how a team interprets the standard will alter both what and how it assesses.

Moving on to step 6 of the unpacking protocol, teams identify the context and content for the assessments that will measure the Common Core Speaking and Listening standard. From the first line, the standard makes it clear that the assessment road map will involve more than one summative assessment, as students must discuss one-on-one, in groups, and in teacher-led situations. Likewise, substandard SL.8.1b indicates that students must have the ability to follow the various rules and roles of different discussion formats. Certainly, teams will need to assess Speaking and Listening standard 8.1 multiple times over the course of many different subjects and possibly even different courses.

Standard to address: SL.8.1

SL.8.1: <u>Engage</u> (discuss) **effectively** in a range of collaborative discussions (**one-on-one, in groups, and teacher-led**) . . . on grade 8 topics, texts, and issues, **building on** others' ideas and expressing their own clearly.

- **SL.8.1a:** Come (prepare) to <u>discussions prepared</u>, having <u>read</u> or <u>researched</u> material under study; **explicitly draw on that preparation by referring to evidence on the topic, text, or issue to probe and reflect on ideas under discussion**.
- **SL.8.1b:** <u>Follow</u> rules for collegial discussions and **decision-making**, track progress <u>toward specific goals and deadlines</u>, and define individual *roles* as needed.
- **SL.8.1c:** **Pose questions** that connect the ideas of several speakers and **respond to others'** questions and comments with **relevant evidence, observations, and ideas**.
- **SL.8.1d:** **Acknowledge new information expressed by others**, and, when warranted, **qualify or justify** their own views **in light of the evidence presented**.

DOK: Collectively, the standard requires DOK levels 3 and 4 tasks. Move from level 3 to level 4 over time.

Source for standard: NGA & CCSSO, 2010a.

Figure 4.3: An unpacked Speaking and Listening standard.

Creating the Learning Targets

When teams are deep into unpacking standards, they can more readily find and name the learning targets. Especially when dealing with modern standards, it's important to note that targets fall into two different categories: (1) specific and (2) strategic. Specific targets are content laden. They identify exactly what the student needs to know (for example, *I can identify the capital cities of all U.S. states or Canadian provinces*). Strategic targets are skill or process oriented. They identify exactly what a student needs to be able to do (for example, *Evaluate resources to determine which best support your investigation*). Many modern standards work to incorporate both specific and strategic learning expectations.

As noted in the unpacking process, targets are not always easy to understand, even for the adults. So, in step 7 in the protocol for unpacking standards, teams must develop student-friendly targets from the unpacked standard. In general, targets begin with the circled or highlighted verbs in a standard or cluster of standards. Too many targets, however, become unwieldy for teachers and especially students to monitor over time. Nicole Dimich Vagle (2015) recommends teams prioritize their learning targets by listing them, placing the easiest at the bottom and the hardest at the top, and then sharing the top targets from the ladder of targets with students. (Figure 4.4, page 80, features a ladder for prioritizing learning targets.) Most often, the targets listed at the bottom of the ladder are embedded in the more robust targets at the top of the ladder.

Step 1: List targets in ladder form, from easiest at the bottom to hardest at the top.

Hardest _____

_____

_____

_____

_____

_____

_____

_____

Easiest _____

Step 2: Select a manageable number of targets (the team determines what it considers *manageable*—usually three to six or so) from the top of the ladder.

Source: Adapted from Vagle, 2015.

Figure 4.4: Ladder for prioritizing, selecting, and framing learning targets.

Many different theories and frameworks for writing learning targets exist (Chappuis, 2014; Fisher & Frey, 2011; Marzano, 2009; Moss & Brookhart, 2012), but in the end, every expert agrees that teachers must write the learning targets in student-friendly terms, making them *visible* to the learners (Hattie, 2009). High-quality learning targets have many different criteria. Some of the more prominent criteria for designing high-quality learning targets include the following.

- Learning targets must be focused and few.

- Learning targets must appear in student-friendly language.

- Learning targets must maintain academic language, so they must clarify key terms in student-friendly ways.

- Learning targets should have enough specificity that they clarify exact expectations for what the learner needs to know or be able to do.

- Learning targets are best framed in robust (multifaceted and increasingly challenging) ways that allow students to monitor growth over time (not just once).

- Learning targets are best when written in generalizable-enough terms that they can be revisited in multiple contexts or settings over time. The targets are *specific* to the standard, but not so specific that they can only be applied once. For example, the target "I can follow the identified rules of a conversation" can be used with debate, Socratic seminar, forums, and so on, whereas the target "I can follow the rules of debate," will only ever be usable in a debate unit, which is seldom repeated.

Note that it's also helpful when learning targets embed the rationale for their importance directly into the target language.

Experts consistently agree that students must be able to see their learning expectations in the form of targets (Chappuis, 2014; Hattie, 2009; Wiliam, 2011, 2018). But this does *not* mean that teachers must always post the target in advance of instruction. In fact, many times the target is best understood when discovered during the learning process and then clarified with student involvement in naming the standard. For example, a teacher might say, "We've been observing the concept of evaporation. What do you think would be most important for us to understand as a class about that concept? How could we write that as a learning expectation to guide our thinking during this unit of study?" Then, the teacher invites students to co-create the target. Even in this scenario, however, individual team members would need to agree *in advance of instruction* what those learning targets would need to be. Toward that end, teams define learning targets together, and then individual teachers work to ensure their students understand those targets in whatever form the teacher would like to use. Varying how learning targets are shared in the classroom can keep the process fresh for students.

Just as there is no one way to unpack a standard, there is no one right way to develop learning targets. What's most important is that teams write the targets so students and teachers alike find them accessible, and teams use them to guide instructional maneuvers as well as assessment design. The following list provides examples of how a team might develop a manageable number of clear and trackable student-friendly learning targets for the standard that figure 4.3 (page 79) unpacks. These targets would permit learners to grow over time and across multiple discussion contexts.

- **I can exchange ideas:** This means I can build on the ideas that others offer by using their words or paraphrasing their ideas before I add my own. When I add my own ideas, I can qualify what I mean and justify my accuracy by using evidence from outside sources that shows I have connected to experts' work.

- **I can come prepared:** This means I will read and research in advance of the discussion and I will show my preparedness by citing the evidence that I encountered when I was preparing.

- **I can propel and maintain the focus in a conversation:** This means I can pose questions and respond to others in a way that invites the conversation to continue or go deeper while always staying on topic.

- **I can follow the identified rules:** This means I will follow the rules that have been set that will guide our discussion.

- **I can use my assigned role:** This means I will use my assigned role to help the conversation remain on track and to interact appropriately with the other assigned roles within the group.

The bolded sections of the bulleted list comprise the actual learning target. Note that they are specific, generalizable, and put in student-friendly terms. Together, the target list comprises the essence of the entire standard. The additional explanation behind each target helps students understand the academic language (like *engage* or *prepare*) while also weaving in significant parts of the standard to lend clarity to what each target must look like in action. The conversation about learning targets can also help teams begin to immediately see the long-term assessment plan as well as the short-term, immediate needs that they must address to help learners succeed.

Steps 8 and 9 of the unpacking protocol require teams to take the long view of the standards over a year's time frame, a semester's time frame, a quarter or trimester's time frame, and even over a unit's time frame. Because the standards incorporate competencies and literacies that can take incredible periods of time to teach and assess, teams must determine where in the curriculum to place summative assessments within the expected time frame before developing them and determining the formative assessment pathway.

Repacking and Bundling Standards

Unpacking a standard helps teachers understand the standard itself while isolating the discrete details. Ultimately, though, teachers must repack the standard to ensure they see the full picture as they design the summative assessments. In the summative assessment, teachers should not be assessing details in call-and-response formats (such as the pencil-and-paper test). Instead, they should be developing more authentic assessments that bring the standards to life.

When teams repack a standard with an eye to the comprehensiveness and the duration of the standard, they can design assessments that scaffold skills over time. And, with modern standards which are heavily process oriented, teams may choose to bundle standards, especially when and where content knowledge would be helpful. Imagine, for example, that the social studies team bundles their content standards regarding the American Revolution with the nonfiction reading standards and the argumentation writing standards. Frankly, there just isn't enough time to teach one standard at a time anymore.

The processes of repacking and bundling standards are critical at the point of designing summative assessments, which precede the development of the formative assessment pathway.

Repacking Standards

Repacking a standard means teachers take the targets they've developed back to the comprehensive standard in order to ensure they will assess the *essence* of the standard. Too often, teachers assess the unpacked standard both formatively and summatively while it is still disassembled into the discrete components. When that happens, learners miss the big picture of the standard, because the unpacked standard outlines details. Teachers can create space for more performance-based assessments in the summative assessment if they opt out of isolating and assessing the more discrete learning targets, especially if they were able to gather evidence of proficiency in the required knowledge and skills earlier in the unit of study. So, teachers must work together to repack a standard so they can design a summative assessment that aligns with the *essence* of the entire standard. Put another way, think of a standard like a pomegranate: the team must break it apart in order for the learner to reap the benefits of the smaller, sweet seeds within, but if the learner never sees the whole pomegranate, he or she will have an incomplete or inaccurate view of what a pomegranate actually is.

During the unpacking and repacking process, teachers examine the whole standard and unpack it into smaller targets (to inform their formative assessment pathway so they can assess the discrete details), and then, once they more fully understand the standard and agree on it, teachers repack the standard in order to design the summative assessment. In the absence of this step, the resulting design for the summative assessment will feel unnatural and long as it assesses every detail, and in the end, neither teachers nor their learners will have any real evidence that the learners can contextualize the learning and solve real-world problems in authentic ways.

If teachers don't repack a standard into the comprehensive standard, they could end up using an entire selected-response assessment to assess each discrete detail of just one loaded standard. The assessment process becomes unwieldy and inauthentic. For example, the fourth-grade Common Core mathematics standard 4.MD.A.2 would seem enormous all by itself:

> Use the four operations to solve word problems involving distances,
> intervals of time, liquid volumes, masses of objects, and money,

including problems involving simple fractions or decimals, and problems that require expressing measurements given in a larger unit in terms of a smaller unit. Represent measurement quantities using diagrams such as number line diagrams that feature a measurement scale. (NGA & CCSSO, 2010b, p. 31)

Instead, a teacher should assess the smaller parts during the formative assessment pathway to ensure the learners understand all aspects of the standard. If the teacher did not repack the standard summatively, he or she would need a sufficient sample size (four or five questions) for *each* operation (addition, subtraction, division, and multiplication) in *each* measure (distance, time, volume, mass, and money), employing fractions *and* decimals, and so on.

Bundling Standards

Bundling standards involves putting key standards together within the domain area or across several domains or disciplines for the assessment. Robust performance assessments typically repack *and* bundle similar or complementary standards in a manner that will generate a more authentic application for the learners, creating the relevance so vital to student interest and motivation. For example, mathematics can feel inauthentic when students only solve algorithm after algorithm on paper. At a very young age, students can likely guess that real mathematicians do not practice algorithms in isolation; instead, they use mathematics to solve real problems. Imagine the fourth-grade team decided to bundle the following Common Core mathematics standards (NGA & CCSSO, 2010b) from the following domains.

- **Measurement and Data:** "Know relative sizes of measurement units within one system of units" (4.MD.A.1; NGA & CCSSO, 2010b, p. 31).

- **Operations and Algebraic Thinking:** "Generate a number or shape pattern that follows a given rule. Identify apparent features of the pattern that were not explicit in the rule itself" (4.OA.C.5; NGA & CCSSO, 2010b, p. 29).

- **Geometry:** "Understand that shapes in different categories (e.g., rhombuses, rectangles, and others) may share attributes (e.g., having four sides), and that the shared attributes can define a larger category (e.g., quadrilaterals). Recognize rhombuses, rectangles, and squares as examples of quadrilaterals, and draw examples of quadrilaterals that do not belong to any of these subcategories" (3.G.A.1; NGA & CCSSO, 2010b, p. 26); "Correctly name shapes regardless of their orientations or overall size" (K.G.A.2; NGA & CCSSO, 2010b, p. 12).

- **Number and Operations—Fractions:** "Understand a fraction 1/*b* as the quantity formed by 1 part when a whole is partitioned into *b* equal parts; understand a fraction *a*/*b* as the quantity formed by *a* parts of size 1/*b*" (3.NF.A.1; NGA & CCSSO, 2010b, p. 24).

Imagine, too, that they also incorporated two additional features: (1) the standard for mathematical practice "Make sense of problems and persevere in solving them" (MP1; NGA & CCSSO, 2010b, p. 6); and (2) the fourth-grade reading informational text standard "Interpret information presented visually, orally, or quantitatively (e.g., in charts, graphs, diagrams, time lines, animations, or interactive elements on Web pages) and explain how the information contributes to an understanding of the text in which it appears" (RI.4.7; NGA & CCSSO, 2010b, p. 14).

Using this bundle, the fourth-grade team might design a multistep task in which students first need to work together to solve the problem before producing an individual product to demonstrate personal knowledge and skill, as in the following example.

- **Step 1:** Use the nonfiction passage provided for guidance on how to build a LEGO robot. (Includes nonfiction standard.)

- **Step 2:** As a team, build a simple LEGO robot that meets the provided specifications for shape and size and that will travel at the given speed and navigate corners. (Includes nonfiction standard, measurement and data standard, geometry standard, operations and algebraic thinking standard, and standard for mathematical practice to persevere to solve problems.)

- **Step 3:** As a team, create a path for the robot to travel that meets the provided specifications. (Includes nonfiction standard, measurement and data standard, operations and algebraic thinking standard, number and operations to solve problems standard, geometry standard, and standard for mathematical practice to persevere to solve problems.)

- **Step 4:** As a team, navigate your simple LEGO robot through the travel path in a given period of time. Make adjustments as needed.

- **Step 5:** Individually, explain your team's mathematical processes in writing. Justify why your mathematical processes did or did not work as intended.

In the simple LEGO robot task, every part of each bundled standard cannot be assessed fully. Fortunately, with clarity regarding the demands of the summative assessment and the specificity of the learning targets from each standard that are not included in the summative task, the collaborative teacher team will now be able to develop the formative assessments they will need to gauge student readiness on the specifics of the standards that will be involved.

Designing the Summative and Formative Assessment Pathway

With summative assessments in place, teachers can then revisit the discrete targets to determine where they might need additional evidence to ensure students understand all parts of the standard *before* they encounter the summative tasks. The unpacked learning targets form the scaffolding to success that allows teachers to gather the required evidence that students have the necessary skills to engage in the final task.

Teams can use the reproducible "Assessment Pathway Planning Template" (pages 115–117) as a bridge between the unpacking protocol and the final assessment road map. The pathway planning template helps teachers use their coding and symbols from the unpacking process to keep all of the assessments (formative and summative) aligned to the standards involved. The tool is only used to help teachers clarify their assessment plans. Students typically do not see the pathway plan—at least in this form. If they have a data-tracking document for the unit of study, the assessments on the assessment pathway may be included on it, but the specificity of which assessments are common, and so on, would not be included on that map.

The bundled and repacked standards form the basis for the summative assessments, which teams design first. After they do that, teams can outline a pathway to lead students to success on the summative assessments. In figure 4.5, the team uses the first column to decide whether the smaller assessments are formative or summative in nature (the pathway to success can include small summative assessments as certification checkpoints, so it is possible to have both along the way), and whether the planned assessments will be common assessments. On the pathway, only key checkpoints need to be common, so the team will have to decide where the key points for checking readiness will occur. The template is set up so the symbols the teachers used during the unpacking step (using the code that figure 4.2, pages 76–78, describes) help the team make informed design decisions as it goes on to map out its assessment pathway. The team can add rows to the template to accommodate as many formative and summative assessments as needed.

Teams have no algorithm or formula when it comes to creating a comprehensive assessment pathway; there is no right answer for the number, frequency, or type of assessments. But because modern standards are so robust, they may require many formative assessments to (1) ensure learners' readiness and (2) sample learners' capacity to do the specific parts that the comprehensive summative assessment might not include.

Likewise, there is no rule or formula for how many of the teams' assessments will need to be common. Teams are tasked with making important decisions at this juncture and, as they do so, they must factor in the content and context for the learning, the readiness of the learners, and even the instructional styles of the team members. The quantity, length, timing, and placement of the assessments all matter greatly—a significant and compelling reason why teachers benefit from operating in teams during the process. Together, they can ensure that their expert opinions of the standards' demands and their individual learners' needs create a supportive, comprehensive, and equitable learning opportunity for students.

Figure 4.5 provides an example of what a completed assessment planning template might look like, but the sample shows only a partial representation, as the map would need far more formative assessments than the sample represents. The sample illustrates an unpacked Speaking and Listening standard; the learning targets that emerged from the unpacking process, which the learners would monitor over time; a bundling of the Speaking and Listening standard with social studies content; a list of planned summative assessments (spread out over the course of a year); and early indications of the formative assessment pathway teachers will employ to ensure students can successfully engage in the summative assessments. Note that the bundled social studies standards portions listed in the example are not actual standards from specific standards documents. Instead, they are created examples that capture the essence of content standards and reflect a numbering system similar to what teachers are familiar with seeing. The sample numbering, meant to reflect an isolated portion of a standard, illustrates how a teacher does not need to assess every detail of a standard cluster summatively.

Once teams have the big-picture map of the summative and the accompanying formative assessments, they can consider the formal design, including the development of all the necessary attending tools, of the individual assessments.

Standards
- **SL.8.1:** Engage effectively in a range of collaborative discussions (one-on-one, in groups, and teacher-led) on grade 8 topics, texts, and issues, building on others' ideas and expressing their own clearly.
- **SL.8.1a:** Come to discussions prepared, having read or researched material under study; explicitly draw on that preparation by referring to evidence on the topic, text, or issue to probe and reflect on ideas under discussion.
- **SL.8.1b:** Follow rules for collegial discussions and decision making, track progress toward specific goals and deadlines, and define individual roles as needed.
- **SL.8.1c:** Pose questions that connect the ideas of several speakers and respond to others' questions and comments with relevant evidence, observations, and ideas.
- **SL.8.1d:** Acknowledge new information expressed by others, and, when warranted, qualify or justify their own views in light of the evidence presented.

Figure 4.5: Sample completed assessment pathway planning template for an eighth-grade Speaking and Listening standard.

continued →

Student-Friendly Target Language

- **I can exchange ideas:** This means I can build on the ideas that others offer by using their words or paraphrasing their ideas before I add my own. When I add my own ideas, I can qualify what I mean and justify my accuracy by using evidence from outside sources that shows I have connected to experts' work.

- **I can come prepared:** This means I will read and research in advance of the discussion and I will show my preparedness by citing the evidence that I encountered when I was preparing.

- **I can propel and maintain the focus in a conversation:** This means I can pose questions and respond to others in a way that invites the conversation to continue or go deeper while always staying on topic.

- **I can follow the identified rules:** This means I will follow the rules that have been set that will guide our discussion.

- **I can use my assigned role:** This means I will use my assigned role to help the conversation remain on track and to interact appropriately with the other assigned roles within the group.

Notes Regarding the Summative Assessment Plan

- Collectively, the Speaking and Listening standards will take a full year and will be bundled with the relevant social studies content standards.

- Different types of discussions with various rules and roles will be required and one major discussion experience will be offered each quarter.

- The content standards can range from DOK level 1–4 tasks, but the speaking and listening tasks will need to be at the DOK level 3, moving to DOK level 4 by the end of the year.

- In each discussion task, there will be two different topics so that the class can be divided in half, making it easier to conduct observations with smaller groups. The topics of those discussions must each be linked to the provided content standards, but the second topic cannot parrot the first. The group of students *not* participating in the topic of discussion will also observe discussion skills (assigned features like number of quotes, paraphrases, academic transitions, and so on) and report their findings regarding the discussion.

Summative assessments for this standard: Connected to our history unit standards; one major speaking and listening task per quarter required

Quarter 1, History standards portions to be included in the speaking and listening task:

2. Explain the historical era and themes from the American Revolution, including the individuals, groups, and ideas, and analyze their relationships between and among one another.

    c. Analyze causes and effects of major conflicts during the American Revolution (DOK levels 1–3).

Summative assessment 1: Debate

- Topic 1: At what point is civil war justifiable?

- Topic 2: Knowing what we know now, is there a way to avoid civil war and improve civil discord navigation?

Quarter 2, Geography standards portions to be included in the speaking and listening task:

2. Explain how both conflict and cooperation can occur over space and resources.

    a. Analyze how patterns of human population, interdependence, cooperation, and conflict are shaped by the interaction of economic, political, cultural, and social processes. (DOK levels 1–3).

Summative assessment 2: Pinwheel discussions

- Topic 1: How might geography divide a community?

- Topic 2: Do racial lines make geographical sense? Where do history and civics fit in the conversation of geographical change?

Quarter 3, Economics standards portions to be included in the speaking and listening task:

3. Understand how various societies allocate scarce resources through analysis of public policy, market interaction, and individual choice.

   a. Identify international differences in resources, productivity, and prices and the impact of those allocated resources on international trade (DOK levels 1–2).

Summative assessment 3: Juried forums

- Inner-circle A discussion: Scarcity thinking with abundant resources
- Inner-circle B discussion: Abundance thinking with scarce resources

Quarter 4, Civics standards to be included in the speaking and listening task:

4. Evaluate and practice rights, roles, and responsibilities of productive and contributing citizens.

   a. Analyze and give examples of the expansion of rights and the ever-changing definition of citizenship. (DOK levels 1–3).

Summative assessment 4: Socratic seminar

- Inner-circle A discussion: Cyberbullying
- Inner-circle B discussion: Digital footprints

Group discussion activities will take place over the course of a semester, and teachers will integrate them with the content of study at that time. These activities include two discussion topics (teachers can add more as needed) so that the group can be divided and pay more specific attention to details and scoring. Teachers will score each group discussion with the same rubrics, and each discussion will conclude with a written essay, which teachers can use to score achievement on the writing standards (not represented here) and which can provide concrete reflection of the ideas the students had during the discussion.

Details of Assessment Role in the Overall Map	Connection to the Standard (such as the specific targets included in the assessment) *See circled and underlined text from the unpacked standard.*	Proficiency Scales, Quality Criteria, Rubrics, or Other Tools Needed to Support Evaluation Processes *See boxed or starred text from the unpacked standard.*
Assessment 1 Will this assessment be *formative* or *summative*? (Circle your answer.) Will this assessment be a common assessment—*yes* or *no?* (Circle your answer.)	**Which parts of the standard will this assessment address?** Target: Engage effectively in a range of collaborative group discussions, building on others' ideas and expressing their own clearly. **Description of assessment:** Assessment 1a: Watch a video of a collaborative conversation and analyze it as a class. Have a small-group discussion, with each group member taking responsibility for a given scale. The whole class debriefs, and the class discusses strengths and opportunities for growth in the conversation. Assessment 1b: Co-create a group discussion rubric to use to judge observed performances.	**What criteria will we employ? What kind of attending tools will we use evaluate the selected criteria?** Data-tracking sheets and scales, including a prepared scale that measures: • Students' ability to express their ideas clearly • Students' ability to ask good questions • Students' ability to qualify and justify their views (Ultimately combine the scales into a single rubric.)

continued →

Details of Assessment Role in the Overall Map	Connection to the Standard (such as the specific targets included in the assessment) *See circled and underlined text from the unpacked standard.*	Proficiency Scales, Quality Criteria, Rubrics, or Other Tools Needed to Support Evaluation Processes *See boxed or starred text from the unpacked standard.*
Assessment 2 Will this assessment be *formative* or *summative*? (Circle your answer.) Will this assessment be a common assessment—*yes* or *no?* (Circle your answer.) *No, but there will be shared artifacts.*	**Which parts of the standard will this assessment address?** Target: Engage effectively in a range of collaborative group discussions, building on others' ideas and expressing their own clearly. **Description of assessment:** Observe another discussion, and practice scoring with the new rubric. Revise and refine the discussion rubric as needed.	**What criteria will we employ? What kind of attending tools will we use evaluate the selected criteria?** Share rubrics from each classroom across the team or grade level so that students and teachers can check for alignment and consistency and eventually end up with a single discussion rubric. *Note: Create alignment with specific targets from the current unit of study.*
Assessments 3–4 Will this assessment be *formative* or *summative*? (Circle your answer.) Will this assessment be a common assessment—*yes* or *no?* (Circle your answer.)	**Which parts of the standard will this assessment address?** Target: Engage effectively in a range of collaborative group discussions, building on others' ideas and expressing their own clearly. **Description of assessment:** Assessment 3: Observe an in-class practice discussion, and practice scoring with the new rubric. Revise and refine the discussion rubric as needed. Assessment 4: Do the fishbowl or philosophical chairs activity; practice scoring with the scales and rubrics. Debrief results, and check for consistency in scoring.	**What criteria will we employ? What kind of attending tools will we use evaluate the selected criteria?** Use scales and rubrics to generate inter-rater reliability. *Note: Create alignment with specific targets from the current unit of study.*

Assessment 5	Which parts of the standard will this assessment address?	What criteria will we employ? What kind of attending tools will we use evaluate the selected criteria?
Will this assessment be *formative* or *summative*? (Circle your answer.) Will this assessment be a common assessment—*yes* or *no*? (Circle your answer.)	Target: Engage effectively in a range of collaborative group discussions, building on others' ideas and expressing their own clearly. **Description of assessment:** Teams practice discussion in small groups using a new formal set of roles and rules. Teams use the class rubric to monitor progress and evaluate performance at the end. Individual students track data on the team's use of the following (one feature to track per student): <ul><li>Academic transitions</li><li>Number of direct quotes with references to author(s)</li><li>Number of paraphrases with references to author(s)</li><li>Number of questions asked of each other</li><li>Number of connections made between ideas, references, and so on</li></ul>	Use scales and rubrics to generate inter-rater reliability. *Note: Introduce formal rules or roles for different discussion formats.*
Assessment 6+ Will this assessment be *formative* or *summative*? (Circle your answer.) Will this assessment be a common assessment—*yes* or *no*? (Circle your answer.)	**Which parts of the standard will this assessment address?** Continue adding the targets and related small formative or summative assessments to support overall mastery and readiness to take the final summative assessments.	**What criteria will we employ? What kind of attending tools will we use evaluate the selected criteria?** Continue adding and creating criteria and tools as needed to align with the added assessments.

Note: This sequence includes many, many more formative assessments. This list simply involves the starting points that a team might use to teach learners about civil discourse and how to self-manage learning-based conversations.

Source for standard: NGA & CCSSO, 2010a.

Applying Criteria for Quality Assessment Design

When external testing or textbook companies design assessments, they have multiple developers, they put the assessments through a review and approval process, and they often field-test the assessments in advance of formal use. Classroom teachers don't have that luxury. They often design and use their assessments on an as-needed basis. Still, teams have some ways they can improve the quality of their assessments during the design phase; they can make certain their assessments meet a list of predetermined quality criteria, and they can seek initial feedback from their peers. Teams can use the following six criteria to determine whether an assessment design meets quality expectations.

1. **Alignment:** The assessment and attending tools match the standards.

2. **Rigor:** The assessment elicits appropriate levels of reasoning.

3. **Relevance:** The assessment matters to the students who will take it.

4. **Fairness and equity:** The assessment and attending tools are as free of bias as possible and allow all students full opportunities for success.

5. **Clarity:** All prompts, questions, criteria, and directions and any other text are written in language that all learners will find clear, direct, understandable, and accessible.

6. **Reliability:** The questions and items are set up in a manner that will generate consistent and accurate interpretations of the results.

Note that these criteria are predictive in nature as teams consider whether the anticipated evidence will produce a result that *proves* a learner's degree of proficiency. Reliability is best checked with the evidence on hand, but in the design phase it's important to work toward creating a question, prompt, or task that will provide clear evidence of what a student knows and can do.

These six criteria for quality assessment designs must be considered *as* teachers are developing the assessments. Of the six criteria for quality, teachers can clearly identify and label two (alignment and rigor) during the design phase because these criteria have precise ways of evaluating that do not involve the learners' interpretations. The final four criteria—relevance, fairness and equity, clarity, and reliability—require that teachers make educated guesses. Teachers constantly use their prior knowledge and experiences of how learners will interpret the directions, questions, prompts, or tasks to develop the clearest, fairest, and most relevant assessments possible. The last criterion, reliability, is the most challenging feature to predict. Each new set of assessment directions, questions, prompts, or tasks will generate new evidence. Teachers must anticipate that the results will provide them with a clear and accurate representation of what a student knows and can do. Teachers plan for the remaining four criteria, but only the evidence that an assessment ultimately produces can determine if the assessment accurately meets those four criteria.

Still, because each criterion is vital to the overall quality of an assessment experience, teachers must consider them during the design phase.

Alignment

All parts of the assessment—the instrument itself and any attending measurement tools—must match the standards' content at the outlined level of demand. If the assessment aligns with the level of demand but the attending tools do not, the entire assessment experience will be flawed. Teams should explore the following questions when seeking alignment to standards.

- Does the assessment experience incorporate the critical aspects (knowledge and skills) of the standards involved?

- Does the assessment incorporate the critical aspects in a manner that matches the standards' integrity? (Teams could easily, for example, look at the standard SL.6.1c, "Pose and respond to specific questions with elaboration and detail by making comments that contribute to the topic, text, or issue under discussion" [NGA & CCSSO, 2010a, p. 49], and assume they could assess it by having students write blogs about their thoughts. However, this would completely miss the integrity of the Speaking and Listening standard, since writing will not work to assess a standard that demands learners pose and answer questions while in conversation with others.)

- Has the team added any extra assessment features (for example, blogging thoughts) or criteria (for example, using eye contact) to the assessment or its attending tools? If so, do they violate or enhance the experience? For example, blogging thoughts might be a wonderful precursor activity to a discussion, but it could never replace the actual discussion or the standard would not be met. And, adding eye contact to the list of criteria for a quality discussion decreases fairness and equity, as some cultures do not make eye contact out of respect during a conversation.

Alignment appears first in the list of quality criteria because assessments are supposed to measure standards. If an assessment misaligns with the standards, the purpose and the resulting evidence will prove fruitless.

Rigor

Rigor is most often identified as a balance of conceptual understanding and procedural fluency during an application-based experience, especially in an unfamiliar context. All modern standards require a shift from students simply knowing content to using content to solve complex problems, create new alternatives, and master discipline-specific skills (Erkens et al., 2019).

There is an increased focus on engaging students as experts in all skills in a discipline, especially communication skills (Erkens et al., 2019; National Education Association, n.d.). But the work has proven rigorous for educators. Education Trust (2015, 2018) has examined ELA assessments and mathematics assessments to see if they appropriately assess the Common Core State Standards. In each discipline, Education Trust (2015) researchers have used a protocol to review a significant sample size of middle school assessments and found the following for ELA:

- Overall, only about 5 percent of assignments fell into the high range on our assessment analysis framework (met 6–8 indicators).

- Fifty-five percent of assignments were connected to a text. However, overall, only 16 percent of assignments required students to use a text for citing evidence as support for a position or a claim.

- Only 4 percent of all assignments reviewed pushed student thinking to higher levels. About 85 percent of assignments asked students to either recall information or apply basic skills and concepts as opposed to prompting for inferences or structural analysis, or requiring author critiques. Many assignments show an attempt at rigor, but these are largely surface level. (p. 4)

Education Trust (2018) has found the following for mathematics:

- Only 9 percent of assignments pushed student thinking to higher levels. The overwhelming majority required low cognitive demand, with more than 9 out of 10 assignments limiting students to recalling a fact, performing a simple procedure, or applying basic knowledge to a skill or concept. This was even more pronounced in high-poverty schools, where only 6 percent of assignments were classified as requiring strategic or extended thinking, compared with 12 percent in low-poverty schools.

- Assignments were more than twice as likely to focus on procedural skills and fluency (87 percent) compared with conceptual understanding (38 percent) or application of a mathematical concept (39 percent). This imbalance meant less frequent exposure to assignments containing multiple representations, a critical indicator for developing conceptual understanding in mathematics. Only 39 percent of assignments incorporated varied types of mathematical representations.

- Less than one-third (32 percent) of math assignments provided an opportunity for students to communicate their thinking or justify their responses. The majority of assignments were answer-focused and did not ask students to defend or explain their thinking at any point within the task. Only 36 percent required students to write anything besides an answer, and 95 percent of assignments showed no opportunity for discussion. (p. 4)

An assessment experience will fall short of its intended goal if it does not elicit the appropriate levels of reasoning. Teachers commonly use Webb's (2005) DOK framework (see chapter 3, page 41) as a tool for gauging rigor. For example, a DOK level 1 task (lowest level of rigor) asks learners to describe the setting of a story they have read and already defined in class (recall-level work). A DOK level 2 task asks learners to use the characteristics of time and place to identify the setting of an unfamiliar story (application-level work). A task reaches DOK level 3 when learners independently critique or evaluate the quality of the story elements (including setting) or modify or create story elements in order to alter the story's intended message so it meets a given purpose (strategic thinking–level work). The most rigorous task, a DOK level 4 task, would have students study story elements and settings across multiple works and synthesize insights or draw conclusions regarding quality in literature development, and then have them use their identified quality criteria to create a story that successfully uses those elements (extended thinking–level work).

No level of rigor is bad. In fact, students cannot get to DOK level 3 if they don't first have knowledge and skill. The general concern is that DOK levels 1 and 2 are often overassessed while DOK levels 3 and 4 are often underassessed. Each level serves a purpose, and each purpose is worth assessing. Sometimes teachers need to be certain that students possess the necessary information to be successful as they advance in their learning, and other times teachers need to be certain that students can put all of their learning together in significant and constructive ways. There are four purposes of assessment. It's important to understand that while are similar to and align with the four DOK levels, they are not the same as DOK tasks.

1. **Possession:** Students demonstrate ownership of declarative and procedural knowledge. They use basic retrieval and understanding.

2. **Execution:** Students use acquired knowledge and skills to solve problems; make informed, strategic decisions; and respond to the demands of daily challenges.

3. **Integration:** Students extend and refine knowledge to automatically and routinely analyze and solve problems and employ solutions. Students must blend knowledge and skills with other disciplines in order to be successful.

4. **Construction:** Students use extensive knowledge and skills in dynamic ways to construct new solutions to current complex problems, to solve unanticipated problems, and to take action. Their efforts inform teachers' understanding of the necessary knowledge and skills.

When considering rigor, teams must explore the following questions.

- Do the questions, prompts, or tasks match the intended levels of rigor that the assessed standards require?

- Do the questions, prompts, or tasks build in complexity over time (easing the learners into rigorous work and ensuring they have knowledge and skills in place before assessing more sophisticated thinking)?

- Do the questions, prompts, or tasks require the learners to use knowledge and skills in authentic applications?

- Overall, has the assessment reached the highest level of rigor that the standards require?

Relevance

Relevance is a measure of connectedness based on the pertinence, interest, value, need, or immediacy of a given context. In other words, when an assessment has relevance, it *matters* to the learners who will engage in it. Relevance is critical. Teachers will have a difficult time increasing rigor for learners who do not find the tasks at hand very relevant.

Like rigor, relevance has degrees. Something has less relevance if it is an isolated experience and far more relevance if it offers knowledge and skills to support lifelong endeavors. Relevance is also contextual. Studying a story's setting has less relevance to a student who hates reading literature than it might to a student who aspires to become a novelist. Fortunately, teachers can increase the relevance of all learning by helping learners find personal value in the studied content or skills. For example, teachers can show disinterested readers that their personal settings or story elements (such as geographical location, family patterns, job history, income levels, or any other trait that currently defines who they are and how they operate) do not define their entire lives and that they can improve their life stories by exploring and ultimately altering these variables. This makes setting and story elements relevant concepts to explore *beyond* literary options. When teachers use content (for example, literature) as a medium (not as the end goal) to explore critical, real-world skills, it maximizes relevance (Erkens et al., 2019).

Multiple theories of relevance (Daggett, 2008; Newmann, Carmichael, & King, 2016; Wiggins, 1989) suggest relevance contains levels of application. The four levels that follow represent a combination of these theories.

1. **Apply in isolation and within discipline contexts:** Items focus on the specific discipline in which concepts and skills are taught.

2. **Apply in multistandard or cross-discipline contexts:** Tasks blend with knowledge and skills from other standards or disciplines.

3. **Apply in authentic, structured challenges:** Tasks are structured for predictable or calculable products that mirror processes beyond school walls.

4. **Apply in authentic, ill-structured challenges:** Tasks are complex problems that require real solutions with no predictable outcome.

Teachers might find it easy to create purposeful tasks for learners to complete, but that doesn't always increase relevance for the recipients. When students deem something not relevant beyond school walls or the here and now, they tend to disengage (Newmann et al., 2016). Indicating that something is important because it's on the test, because it's in the standards, or because students will need it later in life does not increase relevance.

Three very common assessment design flaws decrease relevance for learners.

1. **Assessing skills or concepts out of context:** For example, people compare things many times a day in order to make decisions (such as, "Do I wear these shoes or those shoes today?"), but when teachers ask students to compare for comparison's sake, without allowing them to make decisions with the information, it loses relevance. Teachers can easily incorporate simple things like decision making into assessment designs—for example, *After you create a Venn diagram comparing birds and fish as pets, decide which would be the better type of pet to have if you lived in an apartment. Explain your thinking.*

2. **Under-empowering learners by relying on algorithms or over-scaffolding to facilitate thinking and productivity:** To under-empower learners is to remove thinking—and even creativity—from the process at hand. For example, algorithms like (1) five-paragraph essays or (2) single paragraphs that have a topic sentence, three supporting details, and a concluding sentence provide patterns that become rote. Likewise, scaffolds like graphic organizers for developing an essay also require

learners to follow patterns. Learners do not have to analyze and evaluate their own designs. They do not have to consider possibilities and compare options before making difficult choices. They do not have to *think* critically. Teachers can use scaffolds and algorithms in the early phases to teach general concepts or processes, but they need to gradually pull away from such tools. At the point of assessing mastery, scaffolds and algorithms stifle creativity and critical thinking.

3. **Providing questions, prompts, or tasks that already have known answers:** In the world beyond school walls, adults do not spend time trying to solve problems that have known answers. An assessment that asks students to recall information that they can find on Google hampers relevance for learners. Instead, teachers should have students use the information they find on Google to solve complex problems—for example, *After identifying quality leadership traits that three different renowned leaders have in common, write an essay that outlines how you can become a better leader today in your family or school life.*

When considering relevance, teams must explore the following questions.

- Will the learners find the questions, prompts, or tasks interesting? (Consider their age, their region, and modern trends as variables.)

- Might the questions, prompts, or tasks unintentionally exclude some learners (for example, those who aren't interested in sports, those who don't have access to gardens, or those who don't wish to become historians)?

- Do the questions, prompts, or tasks replicate processes that have authentic, real-world applications?

- Will the learners find the questions, prompts, or tasks fun or engaging? Will the team explain the questions, prompts, or tasks in the context of lifelong application?

Fairness and Equity

The criteria of fairness and equity are about access. Will all the learners have a fair and equitable opportunity to articulate their knowledge or demonstrate their skills? It is impossible to create a bias-free assessment. In a learning environment, *bias*—a predisposition or partiality—has too many agents (the perspective of the employed text, the viewpoint of the test writer, the mindset of the test taker, the ambiance and conditions of the testing experience) to control completely. While teachers cannot possibly have a bias-free assessment, they can minimize bias in an assessment experience. To do so, teachers must factor in cultural differences; varied cultural, spiritual, or religious values; limited access or exposure to content or resources; and even personal challenges.

Katie Novak and Kristan Rodriguez (2018) have transferred the Centre for Excellence in Universal Design's (n.d.; https://bit.ly/2FaeHOa) seven principles of universal design to the educational realm in order to promote fair and equitable educational leadership, curriculum, and instruction. The seven original principles include (1) equitable use, (2) flexibility in use, (3) simple and intuitive use, (4) perceptible information, (5) tolerance for error, (6) low physical effort, and (7) size and space for approach and use (Centre for Excellence in Universal Design, n.d.). In alignment with the concepts of fairness and equity, Novak and Rodriguez (2018) suggest the following principles that support access for all.

- Provide multiple means of *engagement*.
  - Provide options for recruiting interest.
  - Provide options for sustaining effort and persistence.
  - Provide options for self-regulation.
- Provide multiple means of *representation*.
  - Provide options for perception.
  - Provide options for language, mathematical expressions, and symbols.
  - Provide options for comprehension.
- Provide multiple means of *action and expression*.
  - Provide options for physical action.
  - Provide options for expression and communication.
  - Provide options for executive functions (for example, managing information and setting goals).

A quick scan of the list suggests that teachers must design assessments to include *options* that open pathways to learning and understanding for all.

When considering fairness and equity, teacher teams can explore the following questions.

- Will all students have had access to information or experiences that allow them to understand the questions, prompts, or tasks equally?
- Will any learner find any feature of the assessment design problematic? If so, are there feasible changes that could make the question, prompt, or task palatable for all?
- Do any questions, prompts, tasks, or scoring criteria have culture-, gender-, or ability-prohibitive features (for example, requiring a student who is medically unable to run a mile in a given time frame)?

Clarity

Teachers need to write all prompts, questions, criteria, directions, and any other text in language that all learners will find clear, direct, understandable, and accessible. Students can easily misunderstand what teachers intend through any of the following means.

- The directions are unclear.

- The language used is unknown.

- The content of the passage is foreign to the reader.

Test writers can quite easily create a question or a set of directions that they find clear but that the recipients find vague. For example, a simple question such as the following might seem crystal clear to the test writer.

What is the typical length of a boot?

    a. 6 inches

    b. 6 feet

    c. 6 yards

    d. 6 miles

However, such a question could really confuse the test taker who doesn't know whether *boot* refers to a rubber knee-high shoe, an overshoe, a trunk of a car or a receptacle that the top of a convertible car lowers into, a metal device one places on a car tire, or even a U.S. Marine Corps recruit. Clarity is vital to a teacher's success in assessing student comprehension.

When considering clarity, teacher teams can explore the following questions.

- Will students easily understand every direction?

- Are all the directions spelled out?

- Will students easily interpret the questions, prompts, or tasks?

- Do any terms need further clarification?

- Are key words like *not*, *always*, or *most* clearly noted?

Reliability

Designing for reliability raises a bit of a challenge for two reasons. First, teachers can only measure reliability when the question, prompt, or task generates accurate, sufficient, and consistent evidence that will allow them to draw a proper conclusion regarding the students' level of knowledge or skill, or when teachers set up the scoring criteria and tools to measure exactness or clearly and accurately delineate degrees of quality. Second, teachers have to anticipate the types of responses students will provide and then determine whether those responses will reliably indicate a learner's degree of proficiency.

Reliability has many different facets, but on the simplest level, many things, including the following, can interfere with questions, prompts, or tasks generating reliable evidence.

- Providing poorly written or easily misinterpreted directions or items
- Reviewing an insufficient sample size (for example, an insufficient number of items per standard, an insufficient number of assessments on a standard over time per student, or an insufficient number of assessments from an entire grade level of students when calibrating scoring)
- Using only one method to assess a standard
- Allowing students the opportunity to guess by only offering predeveloped selections to choose from (for example, true/false or multiple-choice questions) without requiring the students to explain their thinking or selection process on at least a few items

When teachers do not decide on assessments by anticipating the reliability of students' responses, it puts teachers at risk of generating false positive or false negative results. When considering reliability, teams can explore the following questions.

- Will the team solicit sufficient evidence from each student to ascertain the true level of knowledge or skill?
- Could students score well by guessing?
- Does the team have ways to check for understanding that would help it see students' thinking and draw more accurate conclusions?
- Will the criteria truly measure proficiency?
- Are the criteria clear enough that the team can consistently apply them from one teacher to the next or from one assessment experience to the next?

Ultimately, teachers can best check for reliability by examining the actual evidence that a particular question, prompt, or task generates and determining if the samples provide accurate, sufficient, and consistent evidence to prove each student's level of knowledge or skill.

Creating Summative Assessments

Once teams clarify and agree on the design criteria, they then go on to design the summative assessments. Educators use summative assessments to answer the question, What does the learner know or what can the learner do at this moment in time? The fundamental purpose of a summative assessment is to certify mastery. Certification, or *confirmation*, is significant work, and teachers can rarely be accurate or thorough based on a single data point. Similarly, basing decisions on a single medium, such as a pencil-and-paper test, can only provide a single vantage point regarding the depth and breadth of a student's knowledge or skill set. In other words, summative assessments require ample evidence. Fortunately, the majority of modern standards incorporate a consistent body of knowledge and skills into increasingly more rigorous tasks and hence require assessments on multiple occasions over time. When teachers sample learning and gather evidence over time, they have a more accurate representation of a learner's knowledge and abilities, and the learner has a better chance to succeed. Imagine, for example, that a student must persuade. Teachers can assess the student's understanding of persuasion through a pencil-and-paper test, and the student can show his and her ability to persuade through an analysis of others' persuasive efforts and, more accurately, through his or her own speeches, debates, and essays.

It helps to have a guide or template that supports teachers in thinking through all the many parts of designing effective summative assessments. The reproducible "Summative Assessment Planning Template" at the end of this chapter (pages 118–124) features an assessment-planning tool that teacher teams would best use to construct a summative assessment. This tool requires teachers to consider the key features—context, timing, purpose, content, DOK levels, knowledge and skills, methods, attending tools, and options for student involvement—of designing summative assessments. Teams do not need to fill every box. They should use their discretion in each area.

In general, common *formative* assessments are smaller and less comprehensive than summative ones, but that is not a hard-and-fast rule. Sometimes, teams intend for a common formative assessment, such as a pretest, to look like the final CSA. In that case, teams might wish to use the reproducible "Summative Assessment Planning Template" (pages 118–124) to design the formative assessment. More often than not, however, a common formative assessment is shorter and more focused on the isolated skills or knowledge that the more comprehensive summative assessment will require. In that case, a common formative assessment could comprise a single question on an exit ticket. The reproducible "Common Formative Assessment Design Considerations" (page 125) provides a design template for common formative assessments.

Formative assessments serve as the scaffolding to success on summative assessments. As such, they must *form* the learning and *inform* the key instructional decision makers, students and teachers, of next steps so that the summative assessments simply become public celebrations of how much students have learned. Chapter 5 (page 135) offers ideas for how teams can use formative assessment artifacts to facilitate clear instructional decision making for students and teachers. Teams also commonly use common formative assessments to isolate and make transparent the many types of errors that might block learners from achieving mastery. Chapter 6 (page 155) offers more information about that strategy.

Creating Attending Tools

All assessments, formative or summative in nature, are subject to evaluation, so they likely require an attending tool. *Attending tool* refers to any tool that must accompany an assessment in order to monitor or score the tasks involved. There are four types of attending tools: (1) checklists, (2) scoring guides, (3) rubrics, and (4) proficiency scales. Students have a better opportunity to improve their results when they are aware of the attending tools for an assessment before they respond to the question, prompt, or task. It best helps learners when teachers either co-create some of the tools (such as rubrics) with them or practice repeatedly using the tools during the formative phases so that all learners deeply understand the degree of quality expected.

Teachers most popularly apply attending tools (rubrics or proficiency scales) to constructed-response assessments, such as essays or performance assessments, because they need the tools to clarify how they will score the degree of proficiency in a student's response, which exceeds a simple right-or-wrong judgment. Any assessment that is not binary in nature will have an attending tool to facilitate a clear and accurate evaluation of the assessment's results.

However, they can also use attending tools (checklists or scoring guides) with selected-response assessments when a question requires any elaboration on the student's behalf (for example, "Explain your thinking regarding your mathematical solution"). Even binary assessments, based on right or wrong answers—which teachers typically evaluate based on the total number correct—could provide better data for teams when employing a scoring guide. Scoring guides, like other attending tools, engage assessors in employing a set of cut criteria or decision-making rules such as the following.

- There are no concept or reasoning errors in the wrong answers of the student's work.
- The student has no errors on any DOK level 2 items.
- The student has demonstrated at least a level 2 degree of proficiency on each DOK level 3 item.

Such decision-making rules might help teams make better decisions regarding their results than simply considering the total number correct each student generated.

No matter the attending tool (checklists, scoring guides, rubrics, or proficiency scales), teams need to determine their criteria and share them with students in advance of giving the assessments. Table 4.1 (pages 104–105) offers a comparison of the various attending tools.

Teachers and students can use checklists and scoring guides with both selected- and constructed-response assessments, but these tools generally have less impact when it comes to generating productive responses from learners that lead to future growth, as teachers most often employ these tools at the summative point of the assessment process. Proficiency scales and rubrics are more popular forms of attending tools.

Table 4.1: Comparison of Attending Tools

	Checklist	**Scoring Guide**	**Rubric**	**Proficiency Scale**
Description	A list of expectations (the required conceptual knowledge, skills, or behaviors) for the assessment	The rules for how teachers will score a student response to a task, question, or prompt; used to measure skill level and quality of procedure, process, or end product	A tool with multiple criteria and an accompanying description of each criterion based on levels of quality	A tool aligned exclusively to a specific standard that illustrates the proficiency level achieved based on what parts of the standard students have mastered
Purpose	Indicates the presence or absence of required features; may provide point values for components	Provides clear directions on how teachers should score each item by assigning points to specific features of the task (for example, one point for a supporting graphic representation, one point for clear description, one point for an accurate answer)	Provides descriptors of performance against a specific set of criteria	Provides descriptors for levels of performance against a specific standard by ranking parts of the standard from easiest to hardest
Limitations	Limited to one-time use; does not provide quality indicators; does not clarify for the student how to improve performance over time	Limited to single items and one-time use	Limited to constructed response assessments; can be challenging to determine a final score with multiple criteria when there are so many different levels of proficiency per criteria	Limited to a single standard but may be used every time that standard is assessed

Link to Selected-Response Assessment	Acceptable fit if the checklist highlights key components that must be present in a response requiring explanation or justification	Good fit when specific to the expectations of an individual item	Not a good fit	Acceptable fit if teams develop the assessment to address levels of the standard
Link to Constructed-Response Assessment	Good fit; provides students with a checklist to ensure their work includes multiple features or standards	Acceptable fit if features of the guide delineate which parts of the standards that certain parts of the task score	Good fit; provides students with descriptive information	Good fit; provides students with a level of proficiency against a standard
Use as a Formative Assessment Tool	Acceptable fit; helps students fulfill expectations	Not a great fit; most often used at the point of summative assessment; if used in advance, offers information about what the assessment will score but does not give feedback in advance	Great fit; gives students feedback during the learning process	Acceptable fit; gives students a sense of their score but does not give specific feedback on how to improve
Use as a Summative Assessment Tool	Not a good fit; used to score points for completion rather than quality	Good fit; used to assign points for features of an answer	Great fit; but hard to determine a final score across multiple criteria	Great fit; used to score proficiency levels specific to the completion of the entire standard
Student Use	Used by students to ensure they sufficiently and accurately complete parts	Seldom used by students; can help after the fact to explain what happened	Can inform students what different levels of accomplishment look like	Can inform students of their proficiency level, but does not provide diagnostic information about how to improve

A *proficiency scale* is an assessment instrument that measures a learner's ability to demonstrate competency against a specific standard. Typically, proficiency scales align to learning progressions. Like a rubric, scales articulate the increasingly sophisticated levels of understanding and expertise within a standard. Unlike a rubric, scales allow for partial proficiency on the overall standard. For example, if the standard requires a student to bake a cake, a proficiency scale might indicate which parts of the standard the student accomplished (such as, could read directions, knew how to measure various ingredients, understood vocabulary, and so on). However, every student was tasked with baking a cake, and each student's final baked cake needs to be judged for quality based on the stated criteria (such as smell, taste, texture, visual appeal, and so on). Teachers use a scale as a measurement tool so they can determine the level of a standard (based on the parts of the standard) the student has met. Generally, proficiency scales have four levels that range from *insufficient* to *masterful* for the standard they assess. In Robert J. Marzano, David C. Yanoski, Jan K. Hoegh, and Julia A. Simms's (2013) work defining proficiency scales, each level of proficiency has consistent characteristics, even though grade-level expectations and content will change for the standards over time. For example, level 3 represents proficiency or mastery, and level 4 will always describe work that goes above and beyond, but what goes in the 3 or 4 category will depend on the standard that the scale assesses.

A *rubric*, on the other hand, is an assessment instrument that teachers use to measure a learner's ability to demonstrate competencies against a given set of criteria on a final product. A rubric comprises multiple criteria, and each criterion has proficiency levels that offer very descriptive language to communicate expectations of quality for a performance task. Levels of proficiency in a rubric range from *initiating* to *advancing*. Criteria can apply to multiple standards. For example, a single writing rubric might have criteria like organization, voice, ideas or content, and grammar, and teachers could use it on a persuasive-writing standard, an informational-writing standard, a narrative-writing standard, and so on.

Both scales and rubrics require the following features.

- A focus on measuring learning descriptively and objectively

- Quality criteria based on the standard's expectations and its field of expertise for that standard

- A stated and consistent range of knowledge or skill that outlines developmental sophistication—from *insufficient* to *masterful*

- Descriptions of the specific performance characteristics arranged by levels of developmental sophistication

There are key points to consider as teams develop both proficiency scales and rubrics and ensure attending tools are effective.

Developing Proficiency Scales

Because scales are specific to a standard, the process for developing proficiency scales involves isolating the levels of complexity within the standard and fitting them into the levels of the proficiency scale. The following four levels provide a modified version of the framework that Marzano et al. (2013) recommend.

- **Level 4:** The student has met standard expectations and advances the standard requirements with in-depth inferences, extensive sophisticated connections, and so on.

- **Level 3:** The student is independent and demonstrates accuracy (no major errors or omissions) on all simple and complex standard expectations.

- **Level 2:** The student is independent but demonstrates only partial accuracy on the complete standard expectations. The student has a grasp on the simple features of the standard, but may still have errors and omissions in the more complex standard expectations.

- **Level 1:** The student depends on support (prompts or cues) or scaffolding (formulas, graphic organizers, and so on) to demonstrate minimal, incomplete, or partial understandings of standard expectations.

Figure 4.6 outlines a protocol for developing proficiency scales.

Step 1	Identify all of the targets of the standard (knowledge or skills) to measure.
Step 2	Place the appropriate targets that will represent mastery in the level 3 position. If possible, provide supporting details from the standard to define what quality looks like with those expectations.
Step 3	Move to the level 1 position and list the relevant targets at the lower levels of rigor (simple processes or recall information). Offer clarifying descriptors of what might be happening if the student misses the target altogether, or of the scaffolded support a teacher might offer (such as prompting or cues).
Step 4	Move to the level 2 position and provide supporting details to clarify what quality looks like at this level.
Step 5	Finish with level 4 and provide supporting details to define what advanced work looks like. Make descriptors distinct enough so they differ from those at level 3. *Note: It's always best to define level 4 work based on actual artifacts. In the absence of evidence, generic descriptors (like "in-depth connections") or contrived features (like "incorporates more than one literary device in the composition such as rhymes and onomatopoeia") can create high degrees of inaccuracy and confusion.*

Figure 4.6: Protocol for developing proficiency scales.

Proficiency scales are powerful because they give students a clear indication of what they can and cannot yet do on a specific standard. Scales also help teachers generate a single score at the point of a summative assessment, so determining a final grade does not challenge them as much as it might with a rubric that results in multiple scores—one for each criterion employed.

Developing Rubrics

Teachers can use rubrics to score the products or processes of students' efforts. Rubrics clearly define achievable performance; they offer multiple criteria to consider when scoring a student performance and then detail the proficiency levels within each criterion using very descriptive language. Unlike scales, rubrics are generalizable enough that teachers can use them on multiple assessments, which allows them to employ rubrics in more comprehensive ways than they might employ a scale. Benefits of rubrics include the following.

- Teachers can use them to score students' performance and products on many standards.

- Students and teachers can co-develop them.

- Students can use them in self- and peer assessments.

- Students can use them to track their progress over time.

- Consistent criteria allow for focused revision and a notable trajectory of improvement.

Rubrics work best when targeting process-oriented work because students can use the same rubric over and over for different assessments and watch themselves grow between assessments (for example, using writing rubrics that highlight commonly accepted writing criteria—such as organization, ideas and content, voice, sentence fluency, grammar, and so on—to improve their writing scores as they move from a narrative paper to a descriptive paper, to a persuasive paper, and to a research paper).

Figure 4.7 offers an example of a typical rubric framework, though the number of rows will change based on the number of criteria involved. Rubrics, like scales, have proficiency levels, so the number of columns should remain stationary. In fact, it really helps teams if they keep the exact same number of levels for proficiency on their rubrics as on their proficiency scales so that they do not have to navigate differences between, say, five-point rubrics and four-point scales in their gradebooks when determining grades.

Teachers will find it most helpful to have student work available when identifying proficiency levels, but sometimes, they cannot make that option work. In that case, teachers must anticipate the proficiency levels, often based on past experience with how much progress

Criteria	1 Initiating	2 Developing	3 Achieving	4 Advancing

Figure 4.7: Rubric template.

*Visit **go.SolutionTree.com/assessment** for a free reproducible version of this figure.*

learners have made, and then use student work after the fact to calibrate their levels and make them accurate. When teachers select this route, however, they *cannot* hold learners accountable for an insufficient or inaccurate rubric.

With or without student work to guide the conversation, teachers must develop rubrics with considerable care, as learners must be able to envision success based on the carefully crafted descriptors. The following list offers the six steps of rubric development.

1. Determine your standards (performance or proficiency levels—both descriptors have been applied when discussing rubric development—such as *1, 2, 3*, and *4*, or *initiating, developing, achieving*, and *advancing*). Note that teams control the number of levels and the descriptors of each level. What is provided here is intended to make the connection between scales and rubrics easier, should teams decide to employ both.

   ○ Reduce the number of performance levels. The tighter the range, the more consistent and accurate the scoring.

   ○ Adhere to an even number of levels if possible. Even numbered rubrics increase teacher discretion during the scoring process because the midline forces the choice of which half of the rubric best represents the work being scored. When rubrics have an odd number of levels, teachers *and* learners tend to move their scoring toward the middle.

   ○ Consider each level a *proficiency* level. Rubric scores do not equate to points, so a 2 on a four-point scale does not equal a grade of 50 percent or an F.

2. Identify the criteria for quality and place those criteria in the first column of the rubric, as highlighted in figure 4.7 (page 109).

   ○ Identify criteria (attributes of quality) directly from the standards.

   ○ Vet criteria against the field of expertise (such as what experts define as *quality*), and add to or modify the existing list of criteria as necessary.

   ○ Keep criteria to a minimum (for example, no more than six to eight for any one rubric).

   ○ Make criteria generalizable enough that you can use them on multiple assessments over time and apply them to multiple student assessment options within a single assessment experience.

3. Start with the first criterion, and describe the level of proficiency. What does level 3 look like?

4. Define the criterion's low end. What does level 1 look like? (Frame it in positive language; avoid using *not*.)

5. Fill in level 2 and then level 4 for the criterion.

6. Move to the next criterion, and repeat steps 3 through 5 until all criteria have been described.

Teams should consider the following additional guidelines for writing performance descriptors during steps 3–5 of the preceding list.

- Use specific, descriptive language that explains characteristics of quality work.

- Address the same elements of performance at each level.

- Avoid developing rubrics that are specific to single assessments. While descriptions do need to be specific to the criterion, make sure the language is generalizable to the task, allowing teachers to judge quality across a variety of similar tasks.

- Frame the lowest performance level in positive terms. If a student *earns* a proficiency level of 1 or *initiating*, then he or she must have done something right. Students can only build on something that's right.

- Avoid generic evaluative adjectives such as *good*, *poor*, *weak*, and *excellent*—these terms are nebulous and offer no clarity as to what or why. Instead, work to use descriptive terms or add qualifiers to a term (for example, *uses enough evidence to validate that the idea is widely accepted by other experts writing in the field*).

- Avoid using quantitative language (such as, *must use at least eight resources* or *must have fewer than five errors*).

Ensuring Attending Tools Are Effective

At the point of using attending tools, assessment succeeds when it generates a productive response from the learners, fosters a sense of hope, creates a sense of efficacy, and improves learning overall (Erkens et al., 2017). To ensure those valuable outcomes happen, teams must attend to the following attributes as they develop their attending tools.

- **Accuracy:** We will increase confidence and competence in our accuracy by ensuring the attending tools—
    - Include quality criteria
    - Reflect definitive proficiency or performance levels
    - Include clear, concise, consistent descriptions
    - Provide diagnostic and analytical information

- **Reliability:** We will experience an increase in reliability by ensuring the attending tools support—
    - Internal consistency (Teachers have consistent scoring from beginning to end.)
    - Parallel forms (Tools can apply to multiple or different forms of assessments and generate consistent results.)
    - Inter-rater reliability (This includes reliability from teacher to teacher, learner to teacher, learner to learner, and learner to self.)

- **Achievement:** We will experience an increase in achievement by creating attending tools that ensure—
    - Learners grow between assessments, from the beginning of the unit to the end
    - Learners grow over time, between summative assessments (between units)

- **Student investment:** We will notice an improvement in student investment (activating learners as owners of their learning) by creating attending tools that ensure—
    - Learners make a physical, social, emotional, and psychological investment in themselves as learners
    - Learners self-monitor progress
    - Learners self-regulate for necessary alterations along the way to achieve mastery
    - Learners adopt a growth orientation and leverage errors and mistakes as learning opportunities in the following ways
        ‣ They make consistent choices to reinvest as needed.

> ▸ They exhibit effort-engaged behaviors (studying harder, attempting a different strategy, seeking additional feedback) necessary to face and embrace challenges so learning can happen.

> ▸ Their setbacks most often prompt them to exercise more effort because the intrinsic reward of learning reveals personal strengths and increases capacity.

- **Intellectual and social capital:** Our learners will gain intellectual and social capital (activating learners as instructional resources for one another) by using attending tools that encourage them to—

  ○ Collaboratively increase understanding by engaging in rich dialogue and active debate, challenge each other's thinking, extend current thinking, and create new possibilities

  ○ Provide peer feedback based on inter-rater reliability with the teacher (When teachers have practice consistently scoring strong and weak examples, they can exponentially increase the quantity and quality of feedback each learner receives.)

  ○ Establish a social norm of excellence for all, relying on social pressure and collective support to motivate and encourage all learners to achieve mastery

  ○ Expand their collective insights and repertoire of skills and strategies to address errors and gaps in understanding

  ○ Engage in productive group work as they prepare for a work world full of collaboration-rich opportunities

Vetting and Approving Assessments

Unlike testing companies, teachers may not have the opportunity to field-test assessments they create prior to using them. However, teams can work toward better assessments by reviewing and approving each other's assessments after they design them and before they use them with students. A kindergarten team, for example, might offer its assessment to a second-grade team for feedback, or a mathematics team might offer its assessment to a science team for feedback.

When teams seek feedback before using the assessments, they can work out some potential pitfalls or hazards in their design regarding the six criteria for quality (alignment, rigor, relevance, fairness and equity, clarity, and reliability). Sometimes, teachers from outside the grade level or discipline notice things that the authors themselves could not see. It's important to note that while the authors of an assessment can solicit feedback, they retain the right of authorship to integrate, modify, or ignore the feedback, as they likely know best whether a proposed change would work.

Teams can easily use tools like the reproducibles "Assessment Review Protocol 1" (pages 126–127) and "Assessment Review Protocol 2" (pages 128–133) to gather feedback regarding the quality of an assessment design before implementing the assessment with students. "Assessment Review Protocol 1" offers a simpler form for reviewers to complete and is more appropriate to use in the following circumstances.

- There is limited time available for an in-depth analysis
- The reviewers are less familiar with the content or processes of the assessment and can only offer a general perspective

The "Assessment Review Protocol 2" is the more complex and comprehensive protocol. It works best when the reviewers can have more time with the assessment and are prepared to go a little deeper in their analysis. This protocol works well with educators who share the content and process knowledge embedded in the assessment itself.

Conclusion

Designing quality assessments is not easy, but when teachers follow the proper steps and work collaboratively, they can find the process to be creative and enjoyable. Teachers assess every day as it is. Maybe it's time to work together to ensure that quality designs will generate reliable evidence of learning at the classroom level. And, maybe it's time to put joy and passion and creativity back into the assessment process for students and teachers alike.

Team Reflections

Take a few moments to reflect on the following questions.

- What do we need to do to ensure that our CSAs match the depth, breadth, and comprehensiveness of our standards and that our common assessments inform our formative assessment pathway?
- What evidence do we have that our formative assessments always build a pathway to success for students on our summative assessments?
- What could we do to ensure our assessment road maps are always designed backward and in advance of instruction? What tools or resources do we currently have at our disposal?

- How can we make certain we are both unpacking and repacking our standards before designing our assessments? How will we know that our summative assessments match the essence of the entire standard?

- How might some of our existing assessments (either teacher created or textbook driven) fare on the six criteria for quality assessment design?

- How could we use the six criteria of quality assessment design to become better assessment designers in our collaborative common assessment work?

- How can we be certain our attending tools increase hope and efficacy for our students? Do they help students increase achievement over time?

Assessment Pathway Planning Template

Standards

Student-Friendly Target Language

Notes Regarding the Summative Assessment Plan

Summative assessments for this standard (write a brief description):

Details of Assessment Role in the Overall Map	Connection to the Standard (such as the specific targets included in the assessment) *See circled and underlined text from the unpacked standard.*	Proficiency Scales, Quality Criteria, Rubrics, or Other Tools Needed to Support Evaluation Processes *See boxed and starred text from the unpacked standard.*
Assessment 1 Will this assessment be *formative* or *summative*? (Circle your answer.) Will this assessment be a common assessment—*yes* or *no*? (Circle your answer.) DOK level: _____	Which parts of the standard will this assessment address? Description of assessment:	What criteria will we employ? What kind of attending tools will we use to evaluate the selected criteria?
Assessment 2 Will this assessment be *formative* or *summative*? (Circle your answer.) Will this assessment be a common assessment—*yes* or *no*? (Circle your answer.) DOK level: _____	Which parts of the standard will this assessment address? Description of assessment:	What criteria will we employ? What kind of attending tools will we use to evaluate the selected criteria?
Assessment 3 Will this assessment be *formative* or *summative*? (Circle your answer.) Will this assessment be a common assessment—*yes* or *no*? (Circle your answer.) DOK level: _____	Which parts of the standard will this assessment address? Description of assessment:	What criteria will we employ? What kind of attending tools will we use to evaluate the selected criteria?

Assessment 4 Will this assessment be *formative* or *summative*? (Circle your answer.) Will this assessment be a common assessment—*yes* or *no*? (Circle your answer.) DOK level: _____	Which parts of the standard will this assessment address? Description of assessment:	What criteria will we employ? What kind of attending tools will we use to evaluate the selected criteria?
Assessment 5 Will this assessment be *formative* or *summative*? (Circle your answer.) Will this assessment be a common assessment—*yes* or *no*? (Circle your answer.) DOK level: _____	Which parts of the standard will this assessment address? Description of assessment:	What criteria will we employ? What kind of attending tools will we use to evaluate the selected criteria?
Assessment 6 Will this assessment be *formative* or *summative*? (Circle your answer.) Will this assessment be a common assessment—*yes* or *no*? (Circle your answer.) DOK level: _____	Which parts of the standard will this assessment address? Description of assessment:	What criteria will we employ? What kind of attending tools will we use to evaluate the selected criteria?

The Handbook for Collaborative Common Assessments © 2019 Solution Tree Press • SolutionTree.com
Visit **go.SolutionTree.com/assessment** to download this free reproducible.

Summative Assessment Planning Template

Directions: Use the summative assessment planning template to walk through each step in the assessment design process. The steps are sequential, but it is possible to skip steps at key points (for example, a selected response assessment will not require a rubric while a constructed response assessment will never require multiple-choice items, and so on). The template offers if-then statements to help guide team decision making along the way. Because of the comprehensiveness of this design template, it works best with summative assessment designs.

Overview and Context of the Assessment

Curriculum unit and assessment name: Provide a statement that captures the essence of this assessment: What unit will it assess? What essential question will it address?

Timing and pacing: Where and when in the unit will this assessment take place?

Primary purpose for this assessment: Often, assessments have more than one feature, but what overall purpose does this assessment serve? What is it you are trying to ascertain if students have achieved mastery? The descriptors in the following table provide clarity for each level. Check only one of the following.

	Possession: Students demonstrate ownership of declarative and procedural knowledge. They use basic retrieval and understanding.
	Execution: Students use acquired knowledge and skills to solve problems; make informed, strategic decisions; and respond to the demands of daily challenges.
	Integration: Students extend and refine knowledge to automatically and routinely analyze and solve problems and employ solutions. Students must blend knowledge and skills with other disciplines in order to be successful.
	Construction: Students use extensive knowledge and skills in dynamic ways to construct new solutions to current complex problems, to solve unanticipated problems, and to take action. Their efforts inform teachers' understanding of the necessary knowledge and skills.

Specific Content for the Assessment

Standards being assessed: See state standards, unit objectives, or both. Note that the fewer standards and objectives, the more focused the instrument and resulting data.

Standard Name and Number	Description of the Standard

Targets being assessed: Targets may be explicit or implicit in the standards. Here, unpacking or deconstructing standards comes into practice. When identifying the targets, consider the following.

- Targets must tie to the standards of the assessment.

- The assessment doesn't require a specific quantity of targets.

- Some kinds of targets may not be represented in a particular assessment.

There are two kinds of targets to consider: (1) specific learning targets and (2) strategic learning targets.

1. **Specific learning targets:** These targets are context dependent. They provide the content (facts, details, general understandings, and so on) that students must know, or they outline the details of a process or algorithm that students must do. Specific learning targets are most often measured by right or wrong answers.

2. **Strategic learning targets:** These targets are generalizable. They do not depend on a specific context, specific curriculum, or isolated details because they have a skills or process orientation. As such, teachers can assess strategic learning targets in multiple media over time. Strategic learning targets require quality criteria, scales, or rubrics to score student responses for accuracy because students could answer in many plausible ways.

Record the specific and strategic learning targets that this assessment will address.

Specific (Content) Targets	Strategic (Skill or Process) Targets

Quality of Targets

Select a level of quality (*no evidence, developing,* or *proficient*) for each statement. Use the indicators of quality for learning targets listed in the far-left column to determine if the learning targets listed on the assessment meet the criteria. Check the appropriate box to the right for each statement.

Indicators of Quality for Learning Targets	No Evidence	Developing	Proficient
Targets **align** with required or appropriate standards for the course.			
The identified types of targets reflect the **core processes** of the standards (maintain the essence of the standards' content and processes).			
Targets are **sufficient and accurate** in reflecting all the course objectives and expectations.			
Targets have **endurance** (will be lifelong, required learning).			
Targets have **leverage** (will be required to support other learning in life).			
Targets are **scaffolded** (build on each other).			
Targets are written in **student-friendly** language (framed as *I will, I can,* or *Students will be able to* statements that students understand).			

Rigor of targets: Rigor (a balance of conceptual understanding, procedural fluency, and application) ties to the entirety of the task, not the discrete parts. Rigor has four levels.

1. **Recall:** Recall a fact, information, or procedure.

2. **Skill or concept application:** Use information or conceptual knowledge, two or more steps, and so on.

3. **Strategic thinking:** Develop a plan or sequence of steps with some complexity and more than one possible answer.

4. **Extended thinking:** Investigate and take time to think and process multiple conditions of the problem.

In the boxes below, identify the total number of items on the assessment that are aligned to each DOK level. Once column one is completed, identify the percentage of assessment items at each DOK level.

Total Number of Targets per Category on Assessment	DOK and Mental Processing	Percentage of Total Targets Represented on Assessment
	Level 1: Recall	
	Level 2: Skill or Concept Application	
	Level 3: Strategic Thinking	
	Level 4: Extended Thinking	

Assessment method: Check one of the following, and follow the directions that correspond to the chosen assessment method.

☐ Selected-response assessment

☐ Constructed-response assessment

Selected-response assessment: If the planned assessment will be a selected-response assessment, then map the assessment plan using the following chart. Record targets in the following specification chart, and total the number of items it includes for each target. Alter the chart to add or remove rows or columns as necessary.

If the assessment will be a constructed response assessment, then skip this section.

	Strategic Target	Strategic Target	Strategic Target	Total
Specific Targets (Content Dependent)				
Specific Targets (Content Dependent)				
Specific Targets (Content Dependent)				
Total				

Record what types of items will appear on the selected-response assessment and how many of each type you anticipate the assessment will include.

Type	✓	Anticipated Number of Items
Fill in the blank		
Matching		
Short answer		
True or false		
Multiple choice		
Diagram or chart to label		
Other		

Constructed-response assessment: First, identify if the constructed response will be an essay assessment or a performance assessment. Then, describe the prompt or the tasks that the assessment requires.

If the assessment will be a constructed-response assessment, then determine the proficiency levels and criteria the essay or performance assessment will have. Develop a rubric by taking the following six steps.

1. Determine your proficiency levels in the top row of the following chart (such as *advanced*, *proficient*, *emerging*, and *basic*, or *4*, *3*, *2*, and *1*). Decide if the highest score is expected for all or above and beyond.

2. Identify your criteria in the first column (such as conventions, claim, support, and comprehension).

3. Start with the first criterion, and describe the level of acceptable proficiency (often level 3). What does level 3 look like?

4. Define the criterion's low end. What does level 1 look like? (Frame it in positive language; avoid using *not*.)

5. Fill in level 2 and then level 4 for each criterion.

6. Move to the next criterion, and use the same process.

Extend or abbreviate the provided chart as needed.

Criteria				

Effective Use of the Assessment

As a team, consider the following questions to preplan responses to assessment results regarding teacher learning, student learning and involvement, and interventions.

Teacher Learning

- How will we gather and organize the data for shared learning and a collective and systematic response?

- How will we score the data?
  - External scoring (outside input)
  - Independent scoring
  - Collaborative scoring (recommended for common assessments, with use of the following protocols)

- What protocols might we use to make sure we score alike? (Consider using the reproducible "Protocols for Examining Evidence and Artifacts" on pages 173–177.)

- How will we manage the data once we have scored them for comparative analysis?

- What will be our indicators of student learning? What cut criteria will we have for each target area? What evidence might we seek in students' answers to know they have truly learned?

List your plans for managing data in the following space.

Student Learning and Involvement

- How will we use the results to monitor and promote student learning?

- What strategies will we use to help students identify their strengths, areas of challenge, and next steps based on the assessment?

    - Opportunities and tools for self-assessment

    - Opportunities and tools to set learning goals

    - Opportunities and tools to create plans to address weak areas on the assessment

    - Opportunities and tools for recording and tracking personal progress on achievement targets

    - Opportunities to talk about their growth

    - Opportunities and tools to plan next steps

- How will we offer data to the learners? How will we offer students feedback on their assessments?

Interventions

- What strategies will we use to help students who did not master the content as required?

- What instructional interventions might we consider as we supply extra time and support to address those targets that students have not mastered?

    - Opportunities for reteaching

    - Opportunities for flexible grouping

    - Resources for continued learning

- How will we reassess to know the interventions worked? (Reassessments should be tied to missed targets and employ different questions regarding those targets.)

Common Formative Assessment Design Considerations

Which standard or which part of the standard will the assessment assess? List one target or standard per line. Note: It's important to keep formative assessments small, so it's desirable to have just a few targets. A formative assessment can assess a single target. A formative assessment could be a single question, prompt, or task.

_____

_____

_____

What questions, prompts, or tasks will elicit evidence of student understanding or proficiency levels regarding the targeted knowledge or skills (learning target)? List one item per line.

_____

_____

_____

What are we seeking from the evidence we solicit (for example, common types of errors or misconceptions with the target area, or the number of proficient students)? How will we use the data to inform our instructional next steps? List one idea per line.

_____

_____

_____

How might we use the artifacts (anonymously) or feedback (privately) from this formative assessment to help learners take informed instructional next steps to address their gaps in understanding? List one idea per line.

_____

_____

_____

Assessment Review Protocol 1

Directions:

1. Find a teacher or a team willing to review your assessment.

2. Provide a copy of the standards you are assessing, any texts that the assessment references, the assessment itself, and any attending tools for the assessment.

3. Provide the reviewers with the following criteria for quality and feedback form, and offer them a helpful timeline for providing their feedback.

Criteria for Quality

- **Alignment:** The assessment and attending tools match the standards.

- **Rigor:** The assessment elicits appropriate levels of reasoning.

- **Relevance:** The assessment matters to the students who will take it.

- **Fairness and equity:** The assessment and attending tools are as free of bias as possible and allow all students full opportunities for success.

- **Clarity:** All prompts, questions, criteria, and directions and any other text are written in language that all learners will find clear, direct, understandable, and accessible.

- **Reliability:** The questions and items are set up in a manner that will generate consistent and accurate interpretations of the results.

The Handbook for Collaborative Common Assessments © 2019 Solution Tree Press • SolutionTree.com
Visit **go.SolutionTree.com/assessment** to download this free reproducible.

Assessment Review Feedback Form

Directions for reviewers: In the following space, try to list both a strength and an area of possible stretch (growth) for each criterion provided. Provide your feedback in a manner that will support continued learning and effort on behalf of the assessment architects who are seeking your feedback.

	Strengths	Stretches
Alignment		
Rigor		
Relevance		
Fairness and Equity		
Clarity		
Reliability		

Assessment Review Protocol 2

Directions:

1. Find a teacher or a team willing to review your assessment.

2. Provide a copy of the standards you are assessing, any texts that the assessment references, the assessment itself, and any attending tools for the assessment.

3. Provide the reviewers with the following criteria for quality and feedback form, and offer them a helpful timeline for providing their feedback.

Criteria for Quality

- **Alignment:** The assessment and attending tools match the standards.

- **Rigor:** The assessment elicits appropriate levels of reasoning.

- **Relevance:** The assessment matters to the students who will take it.

- **Fairness and equity:** The assessment and attending tools are as free of bias as possible and allow all students full opportunities for success.

- **Clarity:** All prompts, questions, criteria, and directions and any other text are written in language that all learners will find clear, direct, understandable, and accessible.

- **Reliability:** The questions and items are set up in a manner that will generate consistent and accurate interpretations of the results.

Assessment Review Feedback Form

Name of course: _____ Date of review: _____

Team members reviewing the materials:

Standards addressed:

Specific and strategic targets isolated for assessment purposes:

Number of specific targets: _____

Number of strategic targets: _____

Total number of targets: _____

The Handbook for Collaborative Common Assessments © 2019 Solution Tree Press • SolutionTree.com
Visit **go.SolutionTree.com/assessment** to download this free reproducible.

Quality of Targets

Select a level of quality (*no evidence*, *developing*, or *proficient*) for each statement. Use the indicators of quality for learning targets listed in the far-left column to determine if the learning targets listed on the assessment meet the criteria. Check the appropriate box to the right for each statement.

Indicators of Quality for Learning Targets	No Evidence	Developing	Proficient
Targets **align** with required or appropriate standards for the course.			
The identified types of targets reflect the **core processes** of the standards (maintain the essence of the standards' content and processes).			
Targets are **sufficient and accurate** in reflecting all the course objectives and expectations.			
Targets have **endurance** (will be lifelong, required learning).			
Targets have **leverage** (will be required to support other learning in life).			
Targets are **scaffolded** (build on each other).			
Targets are written in **student-friendly** language (framed as *I will*, *I can*, or *Students will be able to* statements that students understand).			

Rigor of Targets

Review the assessment and note the total number of targets per DOK level. Then, note the percentage of the assessment that addresses each DOK level. Note: Your interpretation of DOK levels may differ from the assessment architect's interpretation. Your input can provide another perspective.

Total Number of Targets per Category on Assessment	DOK and Mental Processing	Percentage of Total Targets Represented on Assessment
	Level 1: Recall	
	Level 2: Skill or Concept Application	
	Level 3: Strategic Thinking	
	Level 4: Extended Thinking	

Is the assessment's purpose clear?

Does it match the essence of the standards involved?

Does the assessment method (selected-response assessment, constructed-response assessment, performance assessment) match the essence of the standards involved?

The Handbook for Collaborative Common Assessments © 2019 Solution Tree Press • SolutionTree.com
Visit **go.SolutionTree.com/assessment** to download this free reproducible.

Criteria for Constructed-Response Assessments: Essay or Performance-Based Assessments

Select a level of quality (*no evidence, developing,* or *proficient*) for each statement. Use the indicators of quality for learning targets listed in the far-left column to determine if the questions, prompts, or tasks listed on the assessment meet the criteria. Check the appropriate box to the right for each statement.

Indicators of Quality for Constructed-Response Assessments	No Evidence	Developing	Proficient
The assessment aligns tightly to the learning targets.			
The assessment focuses on assessing skills worth learning.			
The assessment strives to stimulate real challenges facing people in a field of study or real life.			
The assessment allows for ill-structured challenges (challenges that have more than one right answer).			
The assessment emphasizes questions requiring thought and knowledge.			
The assessment demystifies tasks, criteria, and standards.			
The assessment allows for activities or topics to match students' learning styles and interests.			
The assessment requires evaluations to be based on explicit criteria and standards of quality.			
The assessment involves students in the assessment process in meaningful ways.			

The Handbook for Collaborative Common Assessments © 2019 Solution Tree Press • SolutionTree.com
Visit **go.SolutionTree.com/assessment** to download this free reproducible.

Reviewer Team Feedback

Use your notes from the earlier sections to provide feedback to the assessment architects. Be sure to provide feedback that will help your colleagues continue their learning as they revise and improve the assessment you just reviewed.

Opportunities for Growth	Celebrations of Strength

Team Self-Assessment

Prior to reading the reviewers' feedback regarding your newly designed assessment, list your own identified opportunities for growth and celebrations of strength.

Opportunities for Growth	Celebrations of Strength

Team Reflections: Next Steps

Looking at the feedback your review team provided, draw your own conclusions. As the architects of an assessment, you always have the option to ignore feedback if you deem it inappropriate or inaccurate given your professional expertise of the subject matter or the levels of readiness for your students. Create your own list of what to do next with the feedback, and record your decisions in the space provided.

5

The Delivery Phase

With foundational agreements and common assessments in place, collaborative team members have a clear sense of purpose and direction when working in their individual classrooms. During the delivery phase, teachers employ their best instructional strategies (best first instruction) as they strive to ensure their students are successful in mastering the necessary knowledge and skills. In their individual classrooms, teachers maintain their unique style, add some of their own assessments, modify curriculum as needed, and make decisions regarding next steps based on the emerging evidence before them.

Quality instruction requires the use of quality formative assessments (Chappuis, 2014; Erkens, Schimmer, & Vagle, 2017, 2018; Hattie, 2009, 2012; Wiliam, 2011, 2018). Only some of the formative assessments that teachers use in the delivery phase will be common formative assessments. At those key junctures, the team connects to examine formative evidence and make certain the learners in their various classrooms are progressing as they should be. They make strategic decisions to support each other's instructional maneuvers, sometimes adding additional common formative assessments to monitor an identified area of concern, sometimes slowing or increasing the pace from what they originally planned, sometimes re-engaging students in the learning when a gap is discovered, and so on. They employ an iterative cycle to monitor student learning individually and collectively. They support each other and adjust as needed along the way.

Instructional Agility

When teams use common formative assessments, it allows team members to be reflective so they can constantly strive to improve their instructional prowess in the service of student achievement. Masterful teachers demonstrate *instructional agility*, the ability to use the emerging evidence to make real-time maneuvers that support continued student learning (Erkens et al., 2018). There are four Is of instructional agility.

1. **Instruct:** Provide purposeful directions regarding the learners' acquisition of new knowledge, skills, or abilities.

2. **Investigate:** Seek confirmation of instructional influence by observing emerging evidence in student responses.

3. **Interpret:** Decode the emerging evidence quickly and accurately for indications of effectiveness, confusion, errors, and so on.

4. **Intervene:** Adjust with responsive instructional maneuvers that keep learning moving forward.

These four core processes are neither linear nor discrete; instead, they are interdependent and at times overlapping. While instructional agility is linked to individual prowess, collaborative common assessment plays a role in supporting teachers through each of the four Is.

Table 5.1 indicates how the collaborative common assessment process supports each of the Is involved in a teacher's individual capacity to have instructionally agility.

Table 5.1: The Link Between Instructional Agility and Collaborative Common Assessment

Instructional Agility Core Processes	Link to Collaborative Common Assessment in the Delivery Phase
Instruct	Teams first identify their agreed-on priority standards, curriculum, and timelines for each unit of study.
Investigate	Teams create common formative assessments as well as their own classroom assessments to monitor learning with deliberate focus and intention.
Interpret	Teams use the data and artifacts from common formative assessments to isolate and interpret common errors or misconceptions and collaboratively score student work samples to identify agreed-on proficiency levels.
Intervene	Teams use common formative assessment results to make instructional adjustments immediately.

It might seem counterintuitive that teams would use collaborative processes and agreements to develop their individual instructional agility, but the shared knowledge they co-create during the foundational and design phases empower them to be precise yet flexible.

Teams need to work together in order to develop precision. The degree to which the individual members *accurately* address their standards, *congruently* follow their expectations and timelines for instruction, and *consistently* score student proficiency within their individual classrooms and across the entire team determines precision. To achieve such precision, a team must have intelligent, philosophical, and ongoing conversations.

Teamwork is also critical to developing the individual members' capacity to flex their instructional efforts while keeping their time frame and degree of quality on target. What happens in one classroom can never exactly replicate what happens in the other classrooms, even when teams co-plan the lessons in advance. Individual teachers need flexibility as they respond to the emerging evidence before them. When teams explore evidence of learning together, identify specific errors, strategize appropriate instructional responses, co-create targeted feedback that will generate productive responses, and monitor their effectiveness through results, they strengthen individual members' instructional muscles. It's like going to the gym for a routine team workout; consistent, rigorous practice makes each member stronger.

During the formative phases of learning, teachers are monitoring the evidence that is emerging as they teach. Evidence emerges moment by moment and may happen by design or happenstance. Such evidence can be formal (a quiz, an exit ticket, classwork or practice work, a project, or a mid-unit summative assessment, to name a few) or informal (checks for understanding, student questions, student answers, student conversations, peer feedback, teacher and student conferencing, nonverbal cues, and so on). All of it can inform a teacher's or a team's next instructional steps. This is why formative assessment and instruction are often referenced as synonymous (Chappuis et al., 2012; Hattie, 2012; Wiliam, 2011). And this is how formative assessments are used to *improve* learning before the summative assessment is used to *prove* learning. Formative assessments are pivotal to agile instruction.

Common Formative Assessment Strategies

In most of the literature about common formative assessments, the focus is on the data that can inform instructional decision making (Ainsworth & Viegut, 2006; Bailey & Jakicic, 2012; DuFour et al., 2016). While those data are indeed powerful, that limited perspective can prohibit teams from tapping into the full potential of formative assessments as instruction.

Educators use evidence to draw conclusions about learners, the learning process, levels of readiness, levels of proficiency, and so on. Evidence is a broad category. It is both formal and informal, qualitative and quantitative. It includes the words, nonverbal expressions, and attitudes students share. It includes the data from assessment results. It includes the artifacts—the tangible projects or products that shed light on students' knowledge, skills, and even metacognitive processing—that they create while immersed in learning. All forms of evidence can provide teachers with enlightening glimpses into how a student thinks and feels.

Done well, formative assessments produce the evidence (data and artifacts) that teams can explore to monitor the collective understanding of their students. Experts on formative assessment agree that the ultimate instructional decision maker in every classroom is the student, not the teacher (Chappuis, 2014; Chappuis et al., 2012; Hattie, 2009, 2012; Wiliam, 2011, 2018). So, when done extremely well, formative assessments produce the evidence that teachers can use to guide and inform the instructional next steps that students must take.

Teachers on collaborative teams can use common formative assessments in a manner that mirrors best practice in formative assessment. They need not treat common formative assessments like a major event; likewise, teachers need not see common formative assessments solely as a robust data-gathering exercise. Instead, teams can use the artifacts from common formative assessments to continue the instruction, just as they would in any quality formative practice. Evidence emerges moment by moment and may happen by design or unexpectedly. It includes the words, nonverbal expressions, attitudes, and deliberate assessment results that learners provide while immersed in learning experiences. All of it can inform a teacher's or a team's next instructional steps. Classroom activities produce artifacts and evidence that teams can explore to monitor collective understanding of their students.

When teams seek to design assessments to elicit evidence that will improve learning, they should employ the following strategies of formative assessment and examine the resulting evidence together. The following offers a modified list of the four formative assessment practices Chappuis (2014) highlights. These four formative assessment strategies are used to engage learners in growing through the assessment process.

1. Ensure all learners can see and understand the learning targets and expectations.

2. Engage learners in examining and scoring high- and low-quality artifacts and evidence of the learning expectations.

3. Offer descriptive feedback that generates continued learning and productive responses for learners.

4. Employ strategies, tools, and resources that empower learners to self-regulate their learning.

Each of these formative assessment strategies is integral to best first instruction, and when teams engage each strategy, they create the body of shared artifacts necessary to promote continued learning within their individual classrooms. Teachers can use those artifacts anonymously across the various classrooms represented on the team to help students engage in analyzing learning and identifying next steps in their learning journey.

Ensure All Learners Can See and Understand the Learning Targets and Expectations

According to Marzano (2003), students who can identify the intended learning significantly outperform those who cannot. To guarantee students understand the learning expectations, teachers must present students with manageable, clear targets; help them understand the terminology of those targets; and clarify what high-quality work will look like with those targets (Chappuis, 2014; Chappuis et al., 2012; Wiliam, 2011). Academic vocabulary can challenge learners. Learners need to unpack the language of a learning target and then identify what plausible results might look like if they accomplish that target. Teams can use the activity in figure 5.1 (page 140) to help students clarify learning targets. In every formative assessment protocol appearing in this chapter, the activities that individual teachers would use in their respective classrooms are listed in sequential form in the first column. The Evidence Produced column highlights what individual teachers are striving to produce and monitor in their individual classrooms while engaged in the activities listed. The last column, titled Team-Based Learning From the Collective Artifacts and Evidence, offers the critical questions or processes that teams can explore when reflecting on the artifacts students generate from one classroom to the next. Reflective learning is powerful at the team level.

The evidence of learning in this activity comes from the final list of learning targets. Team members can share the targets that were generated in their individual classrooms and compare them as a means to ensure that the students in *each* classroom truly understand the learning they are to accomplish in the unit of study before them. As a further brush toward clarity, teachers can swap the lists of learning targets with their peers, return to their classrooms with a new set or sets, and invite their students to compare and possibly combine classroom targets into grade-level targets (across all participating classrooms).

Of course, teams can introduce learners to targets and clarify their meaning in more than one way. In another strategy, teachers can use preassessment to expose students to the learning targets early and then use those same preassessments as a feedback tool throughout the unit of study. Teachers can also use those preassessments collectively to guide their understanding from one classroom to the next on what to monitor further during instructional activities.

Activity	Evidence Produced	Team-Based Learning From the Collective Artifacts and Evidence
1. Break learners up into pairs, and have them unpack the language of a target and write it in their own words. 2. Merge two pairs to create a group of four. Have the new group compare the two pairs' answers, agree on key terms, and confirm accuracy. Then have students rewrite the target (if necessary) in order to combine their answers into a single statement, and then create an example of what the target might look like in action. Have teams brainstorm what evidence would suggest they understand or could do the work of the learning target. 3. Merge two groups of four to create a new group of eight. Have them review the target language from both groups and revise or blend their language as necessary. Ask them to share their two examples of what that target might look like in action, and to create one or two test-like questions or tasks that a teacher might use to gather evidence. They should be ready to share with the entire class. 4. Engage the groups of eight in sharing their final products with the whole class. Use the share out process to clarify any misunderstandings and redirect as necessary.	• Variations of the targets (from different teams) in student-friendly language • Early ideas of what students believe the targets might look like in action • Questions or tasks students anticipate that teachers might ask them to answer or do in order to demonstrate mastery of the learning target	• Review the materials produced in the various classrooms. Check for accuracy and consistency (from team to team and from room to room). • Ask the following questions. 　• "Do the learners understand the learning targets?" 　• "What misconceptions or misunderstandings might already require more clarity during our instruction?" 　• "Did any questions or tasks emerge that we could actually employ in our various classrooms?" 　• "Could teachers use any of the resulting materials as artifacts to trade for continued conversation?" (For example, teacher A takes teacher B's anonymous examples back to his or her room to re-engage learners in the discussion if there were points that required further clarity.)

Figure 5.1: Protocol for clarifying learning targets with students.

*Visit **go.SolutionTree.com/assessment** for a free reproducible version of this figure.*

Figure 5.2 outlines the protocol for using preassessment as another means to help clarify learning expectations with students. It is set up the same way as figure 5.1, but the specific student activities, types of evidence produced from those activities, and possibilities for team use regarding the evidence differ.

Activity	Evidence Produced	Team-Based Learning From the Collective Artifacts and Evidence

1. Early in the unit of study, employ a preassessment that provides one or two open-ended questions for each learning target of the unit. Require learners to attempt an answer, even if they don't understand the target yet. Do not accept blank spaces, "I don't know," or "I don't care" answers. Walk around to ensure completion.
 	
2. Gather the assessments, and hold on to them; do not score them. You will return them and gather them again repeatedly throughout the unit of study.
	• Student answers to key questions, target by target	• Examine the artifacts to answer the following questions.
		  • Have students already mastered any target areas that won't require teaching?
		  • Have any mistakes, errors, or misconceptions emerged? (If so, create a list of the things that will require more focused clarity throughout the unit as instruction continues.)
		  • Could we preserve any sample responses and share them anonymously to give students practice with error analysis and collaborative scoring?
		• Create a bank of answers that teachers can use (not in the classroom of the student who generated the response, and never in a way that pinpoints the author of the work or that shames the quality of the work).

Figure 5.2: Protocol for preassessing students' understanding of learning expectations.

continued →

Activity	Evidence Produced	Team-Based Learning From the Collective Artifacts and Evidence

3. After a body of instruction has occurred (for example, after several days or a week), return the preassessment (with no markings) to the students.
 	
4. Have the students revisit the specific questions they should now be able to answer based on the previous learning (for example, you might say, "Please look at questions 3, 4, and 9"). Ask learners to modify their answers if they would like. It shouldn't matter if they erase the first answer or if they use a different color to write the new answer. The point is to determine if they have a more accurate answer to share. (For example, you might ask, "Do you want to change your answers now that we have studied the target in more depth?")
 	
5. Gather the preassessments. Put a dot next to the questions that students revisited *if* they still have wrong answers. Do not return the preassessments until the next round (unless the learning needs to be fixed before you advance; in that case, return them as needed).
	• Student answers to key questions target by target
	
	• New insights into continued misconceptions, errors, or mistakes
		• Examine the specific questions that students had to revise, and answer the following questions.
		   • Have students now mastered the target area in question? If so, can we move on? If not, must we fix the misunderstandings or errors before advancing?
		   • Do students have any persistent mistakes, errors, or misconceptions? (If so, create a list of the things that will require more focused clarity throughout the unit as instruction continues.)
		   • Could we preserve any sample responses and share them anonymously to give students practice with error analysis and collaborative scoring?
		• Add to the bank of answers and artifacts that teachers can use (not in the classroom of the student who generated the response, and never in a way that pinpoints the author of the work or that shames the quality of the work).

6. Continue the process, periodically returning the preassessment (following instruction), and allow learners to fix previous answers, especially those that you have now dotted as errors or misconceptions. 7. Return the completely revised preassessment before the summative assessment. Ask learners to target those areas on their preassessment that they know will require more time and study efforts (or *focused revision*) as they prepare for the summative assessment.	• New answers to key questions, target by target, following focused revision • New insights into continued misconceptions, errors, or mistakes following focused revision	• Continue gathering team insights; isolating common mistakes, errors, or misconceptions; and generating potential anonymous samples to use with students to help clarify what they have wrong and what they have right with each learning target.

Source: Adapted from Mattingly, 2016. Used with permission.

*Visit **go.SolutionTree.com/assessment** for a free reproducible version of this figure.*

According to middle school teacher Ken Mattingly (personal communication, June 2016), when teachers turn targets into preassessment questions and use preassessments to guide students' thinking throughout the unit, students begin to value the assessment process as an opportunity to gather meaningful, personal data to support their own continued learning. Also, when teachers set clear targets, they support students' ultimate success on the summative assessments. Note that neither strategy outlined in figures 5.1 (page 140) or 5.2 (pages 141–142) have involved gathering specific data about individual learners; rather, they are designed so both students and teachers focus on eliciting and monitoring evidence of learning regarding the targets.

Engage Learners in Examining and Scoring High- and Low-Quality Artifacts and Evidence of the Learning Expectations

Clarifying learning expectations also involves defining what high-quality evidence will look like with each target for both students *and* teachers. When students understand what is expected of them to demonstrate proficiency, two things happen: (1) they develop consistency between how they would score their work with how the teacher would score it, and (2) they can dramatically improve their own performance.

The process of collaborative scoring is critical to the individual teachers' success as well. A team can employ a common assessment and not have common data in the end if it has not practiced scoring consistently on an ongoing basis. To identify criteria for quality and desired degrees of proficiency, a team should first create their rubric together. Once the team rubric is completed and individual team members have agreed to what quality will look like, they can facilitate the same process in their own classroom, working to co-create rubrics *with their students*. Because they have a team agreement on what quality will look like, individual team members can guide their own students to notice those same criteria in the sample materials they use to showcase quality. After each classroom has completed its own rubric, the collaborative team can check across all of the rubrics to ensure consistency of criteria and levels of proficiency.

Co-creating rubrics with students might seem like a lengthy process, but in the end it's the best way to help learners understand what is expected in their own work. Moreover, when students co-create rubrics and they better understand what is expected, they can do a much more accurate job of self-assessing and giving peer feedback.

Because co-creating rubrics is powerful but very time consuming, it's helpful if teams have just a few key rubrics that they use repeatedly over an extended period of time. To make that happen, the teacher team should start by naming criteria that are specific to the context but generalizable enough to use in multiple settings or with various assessments (for example, the criterion of engaging in conversations through asking and answering questions, cuing, prompting, or sharing insights is specific to the Speaking and Listening standards but generalizable enough to be applicable in the debate, forum, seminar, or partner-share mediums).

Once the collaborative teacher team has a clear rubric, individual team members set about identifying samples of strong and weak work. Samples can come from outside the classroom via professional- or amateur-developed materials, teacher-created options, and class-generated materials. No matter what, it's always critical, especially in the formative phases, that teams use the samples they select as examples of strong and weak work in a manner that will shield students from public ridicule or shame once they bring those samples to the classroom for student discussions. When teams manage this work in a manner that protects the students' identities, they can also use answers or artifacts produced in classwork from the other classrooms represented on the team. Figure 5.3 outlines the protocol for co-creating rubrics with students. The protocol happens *after* a team has predetermined what their rubric will be. Note that this is *not* an elaborate exercise in guessing what the teachers want. The goal is to elicit student understanding of quality, so individual teachers must know what their team rubric says and then use the appropriate prompts and cues to guide students toward identifying the same criteria and levels of proficiency. Students can use their own language to describe quality, but it must closely match what their teacher expects.

Creating rubrics can lend further clarity for both students *and teachers* regarding what learning will look like when done well, but it is never enough. The next step involves using the rubrics with such consistency that there is inter-rater reliability from teacher to teacher, from teacher to student, and from student to student. When teachers have created inter-rater reliability (everyone scores the same way) with their rubrics, they exponentially increase the quantity and quality of feedback they can provide in their classrooms. In this scenario, teachers have increased confidence that students are able to give each other accurate scores and productive feedback, so students are no longer dependent solely on teacher feedback.

The collaborative scoring process outlined in figure 5.4 (page 146) is virtually the same at the classroom level as it is at the teacher level (see the scoring calibration protocol reproducible "Protocols for Examining Evidence and Artifacts" on pages 173–177). Figure 5.4 (page 146) outlines the process teachers can use to help their students score consistently with the class rubric (developed in figure 5.3).

Activity	Evidence Produced	Team-Based Learning From the Collective Artifacts and Evidence

1. Engage learners in examining various samples of work. Ask them to identify what makes some examples better than others. (Teachers should use the collaborative team-created rubric to guide the types of questions they ask and observations they cue their students to make so the process results in students developing a similar set of expectations.)
 	
2. Generate a list of quality criteria for all to see.
 	
3. Try using the developed list of criteria on some additional samples of work. Do the same criteria still hold up? Modify, add, or delete criteria as needed. (Teachers can use this process to begin asking the guiding questions that will steer the learners toward better understanding of the various degrees of proficiency in each criterion. Again, the goal is to help students match what the teacher team developed in the teacher-created rubric.)
 	
4. Fill in the class rubric by formalizing what the various gradations of quality within each criterion will be. How good is good enough? What do proficiency levels of 1, 2, 3, and 4 look like?
 	
5. Generate a published rubric. Let the learners know they will use the rubric often. *Note: Individual teachers should plan to bring their class rubrics back to the team meeting for verification of alignment to the original source (the team-created rubric).*
	• A rubric from each participating classroom that *matches* the criteria and levels of proficiency on the team-created rubric that was developed in advance.
	
	• Consistent criteria on each rubric (though specific terminology may vary)
	
	• Consistent levels of proficiency on each rubric (though specific terminology may vary)
		• Examine each rubric. Explore the following questions as a team.
		  • Do the rubrics have a consistent message even though the words might differ?
		  • Are some rubrics better than others?
		  • What do the rubrics suggest the learners now understand about the learning targets?
		  • Would it be beneficial to share the rubrics with each classroom so the students can compare the options and make more decisions about quality? Could teachers possibly engage students in generating one classwide rubric, which all classrooms involved in the unit of study could use?
		
		• Consider bringing the rubrics back to class discussions to revise and improve them over time.

Figure 5.3: Protocol for co-creating rubrics with students.

*Visit **go.SolutionTree.com/assessment** for a free reproducible version of this figure.*

Activity	Evidence Produced	Team-Based Learning From the Collective Artifacts and Evidence

1. On a consistent basis, engage student teams in scoring work samples (such as with a bell ringer activity, an exit ticket from the day prior, a single item on the homework, or a sample from another classroom's preassessment). Ask each team to score the work using one or all of the criteria on the class rubric. Require each team to defend its answer with evidence from the artifact it examines.
 	
2. Engage teams in arguing from evidence until the entire class agrees on the score for the work.
	• Team scores for specific artifacts
	• Identified evidence to support the team scores
		• Look at the scores and evidence that emerge from the various classrooms. As a team, explore the following questions.
		  • Do the students and various classrooms have general agreement or consistency regarding what quality is and is not?
		  • Can the learners accurately identify the evidence that supports their scores?
		  • Do the learners' scores match the scores the teachers would give? Why or why not?
		  • Do the learners' responses shed light on any misconceptions or errors that require further clarification? If so, what are they, and how might we address those discrepancies?

Figure 5.4: Protocol for practicing classwide scoring on items or tasks.

*Visit **go.SolutionTree.com/assessment** for a free reproducible version of this figure.*

When learners can score with consistency, it sets them on their way to solving their own gaps in understanding. Once the learners can consistently determine quality as a class, teachers must move the practice to the self and peer levels with the learners' personal assessment products.

Offer Descriptive Feedback That Generates Continued Learning and Productive Responses for Learners

Feedback is one of the most powerful instructional intervention tools teachers have at their disposal. Its primary purpose is to reduce the discrepancy between where a learner is and where the learner is supposed to be (Chappuis, 2014). Teachers use feedback as an instructional tool to ensure every student continually *learns*. But not all their feedback, whether positive or growth oriented, generates a constructive response from learners. The LEARNS acronym offers the following criteria for quality feedback that generates productive responses in learners. Quality feedback is:

- **Learning oriented**—The feedback continues a student's learning, encouraging the student to keep thinking and investigating. Learning-oriented feedback does not generate compliance-based fixes.

- **Error specific**—The feedback explores specific types and patterns of errors and the strategies needed to address those errors, but it does not give away the answers. It must support the learner in finding his or her own fixes by being descriptive, informative, and evidence-based or data-rich.

- **Actionable**—The student can apply the feedback while he or she engages in the learning because the feedback is timely and applicable. If the teacher offers the feedback during the formative stages, the feedback sets the student up for mastery on the summative assessment. If the teacher offers the feedback during the summative stages, the feedback is process oriented for future assessments that will engage similar knowledge and skills.

- **Related**—The feedback relates directly to the learner by connecting three significant areas.

    a. It links directly to the learning targets involved.

    b. It highlights the specific predetermined quality criteria it addresses.

    c. It indicates both success and growth areas for the learner.

- **Narrowed**—The feedback narrows the concerns to address a prioritized and manageable few, helping the learner focus his or her efforts on those elements that will have the greatest impact in a given amount of time.

- **Self-regulation oriented**—The feedback supports self-regulation. It enables the learner to make independent, healthy instructional choices and inspires him or her to continue doing so. Ultimately, the feedback creates a tone that fosters hope and efficacy for the learner.

There are quality indicators that must be employed if the feedback is to work—that is, the feedback reduces the discrepancy between what currently exists and what needs to exist in order to be deemed proficient. Providing a learner with feedback is serious business. It's more challenging to offer descriptive feedback that generates productive responses than one might think. Toward that end, both teachers and students benefit from practicing how to give good feedback. In fact, it even helps them to receive feedback on how well they did at giving feedback.

Teachers can use the protocol outlined in figure 5.5 to teach students the process of giving quality feedback. All of the formative processes build on one another, so as students are practicing giving feedback, they should be anchoring that feedback in the criteria and levels of proficiency they developed in the class rubric.

Activity	Evidence Produced	Team-Based Learning From the Collective Artifacts and Evidence
1. Teach learners the criteria for quality feedback. 2. Create a visible checklist of the criteria for learners to reference. 3. Using strong and weak learning samples (these may include examples that you already collaboratively scored with the class rubric in previous learning opportunities), model giving feedback. Role-play the experience; act as the author or learner in the situation, and invite students to give feedback regarding the artifact. Use the think-aloud strategy to engage learners in discussing whether their comments would promote continued learning for the recipient. 4. Record some of the students' feedback suggestions. Give feedback about the quality of their feedback. Did it produce or would it have produced a productive response in the recipient?	• Samples of class-developed feedback tied to the targets of the criteria for quality outlined in the rubric • Samples of feedback on various assessments • Feedback regarding the quality of the feedback given during the practice activities	• Examine the feedback students generate across the various classrooms. Explore the following questions as a team. • Does the proposed list of feedback options indicate that learners understand how to give quality feedback that will produce productive responses in their peers? • Does the proposed list of feedback options indicate that learners understand the learning targets? Do their comments indicate that they are getting closer to understanding what quality looks like? • Given their feedback and comments, are learners ready to self- and peer assess? What must happen to make certain that learners will benefit from helping each other?

Figure 5.5: Protocol for teaching learners to give quality feedback.

*Visit **go.SolutionTree.com/assessment** for a free reproducible version of this figure.*

Though it is not outlined specifically in the protocol, it's helpful if teachers also teach students how to receive feedback. A simple twist on the role-play experience in step 3 (figure 5.5) can also showcase the various ways to graciously accept or rudely deflect feedback.

When learners can provide quality feedback to each other, not only does it completely remove the burden from the teachers' shoulders, but it also involves learners in the assessment process and supports the critical competencies of collaborating, communicating, and thinking critically. The work activates learners as resources to one another. In figure 5.5, students rehearsed how to give quality feedback. Now it's time to use their learned skills to give authentic peer feedback, using all of the tools they have developed along the way (clear learning targets, quality criteria for their learning targets, levels of proficiency for their learning targets, quality criteria for giving feedback, and so on). Figure 5.6 outlines the protocol students will use repeatedly as they engage in self-assessment and peer feedback.

Activity	Evidence Produced	Team-Based Learning From the Collective Artifacts and Evidence

1. Using the class rubric and the list of criteria for quality feedback, engage learners in peer assessment.
 	
2. Ask the author of the assessed work to write down the feedback he or she receives from a peer. When the author has to write out the feedback, it increases the likelihood that the author will ask follow-up, clarifying questions. Also, he or she will be more likely to understand the peer-given feedback and remember the feedback than if he or she simply read what someone else wrote.
 	
3. Ask the peer assessor to back up his or her rubric scores and detailed feedback with evidence. He or she should be able to highlight sections of the rubric that apply as well as sections of the student's work that correspond to the rubric levels assigned.
	• Student-assigned rubric scores that correlate with the scores teachers would assign
	
	• Highlighted sections of the assessment that provide evidence of the assigned rubric scores
	
	• Qualitative feedback that demonstrates an understanding of the learning targets at hand
		• Examine the artifacts collaboratively. Explore the following questions as a team.
		
		  • Do the rubric scores that the learners assign match the scores teachers would give?
		  • Can the learners accurately identify the evidence that supports their score?
		  • Has the quantity of feedback increased overall?
		  • Are learners providing accurate, quality feedback?
		  • Are learners improving as a result of the peer assessments?

Figure 5.6: Protocol for engaging learners in self- and peer assessment.

continued →

Activity	Evidence Produced	Team-Based Learning From the Collective Artifacts and Evidence

4. Use the same process outlined for peer assessment to move into self-assessment. Have learners highlight on the rubric where they think they are and then highlight sections in their actual assessment that support their self-assigned scores.
 	
5. In addition, consider having learners submit their initial work by indicating with dots or small marks where they believe errors exist. In this manner, they critically look at their submissions in advance and indicate where their questions and concerns still exist.
	• Student-assigned rubric scores that correlate with the scores teachers would assign
	• Highlighted sections of the assessment that provide evidence of the assigned rubric scores
	• Qualitative feedback that demonstrates an understanding of the learning targets at hand
		• Examine the artifacts collaboratively. Explore the following questions as a team.
		  • Do the rubric scores that the learners assign match the scores teachers would give?
		  • Can the learners accurately identify the evidence that supports their score?
		  • Has the quantity of feedback increased overall?
		  • Are learners offering themselves accurate, quality feedback?
		  • Are learners improving as a result of their self-assessments?

*Visit **go.SolutionTree.com/assessment** for a free reproducible version of this figure.*

Learners who can self- and peer assess accurately can begin to activate themselves as resources during the learning process.

Employ Strategies, Tools, and Resources That Empower Learners to Self-Regulate Their Learning

All of the formative work prior to this moment has created the foundational content that allows students to regulate their own learning needs; however, *exposure* is never sufficient for creating reliability. Individual teachers need to constantly re-engage students in the process so that they can become clearer, more consistent, and more accurate in their interpretations of quality. Again, to support an individual teacher's ability to do this work, teams constantly gather artifacts from their joint efforts, practice the same work in advance of sharing it with the learners in their individual classrooms, and swap out samples of artifacts from each other's classrooms to maintain a sense of anonymity and to create consistency from one room to the next.

When students self-regulate, they take charge of their own learning. They can self-assess, describe their learning expectations and the quality criteria that accompany them, score with accuracy, and send and receive feedback. At this point, students should be able to set goals and identify the strategies, tools, and resources they will need to ensure they meet their goals.

When learners have the strategies, tools, and resources to self-regulate, they learn *how* to learn. When learners know how to learn, they can grasp almost any instruction they encounter. They take charge of their learning. They become career and college ready. Figure 5.7 offers a protocol for student goal setting.

Activity	Evidence Produced	Team-Based Learning From the Collective Artifacts and Evidence
1. Using any or all of the students' assessment results, engage learners in identifying strengths and areas of growth. Evidence can include artifacts, feedback, or data from outside sources as well as personal scores or perceptions. 2. Engage the students in goal setting. The language of the goal should be specific and should inform both teacher and student in what comes next in the learning. Direct students to use the current learning expectations as well as the newly created list of strengths and weaknesses. Ask, "Relative to that list, what goal do you have for yourself as a learner?" 3. Engage the students in recording the goal (for example, by creating a goal sheet). It's equally helpful at this point to engage students in anticipating the quantity and quality of evidence they would need to produce in order to best monitor their achievement of the goal.	• Student lists of strengths and opportunities for growth that are backed by artifacts, feedback, or data • Goals aligned to standards and personal needs • Accurate goals that clearly name next steps	• Examine the artifacts collaboratively. Explore the following questions as a team. 　• Can each of our students accurately self-assess strengths and weaknesses with data? If not, why not and what comes next? 　• Do all students' goals match the standards? Are the goals targeted to the specific students' needs? 　• Can each of our students accurately develop meaningful and targeted goals to support their instructional next steps? If not, why not and what comes next?

Figure 5.7: Protocol for setting goals.

*Visit **go.SolutionTree.com/assessment** for a free reproducible version of this figure.*

Goal setting is often a precursor to data tracking. While the two go hand in hand, they are not inextricably linked; one can happen without the other, but the two work best in tandem. Goals are best monitored when the data are tracked over a period of time.

Once students have goals in place, it's important that they become metacognitive as they strive to answer critical questions such as the following.

- Where am I relative to where I am supposed to be?

- What comes next in my learning?

- What are my strengths or assets for the tasks at hand?

- What are my personal challenges or opportunities for growth for the tasks at hand?

- What do I know about myself as a learner in this set of learning expectations?

- What do I like or dislike about this content or process?

- What new strategies might I need to add or what can I refine in order to achieve my goals?

Metacognition can best happen as students monitor progress on their individual goals. There are many different ways or even combinations of ways to do such work. Sometimes monitoring progress takes the form of students documenting and evaluating their assessment results over time on tracking forms or in data notebooks full of various tracking forms. Sometimes it involves engaging students in analyzing their own errors and recognizing patterns within their work. And sometimes it takes the form of engaging students in focused revision activities so they can improve a single product or process over time. As teams engage students in metacognition, they can gather relevant evidence regarding their individual students' success or opportunities to improve in any or all of the following activities.

- Answering reflective questions following an assessment

- Recording and monitoring progress over time

- Analyzing and improving personal errors

- Revising and improving assessments over time

- Adjusting goals as needed and selecting appropriate strategies to meet goals

The team must decide what artifacts to gather and explore together, and their decisions should always be anchored in two key criteria: (1) will the evidence the students produce help them improve their own learning in meaningful and productive ways, and (2) will the evidence revealed within the artifacts help the team make informed decisions that help all students become successful learners.

Conclusion

Collaborative teams can use the common formative assessment process to examine data, but they can also use it to generate tools and processes for empowering students to navigate their assessments successfully. When a team's shared expectations are mirrored in each individual's classroom during the formative phases of learning, the team can be assured it is moving toward fairness and equity. Equally important, when teams use the collaborative common assessment process to generate important teaching materials (learning targets, rubrics, data tracking, and so on), they empower their learners. The process involves a back-and-forth momentum; teams step back to co-create necessary tools and then go forth to bring them to the classroom. Then they step back once more to determine how their individual efforts went by examining the resulting artifacts, to analyze the consistencies or inconsistencies in their students' understanding, and to problem solve collaboratively as they work to close gaps in student understanding and skill throughout their units of study. Team learning from artifacts can be just as significant as team learning from data.

Team Reflections

Take a few moments to reflect on the following questions.

- What evidence do we have to prove we have both precision and flexibility in our instruction as individuals and as a team? If we don't have evidence, what evidence could we gather? Who will do it and by when?

- How have our team conversations and insights supported the ongoing refinement of our individual instructional agility? If they haven't yet, what could we do to ensure our conversation *do* support our individual instructional agility?

- How could we use common evidence from high-quality formative assessment practices to explore learning?

- What do we currently employ or what could we employ (tools, processes, and policies for data interpretation, self-assessment, goal setting, intervention planning, and reflection) in order to allow students to have involvement in responding to their results?

- How do our assessment practices help learners know more about their strengths, assets, and desires and about their needs for growth? How do we know we are developing growth-oriented learners? What could we monitor?

- Do our formative assessment results lead to different instructional decisions on our behalf? On our students' behalf?

6

The Data Phase

In the 21st century, data abound. Advances in technology have generated a hunger for big data across all industries, including education. But do educators collect the right data? And do these data lead to high-quality information? The challenge, experts at the National Research Council note, includes getting the *right* data and then developing the expertise to draw reliable inferences from the data (National Research Council of the National Academies, 2014). When data are too narrow in focus, too far removed from the classroom, or studied in isolation or retrospect, opportunities for powerful solutions dissipate, and learning—for students and educators alike—plummets. Too often, educators receive data from large-scale assessments that are too generalized (leading to inaccurate conclusions), that arrive too late (leading to tardy, ineffective responses), or that disconnect from the previous years' data because of a shift in the testing (leading to unusable information). Unfortunately, sometimes, the conundrums of large-scale assessments find their way into local school settings as well. Teams can use collaborative common assessments, however, to move meaningful, trusted, and just-in-time data closer to the classroom. Fortunately, there are protocols and tools that can help teams make data manageable, ensure they work with common data, establish criteria and guidelines for their data-mining activities, mine data effectively, isolate gaps in understanding, analyze formative data, and isolate errors.

Making Data Manageable

Teams need to collect meaningful data that support teacher decision making. Collaborative common formative and summative assessments provide such data and evidence or artifacts that help teams make informed instructional maneuvers to guarantee student success. In a PLC, data from team-developed common assessments serve as the linchpins of success.

Teachers can find examining data from student work daunting, especially when they have a large number of student samples or a lengthy body of evidence to examine for each student. In such cases, sampling helps make the process more manageable. When they have too many students to score collaboratively, individual teachers can bring a random sample set (such as work from five to eight students) to the table. Teachers should randomly select students, so most often, it's best if a teacher has someone else select the work from his or her classroom. If teachers come to the meeting already having determined the range of ability in their evidence sets, then bias becomes a factor. When the student work samples are lengthy (for example, videos of eight-minute speeches or fifteen-page research papers), teachers can select either a small portion of the assessment to examine (for example, the last two minutes of a speech or the third paragraph of a paper) or a single scoring criterion to use when looking at the sample sets (such as a student's eye contact, a student's mathematical reasoning on a specific test question, or the voice in a student's writing).

Collaborative teams engage in professional learning when they focus on the results of their efforts. This means teams should look at data on a consistent basis. However, many teams complain that most of their meetings get tied up in the planning phases, rather than the reflective phases, because they become bogged down by large data sets and attempts to organize the data. As a result, teams have limited opportunities to gather data, limited meeting time for discussing assessment results, and so on.

Teams can increase the frequency of their data conversations and make the overall process more manageable by having *data moments* in every meeting instead of just waiting for the more formal but infrequent *data meetings*. Unlike a data meeting, which can involve examining a lot of data over a lengthy period of time with a formal protocol, data moments are quick and informal. It's best if data moments (approximately five to seven minutes in length) occur at the very beginning of a meeting for two reasons: (1) the data moments are sure to happen when they are first; if they were the last item on the agenda, they could frequently be skipped as teams fast run out of time, and (2) the focus on student learning early in the meeting can set the appropriate tone for the rest of the meeting to follow. The artifacts for data moments—small sample sizes of data or even a single artifact of one student's work—are predetermined at the end of a previous meeting, and the job of bringing artifacts rotates from one team member to the next. The artifacts that teams create during the formative phases of learning serve as perfect conversation options for data moments.

When teachers share artifacts during data moments, it is for the purpose of taking a deeper look into an area of concern and gathering alternative insights into what might be happening.

For data moments, team members might ask a teacher at the conclusion of the previous meeting to bring an artifact that falls into one of the following categories.

- A single artifact from a student who seems to be falling behind academically

- A single artifact from a student with great potential who does not seem to be motivated

- A single artifact from a student who has overcome hurdles and adversity recently

- A sample of work from a student who has undergone a sudden change in demeanor

- A sample of work from a student who is challenging you

The list of options for evidence and artifacts to bring to data moments is limitless. No matter the sample purpose, the goal of the process is to begin each meeting with a results orientation while helping each other explore student work from new vantage points, develop new insights, and problem solve collaboratively.

Significant learning conversations and planning for targeted next steps can happen during data moments. When teams have data moments with single artifacts, they can explore questions such as the following (Erkens, 2017).

- What score(s) would we give this student based on this work? Do we have a common understanding or an agreement that would generate inter-rater reliability? If not, what could we do to become more consistent?

- What are the students' strengths? Has the student demonstrated growth over time (e.g. from earlier indications with prior assessments)?

- What are the students' opportunities for growth?

- What instruction have we planned and/or delivered that should have addressed the challenges this student is still facing?

- What could we still do to help this student move forward?

- Do we have the right criteria? The right performance descriptors?

- Given this evidence, is there anything we should change about our assessments and attending tools (rubrics, scales, scoring guides, etc.)?

Another option includes having each team member randomly select three pieces of student work from the last common assessment and score one common detail from a predetermined isolated task in each of the selected samples (for example, only score item 6 on a test). In this way, teams can use a more fast-paced, data moment structure to quickly calibrate their scoring systems before individually scoring the rest of their student work from the remaining untouched piles. As teams have data moments with small sample sizes, they can explore questions such as the following (Erkens, 2017).

- What score(s) would we give these students based on the provided work? Do we have inter-rater reliability?

- What has everyone mastered within the sample size?

- What errors and misconceptions are evident in the sample size?

- Based on our collective expertise, is this sample of evidence representative of the larger group? If so, how do we know? If not, what additional evidence might we need to bring to the table at the next meeting?

- Are there artifacts in the sample set that we could use anonymously in our individual classrooms (use anonymous work from someone else's classroom to avoid exposing your own students) to help students understand strong and weak work?

- How else could we use these few artifacts to help all of our students improve?

- What program improvements (curriculum, instruction, and assessment) do the samples suggest we might need to consider?

- What are plausible next steps for the students represented here, and would those next steps be beneficial to the larger group as well?

Teams can learn a lot from a few brief moments of mining data evidence and artifacts, and individual team members can gain new insights into their students when others share their observations about the work. Eventually, as teams become experienced with data moments, they can become more adept in data meetings. Ongoing experience with data moments can provide more focus and clarity for data meetings. It shifts team conversations from the planning mode into the results mode where teachers can feel they are making a difference, and rehearsal with data moments can build trust over time, making it easier for team members to allow themselves to be vulnerable learners of their own craft when at the data table.

Ensuring Common Data

It's entirely possible to give a common assessment and not have common data. Uncommon expectations and scoring may occur among teachers even on a test that is primarily based in right and wrong answers. Teachers may award different point values for different things or have multiple criteria that they weigh differently (for example, how the student set up a problem, the methods used to solve the problem, and the answer's degree of accuracy).

To avoid this, teams must develop very clear and consistent expectations. The protocol for calibrating scoring during data moments is a start, but the full protocol for scoring student work could easily take an entire meeting. Developing a rubric can promote shared expectations, but that process alone never suffices for getting to common data. In order to develop common expectations and consistent data, teams must examine student work together and come to consensus on the scores the work would earn. If teams simply average the various scores each teacher would have assigned, they miss the critical discussion that enables them to consistently calibrate their scoring practices.

Teams look at student work together for three primary reasons: (1) to calibrate scoring so it has consistency, (2) to analyze student errors, and (3) to refine assessments after student evidence clarifies whether they assessed the standards. Teams also require data protocols to support their ability to navigate conversations around data in three ways.

1. **Quickly:** Protocols help streamline the process by outlining all steps and ensuring consistency. The more a team engages in using the same protocol, the faster and more efficiently its members can navigate the process.

2. **Safely:** When teams know exactly what questions they will need to answer and at what point the questions will arise, they are better able to anticipate and prepare. There are no surprises in the process.

3. **Accurately:** No matter what protocol teams design and employ, focusing on the right questions can ensure that teams are addressing the needs of all of their students and specifically identifying what they will do for students who have not yet learned the material, and what they will do for students who have already mastered it.

The reproducible "Protocols for Examining Evidence and Artifacts" at the end of this chapter (pages 173–177) supports teamwork toward ensuring these processes provide common data.

If teacher scoring could possibly lead to uncommon data, then teams must carve out meeting time to examine student work. Once teachers have calibrated their expectations so they have consistency, they can resume scoring the rest of their students' work. If they have any questions about a particular sample or two, then they can bring those few samples to the table for a team conversation. In this way, teams can come to the data meeting with a high degree of confidence that they have common data.

Establishing Criteria and Guidelines

Teams will find it helpful to establish clear criteria and guidelines in advance of all data-mining activities. Clarity precedes competence. If teams are to use common assessments, they must score student work in common ways, and they must have agreements on how to examine the resulting data. Table 6.1 outlines both the wrong and the right ways to look at data.

Table 6.1: Wrong and Right Ways to Look at Data

Wrong Ways	Right Ways
Use percentages.	Use proficiency scale scores with descriptors.
Look at the whole rather than the parts.	Look target by target.
Use grading-based cut scores (such as 80 percent as passing).	Dig deeper to target specific needs and analyze errors.
Provide scores to students for review and acceptance.	Engage students in self-analysis and decision making.
Reteach entire general categories (for example, a student must relearn all of *inference*).	Develop strategic interventions within target areas based on types of errors (reteaching, coaching, error analysis with students, or outside or companion skill teaching, such as vocabulary development if that was the actual reading issue and not just the overarching skill at hand).

Of course, teams need to come to agreement internally on how they will examine their data, but oftentimes it's more helpful to have buildingwide agreements on the protocols and guidelines to do so. Only then can schools begin to move toward more consistent grading policies and practices. Data guidelines might look like the following.

- Mine data for a proactive response to the results.

- Seek to work diagnostically, isolating errors and misconceptions in student understanding target by target.

- Engage students in reflecting on their individual results to improve their learning and give them continued options to achieve mastery.

Once teams have clear criteria and guidelines to facilitate their scoring efforts, they identify a data protocol. In a data conversation, protocols provide team members with a sense of safety because they know the sequence of questions or activities in advance. Familiarity with the steps of the protocol creates comfort, and the consistency of the steps allows team members to anticipate any challenging questions they might face should their student scores be low. In this way, they can prepare and not be caught off guard or embarrassed in the moment.

Many great data protocols exist, and this chapter offers several reproducible data protocols for teams to consider: "Data Protocol 1: Exploratory Dialogue" (pages 178–181), "Data Protocol 2: Structured Conversations for Team Learning from Evidence" (pages 182–185), and "Data Protocol 3: Data Analysis for Team Learning" (page 186). No one protocol is better than another, and each protocol is offered as a resource. Ideally, teams would take any protocol and make it their own. However, in the end, it is less important that teams use a provided protocol and more important that they understand their options for decision making—for example, where they be tight (nondiscretionary) and where will they be loose (discretionary) in their agreements. Teams can feel under-empowered if they are limited to using a given set of tools, but when teams feel they have tools available to support their endeavors and criteria that guide their decisions, they feel empowered. A principal can better serve staff by offering a data protocol as a resource and then outlining the nondiscretionary features that allow teams to create their own protocol if the proffered one will not work for them. For example, a principal might say, "I'm providing a protocol as a resource to make your conversations easier, but you don't have to use it. If you decide to create your own, I'm also offering a list of the nondiscretionary features, but if you do create your own, please be willing to share it with the rest of us so we can learn and grow from your efforts." When it comes to common assessments, the final protocol teams select or create must always be able to answer the following three questions that will help them ensure all students learn at high levels (Erkens, 2016).

1. As a team, which targets from the assessment require more attention?

2. As a team, which students require what support? Organize the data in a manner that identifies the learners requiring intervention, extended practice, and extension (see reproducibles "Response-Planning Template for Students Needing Practice or Enrichment" and "Response-Planning Template for Students Needing Support," pages 187 and 188).

3. As an individual teacher, which area was my growth area, and how can I improve in that area?

Whatever protocol a team chooses or creates, it should ensure every team member leaves a data meeting with *new* insights on what it takes to tackle learning challenges in their individual classrooms.

Mining Data Effectively

Many school systems use common assessments to generate numbers, and they use those numbers to make decisions. The data that they most often produce to measure learning—marks (+ or –), grades (such as C+), and scores (such as $^{12}/_{15}$ or 80 percent)—do not always accurately reflect degrees of proficiency that students generate. Moreover, totaling the points accumulated over time does not accurately reflect the resulting learning. In the collaborative common assessment process, the data conversation might begin with numbers, but teams do not use the numbers as decision points; rather, the numbers give teams or individual teachers windows into where they should look more deeply. Numbers should launch investigations, not decisions.

Analyzing student learning, however, is more than a numbers game. When teams make decisions based merely on numbers, they miss the opportunity to engage in deep learning and to develop the collective instructional insights that will lead to their independent instructional agility.

For example, if a student earned 12 points on a 15-point quiz, or 80 percent, teachers in a traditional setting would consider the $^{12}/_{15}$ or 80 percent sufficient to advance in the learning, and they commonly reference it as *passing*. But is that really passing? Figure 6.1 provides a blueprint for a fifteen-question assessment covering three target areas. Each question in the blueprint serves a purpose. The first two questions in each target area assess DOK level 1 (recall) to ascertain whether students know or understand the important aspects of that target. The third and fourth questions in each target area assess DOK level 2 (skill or concept application) to ascertain whether students can apply algorithms or skills to solve problems with what they know. The fifth question in each target area assesses DOK level 3 (strategic thinking) to ascertain whether students can blend all that they understand conceptually with all that they can do procedurally to solve complex problems, construct, create, critique, and evaluate, along with other strategic-thinking processes.

Test Construct	Learning Target 1		Learning Target 2		Learning Target 3	
	Question Number	Question Type	Question Number	Question Type	Question Number	Question Type
DOK level 1: Identify	1	Multiple choice	6	True or false	11	Labeling
DOK level 1: Describe	2	Short answer	7	Short answer	12	Short answer
DOK level 2: Compare	3	Analogy	8	Matching	13	Venn diagram
DOK level 2: Interpret	4	Data chart labels	9	Short answer	14	Data chart labels
DOK level 3: Construct	5	Model creation	10	Arguing with evidence	15	Critique

Figure 6.1: Blueprint for a fifteen-question assessment.

Now imagine that the following learners each got three questions wrong on the fifteen-question assessment, so each has a score of 80 percent.

- Student A got questions 13, 14, and 15 wrong.

- Student B got questions 5, 10, and 15 wrong.

- Student C got questions 2, 9, and 12 wrong.

Would each learner be ready to advance in the learning? Would 80 percent accurately summarize each learner's proficiency level? Consider the following.

- **Student A:** With questions 13, 14, and 15 wrong, student A has demonstrated a lack of understanding for target 3. In this PLC, students must master the essential learnings that common assessments assess. Student A requires intervention regarding target 3, so 80 percent would not suffice.

- **Student B:** With questions 5, 10, and 15 wrong, student B has demonstrated an inability to think strategically with each target. In this case, the learner *remembers* things (the first four items in each target) but cannot think strategically within the target areas (the fifth item), so student B has not yet *learned* them. Student B requires additional practice and feedback with all three targets in order to get to deep learning, so 80 percent would not suffice.

- **Student C:** With questions 2, 9, and 12 wrong, student C has gotten only one question wrong per target area, and each wrong item appears in the remembering category (DOK levels 1 and 2 tasks—recall and skill or concept application, respectively), so 80 percent *might* suffice. But even in this case, teachers have more to consider. For starters, questions 2, 9, and 12 all require short answers.

Educators must consider the context when examining students' responses in order to judge their proficiency. Assessment work is always contextual. For example, if student C could not answer questions on an ELA assessment that required complete sentences, an ELA teacher might suggest 80 percent is not sufficient, as the student still lacks a significant ELA skill. As another example, if student C could accurately do the mathematics in questions 2, 9, and 12 of a mathematics assessment, but did not employ clear and accurate mathematical language in the short-answer explanations, a teacher might say 80 percent is passing, but then require the student to improve in employing accurate mathematical terminology over the course of future assessments. Still, in this case, student C might have demonstrated sufficient mastery of the mathematics to advance. However, this might not be the case if question 9 required learners to explain their thinking on how to solve this mathematics problem: *Chase had 12 marbles. He gave ⅓ of his marbles to Hakeem and ⅓ of his marbles to Marguerite. How many marbles does Chase have left?* And student C answered correctly (4 marbles), but proceeded to do the mathematics and explain his thinking in the following way.

$$\frac{1}{3} + \frac{1}{3} = \frac{2}{6}$$

$$2 + 6 = 8$$

$$12 - 8 = 4$$

The answer is 4. I knew I was dealing with thirds, so I lined up the fractions and added them. I know that 1 + 1 is 2, and 3 + 3 = 6, and 2 + 6 = 8 and 12 − 8 = 4.

Even though question 9 is a DOK level 2 task, student C has clearly demonstrated a faulty understanding that will cause immediate problems during future instruction. In this scenario, the score of 80 percent should not be sufficient to advance the learner to the next stage of learning.

The bottom line is that when teams look at common assessment data, the use of total points, percentages, and grades can mask substantial gaps in knowledge and skills. Holistic scores are not indicative of learning; worse, holistic scores do not help students understand *what* needs to improve. When teachers use holistic scores to make decisions, they end up working harder than their students to address achievement gaps because the students cannot isolate their own gap in order to join the teachers' effort to overcome it.

Rather than using cut scores to make decisions, teams should use cut criteria that indicate the quality of student learning. Cut criteria should address accuracy, proficiency levels, or both; comprehensiveness of the expectations; and designated levels of cognitive complexity. So, instead of saying a cut score of 80 percent correct is passing, a team might say each student's performance must meet the following cut criteria.

- **Accuracy:** The student functions without scaffolded support (such as teacher prompts or graphic organizers) and demonstrates a high degree of accuracy (such as he or she gets no more than two wrong in a set of six questions or gets a proficiency score of 3 on a four-point scale).

- **Comprehensiveness:** The student demonstrates understanding and ability on the full range of knowledge and skills assessed (for example, a target area does not remain ignored or unmastered).

- **Complexity:** The student comprehends and accurately applies knowledge and skills at the assessment's highest designated level of complexity.

When teachers have data conversations to either certify mastery or identify interventions, they require correct, detailed interpretations of the evidence at hand. Toward that end, collaborative common assessment data conversations require team members to develop and adhere to the following.

- Predetermined quality indicators of learning to guide decision making

- Comparable data arrangements to generate information (for example, data are arranged skill by skill, student by student, and classroom by classroom)

- Accompanying student artifacts or evidence to isolate specific knowledge and skills or gaps in knowledge and skills beyond the numbers

- Qualitative information to move teams beyond inferring and into confirming students' skill and knowledge levels

The more specific and detailed the analysis, the more valid and reliable the interpretation of the results.

Isolating Gaps in Understanding: Misconceptions, Mistakes, and Errors

Whether looking at data and evidence during the formative or summative phases, teachers are always seeking information that helps them address gaps in understanding and improve their instructional efforts. Gaps in understanding can include misconceptions, mistakes, or errors. Isolating gaps in understanding can illuminate the necessary instructional maneuvers for both teams or teachers and their students. Done well, the process leads to the following actions.

- Informs immediate, proactive instructional maneuvers

- Empowers learners to drive personal improvement efforts

- Directs intervention and enrichment efforts

- Guides assessment development

- Advises curriculum improvements

It always helps teachers to use anonymous samples from other team members' classrooms when engaging students in isolating gaps in understanding. When teachers and students alike can identify misconceptions, mistakes, and errors and isolate errors using common formative assessment data, they have a better chance at reducing the gap between what is happening and what needs to happen.

When working to isolate gaps in understanding, teachers must have awareness of the differences between misconceptions, mistakes, and errors (Chappuis, 2014; Fisher & Frey, 2007). Douglas Fisher and Nancy Frey (2007) note, "Misconceptions include preconceived notions, nonscientific beliefs, naïve theories, mixed conceptions, or conceptual misunderstandings" (p. 32). A mistake is the state or condition of being wrong because of a simple accident (such as misreading the directions or missing a key word like *always* or *not*). Clear and consistent additional evidence demonstrates that key concepts, terms, or processes are understood. An error is the state or condition of being wrong because of a clear misunderstanding or misapplication of a practice in concept, skill, reasoning, or any combination thereof. Available evidence demonstrates a visible disconnect between what was taught and what is understood.

In general, *mistakes* don't require interventions because the student who makes a mistake still understands the concepts or skills. But *errors* signify a condition of being wrong, and teachers must address this. When evaluating errant student work, teachers should carefully examine the student work to determine the exact gap in understanding.

Mistakes are easy to spot if there is sufficient evidence from prior work or other problems within the current assessment to indicate that the learner has mastered the skills and concepts. Even if it is a simple mistake, it can help to clarify where the mistake happened. Did the student misunderstand the directions? Did the phrasing of the question or task cause confusion? Did the student skip a key word like *not, always, most,* and so on? Or, did he or she read only the first part of the task and fail to finish following all of the required steps? The type of mistake can inform the feedback a teacher provides. If the mistake is frequently repeated (for example, the student constantly stops short of answering all parts of the task), then the teacher could employ an intervention to heighten the student's awareness of the problem and provide strategies to avoid repeating it. But any intervention for simple mistakes should be low stakes (requiring minimal time and minimal energy to resolve the problem). Students who make many mistakes would qualify for extended practice and feedback during the re-engagement phases.

Errors can be more challenging to identify. When a student doesn't understand something, it's important to understand both what it is that the student misunderstands and why that misunderstanding might exist. To notice student errors, teachers must analyze student *thinking*. Oftentimes, when trying to analyze thinking, teams must work together to explore a series of questions that can help them identify the type of error.

- Does it include a misconception or concept error based in one of the following?
  - Preconceived notions from personal experience (For example, a student might think, "I see the sun move, but you say it stays stationary and the earth moves. My experience hijacks your new information.")

  - ◦ Naïve theories or interpretations
  - ◦ Nonscientific beliefs
- If it includes a concept error, which concept does the error involve? What *does* the student understand about the concept? What understanding is the student missing? Which of the following caused the student to make the error?
  - ◦ Limited vocabulary and lack of background knowledge
  - ◦ An inability to identify individual parts
  - ◦ An inability to explain key processes
  - ◦ An inability to link together the interworking relationships
- Does it include a reasoning error (poor application of a thinking skill applied to concepts) caused by one of the following?
  - ◦ Not understanding the reasoning process
  - ◦ Employing the reasoning process inaccurately or insufficiently due to one of the following
    - ▸ Unsupported claims
    - ▸ Insufficient evidence or sampling errors
    - ▸ Overgeneralizations or oversimplifications
    - ▸ Inconsistency in evidence or application
    - ▸ Omissions
    - ▸ Contradictions
    - ▸ Illogical thinking and non sequiturs

Genuine mistakes should not require interventions unless the student consistently makes them—for example, the student consistently reads too fast and skips key words. Errors, however, require isolation and intervention. However, because errors in the form of misconceptions or reasoning errors are so challenging to identify and address, it is unlikely that students would be able to self-correct, so they often require interventions. Some interventions can be quick and easy—it might just require pointing out what is happening so the student can see the issue and adjust. But some interventions might require considerable time and often require alternatives to how the teacher initially taught the skills or concepts.

Analyzing Formative Data

Teachers can use common formative assessments to analyze errors. For example, a team may plan a single assessment question to use on an exit ticket. When teachers use exit tickets in the formative phases, it gives team members a chance to analyze what might be happening in the varying levels of readiness within their classrooms—what are the most common types of mistakes they will need to address instructionally so learners are ready for the summative assessment? Figure 6.2 provides the error-analysis protocol that the team could use with its exit tickets to identify, label, and address errors.

Protocol Steps	Process for Analyzing Right and Wrong Answers	Process for Analyzing Rubric- and Proficiency-Scored Answers
1. Create stacks of answers.	Create two stacks of answers—(1) those that are completely right and (2) those with errors.	Create the number of stacks of answers that aligns with the predetermined proficiency levels.
2. Identify types of errors (such as reading errors, concept errors, and reasoning errors).	Examine the error stack, and subdivide it into smaller stacks of alike errors.	Examine each stack, and identify common errors or isolate the components that would move work into the next-highest level if addressed.
3. Label common errors.	Give each type of error a label that describes the error.	
4. Determine interventions.	**Step 1:** Design instruction to help learners understand the type of error and the strategies to fix that type of error. **Step 2:** Engage learners in focused revision of that type of error in their own work.	
5. Use artifacts as teaching tools. *Note: Never reveal student names in this process.*	**Strategy 1:** Swap exit-ticket sets with a colleague. In your classroom, give the tickets to students, and have students repeat the process you used to create stacks. Create a class-generated list of types of errors that students made when they engaged in given concepts or processes. **Strategy 2:** Pull a few significant example exit tickets from other classrooms, and use them as class teaching tools, naming the errors, identifying the strategies to fix or avoid such errors, and collectively modifying or altering the examples with classroom input.	

Figure 6.2: Error-analysis protocol.

*Visit **go.SolutionTree.com/assessment** for a free reproducible version of this figure.*

After giving students the assessment and following the error-analysis protocol, teams should hold a ten-minute *standing meeting* to analyze their results. A standing meeting is called *standing* for two reasons: (1) the team has a standing expectation that, after every quick formative assessment, it will gather to analyze the results, and (2) no one sits down. The agenda for the ten-minute standing meeting would look something like the following.

1. Have the team leader or facilitator state the meeting's purpose and desired outcomes. (thirty seconds)

2. Have team members switch cards, sort them into like categories, and name the type of error represented in the cards within each pile, as outlined in the error-analysis protocol (figure 6.2). (five minutes)

3. Count exit tickets per pile, and enter the data in a simple table like figure 6.3 (page 171) that names the types of errors and mistakes and indicates how many students made each type of error. (two minutes)

4. Have members brainstorm and discuss possible solutions. (two minutes)

5. Close the meeting with confirmation of the solution the team agrees to implement. If time permits, ask for a quick thumbs-up or thumbs-down response on the team members' feelings about the quality of the standing meeting. (thirty seconds)

At first, it might take more than ten minutes to figure out how to use the protocol, but as teams become more familiar with the process and more experienced at isolating errors, the process can move quite quickly. In general, educators can quickly identify common mistakes or errors once the evidence is before them. Sometimes, it can take a little longer to identify the root causes, but the conversation is rich and always expands team understanding of what they see on the cards.

Using Common Formative Assessment Data for Error Isolation

As noted previously in this chapter, isolating errors enables educators to provide immediate, proactive instructional responses. Imagine, for example, a team uses a small common formative assessment to assess the learning target, "I can assess evidence. This means when reading, writing, listening, or speaking, I can identify and examine the evidence I provide or receive to determine its quality." Content- and grade-specific samples outlining possible exit-ticket prompts for that type of learning target follow.

- **Elementary ELA:** Simone put a period at the end of her sentence, but Bill told her she needed a question mark instead. Read the sentence and tell me who is right. What clues tell you the answer?

- **Elementary mathematics:** Alissa argued that the sum of two odd numbers will always be even. Hakim argued that the sum of two odd numbers will always be odd. Look at the arguments that each provided. Who provided the most accurate evidence? Explain your thinking.

- **Middle school science:** In the text about voltage and currents, the author said that vegetables could be turned into batteries. Name the most compelling evidence she provides to prove her claim is true. Use her evidence to explain why it makes her right or wrong.

- **High school social studies:** Deconstruct the news reporter's argument that the government should mandate every citizen over the age of eighteen to vote when living in a democratic society. Use evidence from the primary sources we have studied in class (Declaration of Independence, the Constitution, and so on) to prove him right or wrong.

Then, the team gathers and sorts exit tickets, identifies common types of errors, and plans instructional responses based on those errors. Table 6.2 offers examples of errors that students commonly make when they struggle on a learning target aimed at assessing evidence.

Table 6.2: Common Student Errors When Assessing Evidence

Evidence Identification Errors	Evidence Quality Errors
<ul><li>**Omission error:** The student skips details.</li><li>**Misrepresentation errors:**<ul><li>The student takes details out of context.</li><li>The student adds details that were not provided.</li></ul></li><li>**Overgeneralization error:** The student assumes everything in print is accurate and logical.</li><li>**Faulty logic error:** The student confuses claims with facts.</li></ul>	<ul><li>Evidence is inaccurate.</li><li>Evidence is insufficient.</li><li>Evidence is irrelevant.</li><li>Evidence is not representative of or generalizable to a greater reality.</li><li>Evidence does not build a cohesive and whole logical argument.</li></ul>

Of course the complexity and the number of errors will vary based on the age of the student and the complexity of the question, but in general, students make common errors when they struggle to assess evidence. Once a team labels the errors, members can gather the data in a simple table. Figure 6.3 shows an example of a simple data arrangement that a team might generate when using small common formative assessments to isolate errors. The data still provide the team with clear indications of where, how, and with whom to target an intervention response.

Each type of error is unique and requires its own type of intervention. It would be inappropriate to make students who have inaccurate or insufficient evidence engage in an intervention about evidence being generalizable to a greater truth. So, once teams have identified trends regarding types of errors, they can organize their findings and begin to plan instructional responses. Teams can use the reproducible "Response-Planning Template for Students Needing Practice or Enrichment" (page 187) to create and organize instructional plans for students who need practice or enrichment. Teams can use the reproducible "Response-Planning Template for Students Needing Support" (page 188) to engage in more detailed planning for students who need support.

Results of the assessing evidence exit ticket: • Four participating classrooms with one hundred completed exit tickets • Seventy-four accurate exit tickets • Twenty-six inaccurate exit tickets containing five different types of errors			
Number of Exit Tickets Reflecting This Mistake	**Description of Mistake or Error**	**Classrooms Involved**	**Students Involved**
4	Misunderstood the question	A, B, C	JN, BV, RE, HY
5	Singular or insufficient evidence	A, C, D	KL, MN, SA, FR, CV
7	Weak reasoning or faulty logic	A, B, C, D	KJ, OP, BR, CD, BG, LO, TG
8	Inaccurate evidence	A, C, D	BT, AG, WN, JT, LI, EF, BY, FS
2	Overgeneralization error	B, D	KL, TR

Source: Adapted from Erkens, 2016, p. 122.

Figure 6.3: Example of isolating errors in common formative assessments.

Collaborative teams focus on learning by examining the results of their effectiveness. In order to do that, they must constantly isolate the appropriate information to guide their instructional maneuvers as they work to increase achievement for all students. There are technical and sophisticated options to support those endeavors, but sometimes a simple grid that categorizes who needs what is sufficient. Response-planning templates like the reproducibles offered on pages 187 and 188 help teachers quickly identify needs so they can go about the business of planning re-engagement strategies.

Conclusion

Common assessment data provide the results teams need to study their effectiveness, improve their instructional practices, and close significant gaps in student understanding, making the common assessment process the core of collaborative team work. Unfortunately, the data process can feel time consuming and overwhelming, prohibiting many teams from engaging in the process frequently. When teams develop the appropriate templates, protocols, and procedures, they can maximize their effectiveness and efficiency. Because results are so critical to a team's success, data and artifacts should be present, to some degree, in every meeting. A data moment conversation about a single struggling student can change the tenor of the entire meeting that follows to plan the next unit of instruction.

Team Reflections

Take a few moments to reflect on the following questions.

- How might we arrange our data in comparative ways that feel safe for us but that also create the information we need to make better decisions?

- How could we organize our data in a very targeted, skill-by-skill manner that would target our learners' specific learning needs?

- What would we have to do to ensure that our data conversations regularly lead us to new insights for our instructional planning?

- What could we do to be more timely and responsive in our data meetings?

- How could we ensure we have productive, efficient, and collegial data conversations? Do we mine the data in the right way? Do we have helpful data-analysis tools, protocols, templates, and processes?

- Do our current data protocols eventually lead us to identifying appropriate program curriculum, instruction, and assessment modifications? If so, how do we know we are making quality improvements in those areas? If not, what could we do to ensure that happens?

Protocols for Examining Evidence and Artifacts

Teams can use these protocols to ensure their work toward three purposes—(1) to calibrate scoring so it has consistency, (2) to analyze student errors, and (3) to refine assessments after student evidence clarifies whether they assessed the standards—produces common data. These protocols involve seven steps.

- Universal components (steps 1 and 2)

- Scoring calibration protocol (steps 3–5)

- Error-analysis protocol (steps 3–5)

- Assessment and measurement tools refinement protocol (steps 3–5)

- Universal components (steps 6 and 7)

If a team wants to focus on only one of the three protocols' purposes, it would use universal components steps 1 and 2, then jump to the specific protocol (each of which provides a different set of steps 3–5), and finally conclude with universal components steps 6 and 7. If, however, the team wants to engage in all three purposes, then it would follow the entire process from start to finish, addressing universal components steps 1 and 2, steps 3–5 for each individual protocol, and universal components steps 6 and 7.

Universal Components

Complete these steps every time.

Step 1: Make key decisions. If this is not done before the meeting starts, then quickly address it at the start of the meeting.

- How much time will be available for collaborative scoring? Availability of time will dictate the quantity of work the team can review.

- How large will each student sample be? What item, feature, or specific criteria will the team review? Oftentimes the entire assessment is too big to review, so a team might say, "We're only examining item 6 on the last test," or "We only want to look at academic transitions in the students' writing," or "We will only look at the second paragraph in each paper we review for our criterion of sentence fluency."

- Given how much time is available and the quantity of what the team needs to review, how many samples will we examine per teacher or per classroom? Note: Pragmatically, teams determine sample size by the length of each student project (fifteen-page research paper versus item 2 on the test), the amount of time available for the review, and the number of educators involved in the review process. This process is informal, so statistical reliability is not part of the equation. It is a best-guess situation.

- Teachers should not identify their own student work for review. Instead, team members should randomly select a range of quality work (for example, low-, medium-, and high-quality examples) from each others' student work piles.

- Have team members remove or hide students' names from the set of unscored samples they bring.

The Handbook for Collaborative Common Assessments © 2019 Solution Tree Press • SolutionTree.com
Visit **go.SolutionTree.com/assessment** to download this free reproducible.

Step 2: During the meeting, review the assessment, its context, the standards, and the scoring tools, highlighting any clarifying questions or details that emerged during the assessment process.

- Decide if any changes in the scoring process need to happen at this juncture, but only make changes to the scoring criteria or proficiency levels that will benefit learners.

- Select which scoring criteria the team will use.

- Trade student work samples to start the scoring process. No teacher should begin with his or her own students' work.

- Distribute small sticky notes for easy scoring.

Scoring Calibration Protocol

Use these steps (continued from the Universal Components) to make sure the common assessment data are truly common.

Step 3: The team scores several samples of student work from each classroom collaboratively (as determined in step 1).

- Swap student work with each other so team members begin with someone else's student work.

- Individual team members review each sample before them and then place the preferred score (from the predetermined criteria or attending tool) for that sample on a sticky note. He or she places a sticky note on the student's paper or test in a place where it cannot easily be seen (such as on the back of the paper) and passes the paper to the next person to review and score (preferably without reading the previously assigned scores from other teammates). All papers rotate around the table until every paper is scored by each participating teacher in the process.

- Once all of the papers have gone all the way around the table to be scored, turn them over to reveal the collection of scores.

Step 4: Sort and stack results.

- Sort the work into similar stacks (all 3s, all 1s, and so on), adding a mixed number stack. If a paper has even one mixed number on it (such as five 2s and one 1), it goes in the mixed-number stack.

- During the sorting process, there is little discussion. Simply move the papers as quickly as possible to the appropriate designated stack.

Step 5: Go directly to the mixed-number stack to engage in a calibration discussion. This discussion is the most critical component of this protocol. The conversation is necessary to create shared understanding of common expectations so teachers can return to their classrooms and successfully score the remaining work that their sampling did not include.

- Discuss one sample at a time using the rubric or proficiency scale.

- Come to consensus as a team on what score to give the sample.

- Note the first few samples will take more time to score than the remaining samples.

The Handbook for Collaborative Common Assessments © 2019 Solution Tree Press • SolutionTree.com
Visit **go.SolutionTree.com/assessment** to download this free reproducible.

- Review as many assessments in the mixed stack as possible. Once the team reaches shared understanding of how to interpret quality using the attending tools with a high degree of consistency, teachers can score the rest of the student work from their individual classrooms as they normally would have.

- The more this protocol is used, the faster the process goes and the more consistent the scoring becomes until eventually, there will be few disagreements on what a score should be. Consider using this protocol with frequency to ensure scoring remains consistent.

Note: It can be helpful at this point to identify anchor papers—sometimes identified as exemplars—for each designated level of proficiency. The identified sample of what each level looks like becomes the "anchor" that students can reference to more fully understand what each level of proficiency entails. Anchor papers can help students better understand the attending tools.

Error-Analysis Protocol

Use these steps (continued from the Universal Components) to identify and problem solve types of error in student work.

Step 3: Sort cards into appropriate categories.

- If the results of the assessment are binary, then quickly sort the student work into two piles: a right-answer pile and a wrong-answer pile.

- However, if the results of the assessment involve gradations of quality, then quickly sort the student work into the perceived level of proficiency; try not to get lost in the need for accuracy during the sorting process.

- Go quickly and trust that follow-up discussions might lead to moving student work into different proficiency-level stacks later.

Step 4: Isolate and categorize the errors the team finds.

- In the right-and-wrong sorted piles, take the wrong-answer stack and subdivide the answers into new stacks by common error. During the sorting process, do not get lost in the need for accuracy.

- In the proficiency-sorted piles, sort cards for proficiency levels 1 and 2 by category of error (proficiency levels 3 and 4 should be error free). During the sorting process, do not get lost in the need for accuracy.

- For each stack, name the type of errors found. Examine the samples in the error piles and discuss them as a team until an appropriate label for that type of error is selected. Move cards to alternative stacks if discussion reveals the error is something other than the team previously thought when they placed it in the initial stack.

Step 5: Generate ideas for corrective instruction (this step's time frame depends on the number of samples involved).

- Discuss one error at a time, identifying the instructional tools and strategies, time frames, and so on that team members will use to support corrective instruction.

- Identify all the learners who will require a specific instruction.

The Handbook for Collaborative Common Assessments © 2019 Solution Tree Press • SolutionTree.com
Visit **go.SolutionTree.com/assessment** to download this free reproducible.

- Review work samples in the *right* pile and the proficiency levels 3 and 4 piles to identify the consistencies that team members can further enhance or refine with extension or enrichment activities.

- Identify all the learners who will benefit from the extension or enrichment activities.

Assessment and Measurement Tools Refinement Protocol

Use these steps (continued from the Universal Components) to improve the quality of the assessment design or the attending tools based on the real-time evidence that emerged in the student work.

Step 3: Identify the trouble spots in the assessment (the places where many students got the answer wrong or misread the directions, or where the errors may have been particularly egregious).

- Name each area of the assessment that requires improvement.

- Isolate the issue that requires resolution.

Step 4: Identify next steps for assessment design.

- Have all team members answer the following questions to offer ideas for the next design steps that will improve alignment to the standards, cognitive demands, and critical competencies and literacies.

  - Is alignment the issue? Does the question, prompt, or task match the standard expectations?

  - Is clarity the issue? Are the directions or the expectations of each item easy to understand?

  - Is terminology the issue? Were students confused by the terms employed or the vocabulary in the text?

  - Is rigor the issue? Were all of the items created at the appropriate level of rigor?

  - Is relevance the issue? Did students seem interested? Engaged? Concerned?

- Identify the greatest areas of concern for improving the assessment, and target those areas first.

Step 5: Modify the assessment or attending tools.

- Question by question, prompt by prompt, or task by task, discuss, review, and improve the assessment.

- Criterion by criterion, review and improve the attending tools (scales, rubrics, or other measurement tools) for their clarity, accuracy, and overall impact on student motivation and efficacy.

Universal Components

Complete these steps every time.

Step 6: Reflect on the experience, and identify next steps, if there are any.

- ○ Identify any additional learning needs for the team based on the findings in the meeting. If something more needs to happen, identify who will do which parts and by when, sharing responsibility whenever possible.

- ○ Identify any needed resources for the team based on the findings in the meeting. If something more needs to happen, identify who will do which parts and by when, sharing responsibility whenever possible.

- ○ Schedule the team's next review of student work; identify the purpose, content area or standard, and kind of work.

Step 7: Provide closure to the meeting. Review and debrief the following.

- ○ **Process:** What worked? What could we have done better or differently to streamline the process? Are there things we need to change in our protocols?

- ○ **Discoveries:** What did we learn? How does that learning inform our future work?

- ○ **Decisions:** What decisions did we make? Who will enact them and by when?

Data Protocol 1: Exploratory Dialogue

This protocol requires that teams have common assessment data that is already aggregated in a comparative format and that individual team members can speak to their instructional strategies or efforts leading up to the data. The protocol guides teachers through a sequence from predicting to problem solving.

Directions: After giving the common assessment and aggregating the data and creating visual tools (run charts, pie graphs, bar charts, and so on) to display the results, use the following protocol in your team data meeting. Make certain every team member has all the important materials (such as copies of the data, copies of the protocol, team norms, and so on) to support the conversation.

Predicting

To begin, *do not look at the data*. From your personal experience or observations in the assessment process, and from your experience with your own classroom results, begin predicting what might show up in the team's common assessment results. As a team, anticipate the outcome of the common assessment, and jot your shared thoughts down in the space provided. What do you predict the data and results will show? (This category is wide open, and team members should be able to explore all options, from the number of students who might be successful to the resulting levels of proficiency to the most significant trouble spots in the data, and so on.) List your shared predictions.

Exploring and Discovering

Now it's time to dig into the actual data. As you explore the results (looking at the data charts as well as the student artifacts behind the data charts), begin trying to interpret what you see. Try creating only statements of fact. Avoid rationalizing, deflecting, explaining, or any other interpretation strategy.

Try to avoid *because* statements or attempts at explaining why the data are what they are. You will do that next. Here, just observe and note the patterns, trends, and so on that have emerged. List your shared discoveries and team observations (statements of fact) in the space provided.

Organizing

After creating the statements of fact, it's time to make meaning of the findings (rationalize and explain the results and identify the plausible causes for the results). An important first step is to arrange your statements of fact into categories. Bruce Wellman and Laura Lipton (2017) suggest there are five key factors to consider at this point. Add your statements of facts as appropriate under the five factors listed in the following table, or add your own categories (for example, testing conditions). At this point, the team draws upon the history of what led up to the results, considering what instructional strategies and curriculum they used, and so on.

What are the possible causes for these data and results? List your statements of fact under the corresponding categories in the following table.

Student Knowledge, skills, and dispositions	Infrastructure Schedules, programming, and resources	Curriculum Design and implementation	Instruction Methods, materials, and resources	Teachers Knowledge, skills, and dispositions

Source: Wellman & Lipton, 2017.

After categorizing the information, begin identifying your team's theories behind the results. What theory (or rationalization that addresses the causes behind the data) can you offer for why the data are as they are? While there is space to record three theories, the number of theories the team generates may be more or fewer.

Theory 1:

Theory 2:

Theory 3:

Researching

If the team's exploration into the data revealed specific instructional strategies that generated significant positive results, the rest of the team members can agree to employ those same strategies in their own classrooms. If, however, current practices *did not* lead to positive results, then the team must turn to the best-practice research to determine what teachers should do to address a particular skill or concept. If there isn't enough time during the team meeting to explore research, individual team members can explore research-based options between meetings, sharing their findings along the way, or reconvening within a short time frame to explore their findings and select strategies to employ to address the known achievement gap.

Only fill in the researching section of this protocol *if research was required*. Begin by naming the theory of causation, and then identify one or more best practices to address the identified cause. Be certain to cite all research the team identifies.

What does the best-practice research recommend for the situations and issues at hand?

Theory of Causation	Best-Practice Strategy as Found in the Research	Citation for Research

Brainstorming Solutions

With all potential strategies now identified for use, it's time to brainstorm the possible solutions the team will employ. What can you do individually and as a team to address the data issues that you noted previously? Keep in mind your theories of causation. Work to explain how your solutions will address the data and results.

Making Decisions and Determining Next Steps

Now it's time to make final decisions. Create an action plan for next steps. What actions will you and your team take? What is your timeline? What criteria will you use to determine success? What links do these actions have to the best-practice research?

Cause	Action Step	Timeline	Success Criteria	Link to Best-Practice Research

Source: © 2016 by Adlai E. Stevenson High School, Lincolnshire, Illinois. Adapted with permission.

References

Wellman, B., & Lipton, L. (2017). *Data-driven dialogue: A facilitator's guide to collaborative inquiry* (2nd ed.). Charlotte, NC: MiraVia.

Data Protocol 2: Structured Conversations for Team Learning From Evidence

This protocol ensures teams focus on data norms and provides a form to guide structured data conversations. The simplified clock images appearing in this protocol provide a quick reference for teams, indicating how much time they should allot to each part of the protocol during a data meeting.

Data Norms

It's always important to make the team's predetermined data norms visible and available during the data conversation. If your data norms differ from those listed in this protocol, substitute them here. Once a team is familiar with its norms, members may not need to read them each time, but it's still important to have them be available should the need arise to invoke them during the meeting.

- We believe that all students are our students.

- We come prepared, ready to share and discuss data.

- We analyze our data to improve instruction.

- We focus discussion on instruction and its effect on student performance.

- We imagine that the students are in the room during our discussions, and we do not use data to blame students or their circumstances.

- We seek first to understand and do not jump to conclusions without ample data and an understanding of context.

Orient yourself to the data. Ask yourself:

- "How are these data organized or sorted?"
- "What are the most important components?"
- "What do I notice or wonder?"

	Strengths	Concerns
Step 1: Analyze strengths and concerns in the organized data. Consider the following. • What are our celebrations? What went well? What are we proud of? What pleasantly surprised us? • What is our greatest area of growth? • What questions did students scoring at the highest level miss? • To what classroom instructional practices can we attribute the change (positive or negative)? • Do the data show a trend or pattern? • What misconceptions did we uncover?		

Below Target	On Target	Above Target
List names of students who have not yet mastered the learning expectations.	List names of students who are working toward meeting the expectations and simply require additional coaching, feedback, or practice opportunities.	List the names of students who are excelling with the learning expectations and qualify for extension activities.

The Handbook for Collaborative Common Assessments © 2019 Solution Tree Press • SolutionTree.com
Visit **go.SolutionTree.com/assessment** to download this free reproducible.

	Students (For whom?)	Learning Goals and Skills (What?)	Instructional Strategies (How?)	Time Frame (When?)
Step 2: Establish goals and select instructional strategies. Consider the following questions, and record the What, How, and When for each group of students listed in the rows to the right. • What student learning goals will we set based on the data analysis? • What small-group and whole-group implications do the data have? • What data did we use to make these instructional choices? • What do I need to learn in order to deliver instruction in response to the data?	Students Below Target			
	Students On Target			
	Students Above Target			
	All Students (Reteaching)			

How will we know the instructional strategies are working?	How often will we monitor student progress?	What data will we collect?
Step 3: Plan to monitor student growth. Consider the questions in the columns to the right, and record your answers in the space below each question.		

Source: © 2017 by Leander Independent School District, Leander, Texas. Adapted with permission.

Data Protocol 3:
Data Analysis for Team Learning

This protocol is designed to help teams focus their work and guide their conversations. It incorporates the team's predetermined agreements regarding proficiency and links the data conversation to the SMART goal work the team did in advance of instruction, tying team decisions directly to the four critical questions of a PLC.

Date:	Team:	Academic area:

Step 1: Bring prepared data (from common formative assessments or districtwide benchmarks). Which specific students did not demonstrate mastery on which power standard?

Power standard:

Students who did not meet proficiency:

Students who need enrichment:

Step 2: Answer the questions, "What patterns can we identify from the data? Where did our students do well?"

Step 3: Answer the questions, "Which instructional strategies worked best? What should we retain, refine, or replace?"

Step 4: Answer the questions, "How effective was the assessment? Should we make any changes to it?"

Step 5: Answer the questions, "What intervention or enrichment activity will we provide to address the unlearned skills, and how will we check for understanding?"

Source: © 2016 by Hortonville Area School District, Hortonville, Wisconsin. Adapted with permission.

Response-Planning Template for Students Needing Practice or Enrichment

Directions: Use this template to group students based on the broad areas for re-engagement (interventions, practice, and extension) and plan instructional responses.

Learning target: _____		
Needs Support	**Needs Practice**	**Needs Enrichment**
Jot down the names of students who need support. Use the reproducible "Response-Planning Template for Students Needing Support" (page 188) to explore this more.	Students:	Students:
	Instructional plan:	Instructional plan:
	Resources needed:	Resources needed:
	Who will facilitate the instruction or process:	Who will facilitate the instruction or process:
	Date initiated: _____ Date completed: _____	Date initiated: _____ Date completed: _____

Source: Adapted from Vagle, 2015.

References

Vagle, N. D. (2015). *Design in five: Essential phases to create engaging assessment practice*. Bloomington, IN: Solution Tree Press.

Response-Planning Template for Students Needing Support

Directions: Use this template to categorize students by error and plan instruction for learners who need targeted intervention.

Learning target:		Learning target:		Learning target:	
Number and names of students:		Number and names of students:		Number and names of students:	
The types of errors students made with this target (list the number and categories of errors):		The types of errors students made with this target (list the number and categories of errors):		The types of errors students made with this target (list the number and categories of errors):	
Error:	Instructional fix:	Error:	Instructional fix:	Error:	Instructional fix:
Error:	Instructional fix:	Error:	Instructional fix:	Error:	Instructional fix:
Error:	Instructional fix:	Error:	Instructional fix:	Error:	Instructional fix:
Error:	Instructional fix:	Error:	Instructional fix:	Error:	Instructional fix:

Source: Adapted from Vagle, 2015.

References

Vagle, N. D. (2015). *Design in five: Essential phases to create engaging assessment practice.* Bloomington, IN: Solution Tree Press.

The Re-Engagement Phase

7

Best first instruction requires teachers to give the first round of instruction their finest attempt by employing strategies that research identifies as best practice. Because every moment counts, instruction requires considerable preparation and careful application. Still, all the planning in the world cannot completely eliminate the surprises, eradicate the challenges, or predict the spontaneous tangential learning opportunities that teachers might encounter mid-instruction. When it comes to teaching, it's imperative to plan with precision and then implement instruction as if the best plans will not work.

Moreover, it's important to note that *all* students qualify to continue engaging in the learning. There is always a next step for every learner, even when each learner is at a different level of understanding or readiness. Done well, learners are engaged in flexible groups—not ability-based groups. In that case, a single learner might be in the advanced group and ready for challenge on one concept but in the struggling group and ready for additional support on another concept.

Master teachers are quick to note that one or more students will struggle to understand even their best lessons. Planning with the realization that there will always be some students ready for stretch and challenge just as there will always be some students who struggle to grasp the learning constitutes a more strategic alternative than just planning a one-size-fits-all lesson for the general population of learners. So, the best plan to eliminate extensive intervention work is always re-engagement in the middle of instruction, before results from the summative assessment indicate that a student missed much of the learning. University of British Columbia PhD candidate Shelley Moore suggests the bowling analogy of the 7–10 split applies to classroom instruction (Social Sciences and Humanities Research Council of Canada, 2016). When teachers teach to the middle, they will likely generate the 7–10 split: the pins on the farthest corners remain standing. These might be the students who need extensions and re-engagement strategies. At that point, only the most talented bowler can get both pins down. Instead, Moore (Social Sciences and Humanities Research Council of Canada, 2016) recommends teachers operate like master bowlers, aiming for the back row, arcing the ball to hit pins 7 and 10, thereby knocking down all the others. When teachers enter a lesson already having strategies for re-engaging students in learning—from the challenged to the wanting-to-be-challenged students—all students in the room will benefit. If teachers plan instruction with the full range of learning in mind, they have a better chance of reaching the full range. Figure 7.1 outlines the three categories of continuing engagement for all learners following a common assessment: (1) extensions, (2) practice, error analysis, and feedback, and (3) interventions.

Figure 7.1: Tiered instructional responses to collaborative common assessment results.

All three categories of re-engagement are likely happening simultaneously in a differentiated setting. There will be some students who are ready for stretch and challenge (extensions), some who just need more supportive feedback to overcome small hurdles in their learning and practice with opportunities to isolate their errors, and some who require an entirely new approach to the instructional material (interventions). Each level can pose challenges for teachers, so collaboration is key to their ability to handle this work in fresh, creative, and targeted ways.

Planning Re-Engagement Responses

Re-engagement creates space for all learners to move to the next step. When teams anticipate that some learners will not learn the first time around and some will be ready for advanced opportunities, they weave time for re-engagement opportunities directly into their unit of study. Moreover, re-engagement addresses the needs of *all* learners differently, and in highly engaging and respectful ways for the learners.

Even though the re-engagement phase typically occurs *after* the best first instruction, there is no reason why teams cannot proactively plan it. When teams lay out plans in advance, they reduce stress as they near completion of instruction and it becomes evident some learners did not succeed the first time around. Granted, it's impossible to create perfect plans in the absence of student evidence that informs the instructional responses, but teachers can base general frameworks for their responses on their knowledge of and experience with the types of mistakes, errors, or misconceptions that occurred previously when teaching the concepts at hand. Figure 7.2 (pages 192–193) features a unit-planning template that teams can use, embedding their predeveloped assessment road maps and then proactively planning for the differentiated contingencies that will likely occur during or at the end of the unit.

Note the different levels of shading in the unit-planning template. Each shaded section highlights a different part of the instructional process during a unit of study. The first section highlights *what* to learn. The standards always lead in quality unit planning. Those standards are translated into specific learning targets to be shared with students during the unit. Together, standards and targets outline the skills and concepts to be learned that must be embedded in the curriculum. The second section names the assessments teachers will use to ensure students learn the concepts and skills. Just as standards are apparent heading to learning targets, summative assessments are apparent heading to formative assessments. When teachers plan for the evidence they must monitor in advance, it informs their instructional efforts. With the assessment system named, teachers can better determine the instructional strategies they must employ to elicit such evidence. It is in the final column, preplanned re-engagement strategies and tools, that teachers can begin to anticipate what they could do for students who require challenge, students who simply need more instruction and practice along the way, and students who will need to engage differently in the learning at hand. Experienced educators know that even their best lessons can leave some students confused or lost while not meeting the needs of their advanced learners. Planning to target the various needs of all learners in advance can mitigate the challenges that are often revealed after a unit of instruction has been assessed summatively.

Re-engaging students in learning at all levels—from extensions to interventions—happens throughout the unit of study as well as at the conclusion of the CSA if necessary. Again, anticipating and preplanning for instructional responses at the end can be helpful. Imagine, for example, that a team filled in the reproducible "Response-Planning Template for Students Needing Practice or Enrichment" (page 187) from chapter 6, outlining what it would do for extension options, practice options, and intervention options. The team's anticipated plans might look like figure 7.3 (pages 194–195), which addresses the needs of all three groups.

Grade level and department:

Contributing team members:

Subject:

Unit:

Start and end dates:

Explanation of why or how the content will be made relevant to the students (do not include testing or credit requirements):

Priority Standards (List one standard.)	Learning Targets (List all targets that align with the standard.)	Summative Assessments (List assessments that will comprehensively cover all the required learning expectations.)	Formative Assessments (List all anticipated formative assessments that will support success on the summative assessment.)	Preplanned Re-Engagement Strategies and Tools
		Provide the appropriate DOK level for each summative assessment (DOK level 1, 2, 3, or 4):	Provide the appropriate DOK level for each formative assessment (DOK level 1, 2, 3, or 4):	Extension options:
				Practice, error-analysis, and feedback options:
		Instruction to support:		Intervention options:
Curriculum to support:				

Curriculum to support:	Provide the appropriate DOK level for each summative assessment (DOK level 1, 2, 3, or 4):	Provide the appropriate DOK level for each formative assessment (DOK level 1, 2, 3, or 4):	Extension options:
			Practice, error-analysis, and feedback options:
	Instruction to support:		Intervention options:

Figure 7.2: Unit-planning template for re-engagement strategies and tools.

Visit go.SolutionTree.com/assessment for a free reproducible version of this figure.

Grade 5 mathematics, order of operations PEMDAS (parentheses, exponents, multiplication, division, addition, subtraction)

Learning targets:

- I can name the standard order of operations and explain why it is necessary.
- I can demonstrate the impact that changing the order of operations has when performing a series of operations.

Needs Extension	Needs Practice	Needs Support
Students: JT, RW, BV, PO, AR, BN, MN, MY, CG, JK	**Students:** Whole class with the exception of students listed in Needs Support and Needs Extension	**Students:** GJ, LO, BF, FA, TK, NH, CD
Instructional plan—PEMDAS (parentheses, exponents, multiplication, division, addition, subtraction) puzzles: Invite students to work with a partner or in a small team. The goal is to solve as many PEMDAS puzzles (out of ten) correctly in the shortest amount of time. The winning team solves the most puzzles accurately first. One PEMDAS puzzle will use the same series of six to ten numbers in the exact same sequence, and there will be five lines for each series of numbers. For example, puzzle one might appear as follows. 1. 3 4 2 3 3 = 24 2. 3 3 4 2 3 3 = 27 3. 3 3 4 2 3 3 = 36 4. 3 3 4 2 3 3 = 54 5. 3 3 4 2 3 3 = 60 Notice that each line is the same except for the different sums at the end of the line. Students only need to fill in the correct operations to get to the prescribed sum.	**Instructional plan—Jeopardy game:** Draw a Jeopardy board at the front of the room—column 1 is P for *parentheses*, column 2 is E for *exponents*, and so on—until PEMDAS. Create boxes for $100, $200, $300, $400, $500, and Bonus ($1,000) under each column label. Obtain three- by five-inch note cards. On each card, create an equation that highlights the focus of its column (for example, exponents) and has a level of difficulty that corresponds to the value of its row (for example, the $500 row is more difficult than the $100 row). Within the classroom, create two teams, and rotate through the teams so they answer in a relay fashion. Have the first participant of team 1 call for a column and row of preference (for example, M for $200) and then solve the equation hidden there within one minute. Let the answering player call on one friend from his or her team for help if needed, keeping in mind that speed will matter.	**Instructional plan—Direct instruction:** First, have the group develop it's own localized mnemonic device for PEMDAS that would fit the school (for example, the school motto, theme, or mascot), replacing the traditional device *Please Excuse My Dear Aunt Sally.* A localized option can help students personalize and own the acronym. Second, draw a PEMDAS table together, inviting students to name the rules and co-create the image that shows the rules. Third, when teaching the PEMDAS process, have the students use their whiteboards to complete each step (the P, then the E, then the M, then the D, then the A, and finally the S) three times. In each rotation, use the same sequence: first as a whole class, second with a partner, and third individually (using different numbers for each step and each rotation to make sure they learned the step).

So, in order for line 1 to equal 24, the order of operations would be as follows.

$3 + (3 × 4) + (2 × 3) + 3 = 24$

The key to this problem follows.

1. $3 + (3 × 4) + (2 × 3) + 3 = 24$
2. $3 + (3 × 4) + 2 × (3 + 3) = 27$
3. $(3 + 3) × 4 + 2 × (3 + 3) = 36$
4. $(3 × 3) × 4 + 2 × (3 × 3) = 54$
5. $3 + 3 × (4 + 2) × 3 + 3 = 60$

Provide students a worksheet that includes ten different PEMDAS puzzles, each full puzzle comprising five different lines. Try to make sure each puzzle gets increasingly more complex.

The winning team must solve all of the puzzles correctly and in the shortest amount of time.

Resources needed:

A worksheet with ten PEMDAS puzzles

A competition scoreboard (if desired) to show how many each team solved accurately and the amount of time it took

Who will facilitate the instruction or process:

A teaching assistant or paraprofessional, if given the answer key and a timer

Date initiated: 9/6
Date completed: 9/6

If he or she solves it, his or her next teammate gets a turn; if he or she doesn't, the turn passes to the next team.

Resources needed:

Three- by five-inch note cards (two per question—one to cover the actual question)

Six questions of increasing difficulty ($100–$500 questions) per P, E, M, D, A, and S category

Who will facilitate the instruction or process:

Two classroom teachers from the collaborative team

Date initiated: 9/6
Date completed: 9/6

---

1. Write the problem.
2. Simplify any parentheses first, starting with the innermost group, and check off the P box.
3. Simplify any powers (exponents), and check off the E box.
4. Perform the multiplication and division in order from left to right, and check off the M and D boxes.
5. Do the addition and subtraction last. Remember, if the operations are written next to each other, work from left to right and check off the A and S boxes.

Resources needed:

Curricular resources

New worksheets or problems

Classroom whiteboards

Who will facilitate the instruction or process:

The classroom teacher who had the best results from the common assessment

One teaching assistant or paraprofessional who will provide support

Date initiated: 9/6
Date completed: 9/8 (one-on-one with two remaining learners)

Figure 7.3: Sample plans to re-engage learners following a fifth-grade mathematics unit on the order of operations.

When teams know the re-engagement plans in advance, they have the benefit of the following.

- Forecasting the extensions opportunity early in the unit to pique student curiosity and motivation

- Brainstorming plausible intervention ideas that can inform their own classroom interventions during the unit of instruction (while team members would not appreciate duplicating the team interventions prematurely, the idea of the strategies to employ can easily help teachers see the possibilities to try in their own classroom; the idea of carefully and specifically deconstructing the PEMDAS process, for example, can happen in a host of different ways)

Designing High-Quality Re-Engagement Responses

Re-engagement means to engage *differently*. During one of his keynotes, Richard DuFour (n.d.) calls for educators to use the data from CFAs to *rethink* instructional options—to go beyond what's *been tried* and into what's *not yet* been tried. He states, "Effective formative assessment informs us about changes we [as educators] need to make; not just the changes the kids need to make." He further asserts that if teams don't use the data to actually do something differently, they are not truly functioning as a PLC.

Learning takes time. It requires clarity, discovery, repetition, rehearsal, challenge, trial, error, feedback, support, and even a little fun. Re-engagement actually just continues learning in a far more targeted way. Done well, classroom re-engagement efforts can rejuvenate teams as they play with instruction and identify alternative ways to ensure all learners meet high proficiency levels. Teams should plan re-engagement responses for each of the three re-engagement tiers: (1) extensions; (2) extended practice opportunities, error analysis, and feedback; and (3) interventions.

Designing Extensions

Traditionally, conversations about enrichment activities have exclusively focused on working with gifted and talented learners and have most often appeared in the literature about differentiating instruction. Unfortunately, this literature includes very little about how to develop enrichment or extension opportunities for learners who advanced in a concept or unit of learning faster than their peers. As a result, opportunities for extension usually fall into one of two categories: (1) long-term projects that only a few learners will have access to over time or (2) short activities that fill time but do not extend learning (for example, watching a movie, reading a book, or playing a game). While such activities can be fun, they do not necessarily tie directly to the learning expectations at hand, and they do not actually extend the learning in rigorous and enjoyable ways for the learners.

Learners who qualify for enrichment activities have already certified their proficiency in an assessment-based experience. This means they have no major concept or reasoning errors or omissions in their work. The evidence they have generated indicates that they understand all the critical concepts and can engage in all the necessary skills at the appropriate proficiency levels. As such, they do not require an additional assessment experience. Their extension experiences can expand learning opportunities without requiring another level of certification.

Extension activities should deepen or broaden learning in a manner that the learners involved find desirable. If learners who qualify for extension simply earn more work, they may not strive for future opportunities, and if they simply advance in the curriculum at a faster pace, the chasm between the learners within the classroom widens, and the process turns into ability grouping rather than flexible grouping based on unit-by-unit evidence. It stands to reason that if students knew there was something rewarding and enjoyable awaiting them on the other side of proficiency, they'd be far more motivated to pass a unit of instruction on their first attempt.

Figure 7.4 (page 198) provides a checklist that teachers can use to brainstorm options for their extension activities or to review the quality of their plans once they complete them. All extension opportunities must be designed to meet the required criteria if they are to deepen the current learning in motivating ways. The additional desirable criteria help educators consider more enticing options within the extension experiences.

Extension should be fun and engaging. It should invite joy and a sense of accomplishment for the learners involved. When learners truly enjoy the opportunity before them, they do not worry about how many points an activity will accumulate, especially if the work they produce will actually be employed or shared in some public way. The issue of grading moves off the table.

Designing Extended Practice Opportunities, Error Analysis, and Feedback

Some learners do not qualify for extensions quite yet, but they do not require direct instruction either. These learners have generated evidence on previous assessments that, although they might still make minor errors, indicates they grasp the majority of the concepts and skills with a small margin of error or inconsistency. They may not have fully reasoned with the content yet, but they independently understand the details involved. Instructional responses

Check all that apply.	Criteria for High-Quality Extensions
Required Criteria for Extensions	
	It links directly to the learning targets of the unit.
	It requires the learner to apply knowledge and skills from the unit.
	It inspires fun and creativity.
	It increases the level of challenge.
	It can be accomplished in the provided time frame.
Desirable Criteria for Enhancing Extension Designs	
	It is based in collaboration.
	It provides opportunities for learners to work with a wide variety of their peers over time.
	It invites multiple perspectives.
	It integrates multiple concepts within the discipline or becomes interdisciplinary.
	It involves a degree of student choice or authorship in the experience.
	It provides opportunities for open-ended, inquiry-based, or problem-based investigations.
	It generates authentic learning experiences.

Figure 7.4: Checklist for designing enrichments.

*Visit **go.SolutionTree.com/assessment** for a free reproducible version of this figure.*

for these learners vary; some might require more rehearsal to generate a high degree of automaticity, while others might benefit from error analysis to avoid repeated error patterns within their control, and still others might benefit from a little more strategic feedback on how to reason differently or form stronger, more comprehensive answers on their own.

Teams must analyze the artifacts of student learning to make appropriate decisions for the learners involved. The type of error, misconception, or simple mistake a learner makes fairly consistently will determine the instructional response a team should ultimately employ. Table 7.1 offers ideas about the necessary classroom tone as well as some ideas for rehearsal, error analysis, and feedback options.

Table 7.1: Classroom Tone and Instructional Considerations for Supporting Rehearsal, Error Analysis, and Feedback Responses

Ideas for Setting the Tone	Rehearsal Ideas	Error Analysis Ideas	Feedback Ideas

• Create an environment of safety—no judgment, just opportunities to grow and improve.
• Focus on learners' desires and assets as much as if not more than their specific needs.
• Allow for risk taking and mistake making in the process.
• Build a culture of support.
• Make learners do the thinking.
• Employ metacognition strategies so learners must think about their own thinking.
• Celebrate successes, and remain focused on the positives.
	• Review current work to observe strengths and opportunities for growth.
	• Set learning goals—these may be incremental goals if chunking is needed.
	• Chunk the work into manageable portions.
	• Establish a purpose for the practice that ties directly to the learning targets and learners' needs.
	• Elicit think-alouds from learners (talking about their thinking).
	• Frame and reframe as needed to help learners view content from multiple lenses.
	• Establish a routine or protocol for all rehearsal work.
		• Engage learners in examining and analyzing samples of strong and weak work.
		• Isolate common types of errors or misconceptions that have shown up in class work (anonymously).
		• Isolate with specific details the *types* of errors or misunderstandings that individual learners demonstrate privately.
		• Identify evidence of success, and name the quality indicators of that success to support continued self-monitoring.
		• Engage learners in tracking their improvement data, and then celebrate incremental successes.
		• Teach focused revision—do not leave revision to chance.
			• Follow best practices in providing feedback:
			  • Feedback feeds forward in a learning orientation.
			  • Feedback is diagnostic and isolates errors or misconceptions.
			  • Feedback is actionable (timely, limited, and doable).
			  • Feedback connects to the strengths and opportunities for growth of the individual.
			  • Feedback is narrowed, with focused and few details.
			  • Feedback supports self-reflection and decision making.
			• Employ metacognitive reflection strategies.
			• Employ self- and peer review.

When working with learners who need more practice to get to automaticity or more error analysis or feedback in order to carefully examine their understanding and reasoning, teams must design opportunities for high-level student engagement. Even though the core instruction may have involved active learning strategies, the follow-up efforts—especially for learners who did not grasp instruction the first time—must be equally if not more engaging. Fisher and Frey (2010) define *guided learning* as "saying or doing the just-right thing to get the learner to do cognitive work" (p. vii). In other words, it's even more critical now that the re-engagement work challenge the learner, interest the learner, and invite the learner into deeper investigation and application.

Designing Interventions

If any student needs a sense of hope and efficacy, it's the struggling learner. Students who haven't grasped the learning the first time around need care and support, not judgment or punishment. Toward that end, intervention work is not reteaching, or the proverbial do-over. As such, it should never involve the following.

- Repeated instruction (same, but louder, slower, or broken into smaller, discrete bits that can distort or distract from the larger conceptual understanding)
- A delivery tone that is punitive or pedantic
- Independent study (self-taught by study packet)

When it comes to interventions, it's time to take a second look at learning. First, relevance matters. Fred M. Newmann, Dana L. Carmichael, and M. Bruce King (2016) assert that relevance is best placed in the present for learners—why they need to know or be able to do something *now*. Relevance creates meaning and purpose. It gives context. Students who don't grasp something right away most definitely benefit from understanding meaning, purpose, and context as they continue to grapple with the learning. Without those components, learning can feel forced, tedious, and unnecessary. If students don't care, it can be easy for them to ignore a teacher's best efforts to engage them.

Second, tone matters. If re-engagement is truly an extension or next step for all learners, then there is no bad place to be; rather, there is only *what comes next* for each learner. A learner's need to be re-engaged is not immediately indicative of laziness or disinterest. Even adults don't always learn at the same time or in the same way. Beginning with a positive presupposition that the learning *will* happen can generate a degree of optimism and confidence in learners who hover of the cusp of giving up.

Finally, engagement matters. Done well, structured learning experiences are intriguing and gratifying. They challenge and captivate. Struggling learners are more likely to re-engage when the learning is interesting, thought provoking, or even *fun*. It should *never* involve self-learning, wherein students are handed study guides and told to fill in the packet without any more instruction. If students didn't grasp it *with* instruction, how are they supposed to grasp it without instruction? It's important to contextualize this work as educators; *all* learners—even the educators themselves—benefit from highly engaging experiences that occur more than once and in more than one way.

When learners struggle, it's essential to tap into the natural curiosity, intuition, insights, and creativity that all learners bring to the learning process. It helps to design interesting tasks that begin from a place of wonder and allow students the opportunity to start from a place of natural intuition, make observations, share what they already know, or frame the questions they have in that moment. Equally, it's important to build on each student's strengths, talents, and interests rather than launch by providing feedback that only spells out his or her deficits. The old adage *Success breeds success*, applies.

Likewise, it helps to keep sight of the big picture regarding the concepts or skills at hand. Sometimes, if concepts are broken into discrete components too early, learners can miss the greater context, which makes grasping concepts even more challenging. Using a wide array of strategies can keep the learning fresh and interesting. Strategies like the following can help.

- Use stories to make meaningful connections. Stories activate both imagery and emotion—two triggers that can help learners understand something.

- Set the learning to music; have learners create jingles, acronyms, raps, and so on. Music, rhythm, and rhymes also activate emotion and provide mnemonic hooks for easy recall.

- Create graphic organizers or visual tools to represent relationships in and among concepts. Visual representations can help students make new connections by exploring relationships.

- Engage students in developing metaphors and analogies or charts that reveal similarities or differences. Understanding relationships between what is already known and what is yet to be learned can give context to understanding.

- Employ kinesthetic or tactual mediums to explore learning. Using body movements, manipulatives, flash cards, or any other features can help the learners experience the learning differently. The mental pegging involved can help ideas remain in the learners' memories.

Ideally, in the intervention tier, learners engage in some degree of guided instruction. *Guided instruction* is small-group instruction that the teacher facilitates or *guides* for a short period of time to develop meaningful understanding of concepts (Fisher & Frey, 2010). Most frequently occurring in reading and mathematics, guided instruction can actually occur in any content area. Guided group sessions often last for short time frames (typically fifteen to thirty minutes), and groups tend to feature eight students or fewer. Because the focus of the instruction is narrowed to one or two topics or skills in guided instruction, all of the learners at the table share a common gap in their understanding or ability. Following guided group sessions, the students frequently have an independent or nonteacher-led experience (like reading privately to practice the reading skills they just discussed or doing a mathematics worksheet to practice the mathematics skills) so the students have more experience or practice. The teacher can also conduct a one-on-one formative assessment to glean additional insight into the current level of proficiency of each learner following the guided instruction (Fisher & Frey, 2010). For example, imagine a teacher conducted guided instruction during a social studies unit for students who struggled to identify the evidence used to support a strong argument. The only way the teacher can verify what each individual student now understands as a result of the instruction is to check for understanding through an assessment task in which each learner must independently identify the evidence behind a different strong argument than the one studied by the group.

Guided instruction groups target specific needs. Done well, they can be powerful, flexible, and responsive intervention opportunities. Done poorly, guided instruction serves as a disguise for ability grouping in which short shots of core instruction are offered to the same students who are always with the same groups, doing the same kinds of tasks.

Guided instruction is not the only option. Another option involves forming mixed groups in which learners of all abilities work collaboratively to solve complex problems. Heterogeneous groupings can be powerful when structured with care so everyone has a contributing role, the problem-based task offers complexity for everyone involved, and knowledge and skill are built collaboratively over time (Frey, Fisher, & Everlove, 2009). When struggling learners have the opportunity to watch effective learners struggle productively, they realize all learners are sure to face struggle at some point, and they observe additional strategies for navigating complex tasks they can begin adding to their own repertoire of strategies (Fisher, Frey, & Hattie, 2016).

No matter the strategies or groupings employed, intervention work is challenging. Teams have a better chance of closing significant learning gaps when they explore classroom data to carefully consider and strategically deliver targeted responses to specific gaps. Likewise, individual team members have a much better chance at improving their own instructional efforts when they explore best-practice research, challenge their own preconceived notions, and co-create original and imaginative alternatives.

Employing Best-Practice Responses

Gaps in understanding can be challenging to address. What's always been done may no longer work to solve complex problems, so collaborative teams turn to the research to explore best-practice alternatives. *Best-practice strategies* are those strategies that a significant body of research and evidence has deemed consistently and highly effective practices. In education, meta-analysts—those who find common threads across multiple bodies of primary research, such as Marzano and Kendall (2007) and Hattie (2009)—note that educational findings are always contextual. What is considered best practice might work in some circumstances, but not necessarily in all circumstances. Moreover, Andy Hargreaves and Michael Fullan (2012) state that best-practice research is based in what *was*, but educators need to always search for *next* practices and *what could be*. In a collaborative culture, they note, deprivatized classrooms open conversations across the building and even across the larger organization, creating the space for shared understanding where research and practice meet (Hargreaves & Fullan, 2012). They state, "We have a golden opportunity to sort out good from bad practice" (Hargreaves & Fullan, 2012, p. 49). Teachers themselves must act as researchers in their classrooms, clarifying with evidence what works and what does not. But they should always explore such findings collaboratively in order to remove personal bias in the results.

PLCs engage in both collective inquiry and action research. In other words, they explore best-practice research as a means to inform their own practices and then employ action research strategies to confirm the effectiveness of their collaborative choices. Hargreaves and Fullan (2012) offer the following perspective:

> What is needed is a profession that constantly and collectively builds its knowledge base and corresponding expertise, where practices and their impact are transparently tested, developed, circulated, and adapted. There needs to be a continuous amalgamation of precision and innovation, as well as inquiry, improvisation, and experimentation. The sorting process involves one's own and other teachers' practice informed by the research base and interpreted together. And there needs to be a mix of committing to *best practice* (existing practices that already have a good degree of widely agreed effectiveness) and having the freedom, space, and resources to create *next practice* (innovative approaches that often begin with teachers themselves and that will sometimes turn out to be the best practices of the future). (pp. 50–51)

Only when teams combine the two traits of collaborative learning teams—(1) collective inquiry and (2) action research—can they accurately identify next practice to address the learning gaps they discovered in their common assessment data. They can also then track effectiveness of their practice to ensure they are truly using best practices.

Collective Inquiry

When learners need to re-engage in learning, they require something different from the original instruction. Teachers must think outside the box to find new instructional alternatives. Teams need to engage in collective inquiry in order to bring new thinking to their craft knowledge.

Richard DuFour (2008) defines *collective inquiry* as:

> the process in which educators engage as they make significant decisions. Rather than making decisions on the basis of mindless precedent ("This is how we have always done it.") or personal preference ("This is how I like to do it."), they begin by building shared knowledge or learning *together*, thus it is a *collective* endeavor. *Inquiry* simply means we are asking and answering questions together.

Teams must engage in collective inquiry, or collaborative research, to answer complex problems. When they don't look to the research to identify best practice, they can miss opportunities to improve their professional knowledge and skills, and worse, they can eliminate possibilities to support student learning differently than they have in the past. Education is a profession that must remain current in best practice, and teachers must constantly train and retrain their instructional muscle. Figure 7.5 offers a protocol to guide team learning in the research process. The protocol may take several meetings; it will require two meetings at a minimum so team members have time to gather information before returning to discuss their findings.

Protocols lend clarity to the steps in the process. When teams have guidelines for how to go about the work in advance, individual members can be more successful and consistent as they strive to answer the questions or complete the tasks involved.

The reproducible "Annotated Research Notes Template" (page 212) provides a note-taking form that team members can use when gathering research. Teams should use one form per research source. The form provides team members with the opportunity to process their thoughts by asking questions and questioning their findings.

Steps	Activities	Resources
Meeting 1		
Step 1	Identify the area of study.	
Step 2	Brainstorm a list of subtopics within the area of study that require further investigation. What questions does the team have that require answers? (Note: The team can brainstorm general ideas together and record them during the discussion, or team members can first brainstorm their own ideas on sticky notes and then post them in a central location so they can cluster them into like categories and then name each cluster.)	Sticky notes for individual brainstorming A writing board for clustering and labeling ideas
Step 3	Generate a collective list of criteria that the research the team members will study must meet. A list of sample criteria follows. • It uses current research. (If possible, the research should be less than ten years old.) • It is backed by multiple sources. • It is applicable to the target audience and identified needs. • It includes practical ideas for classroom applications. Confirm the criteria that team members should use before they leave the meeting to begin individual research efforts.	A shared document or a public writing space like Google Docs to generate and document conversation
Step 4	Brainstorm a list of potential resources to study.	A shared document or a public writing space like Google Docs to generate and document conversation
Step 5	Bring closure to meeting 1 by doing the following. • Divvy up research responsibilities so everyone gathers information. • Establish timelines for conducting the research. • Provide team members with tools needed for recording (see figure 7.6, page 210). Have team members bring annotated findings to the next meeting.	Research-recording templates or online tools

Figure 7.5: Protocol for team-based research of best practice.

continued →

Steps	Activities	Resources
Meeting 2		
Step 1	Identify the various sources that team members studied. Create a list of them.	A shared document or a public writing space like Google Docs to generate and document conversation, or a shared folder in which to place some of the discovered reading materials
Step 2	Share the findings from each source in a round-robin discussion. Share quotes, data, or important information that informs the team's future decision making.	
Step 3	Share specific application ideas. You may find it helpful to transfer specific ideas onto sticky notes so that the team can cluster the ideas into like categories.	Sticky notes A shared document or a public writing space like Google Docs to generate and document conversation
Step 4	Identify any questions or concerns the team still has before launching into next steps. (Note: If the team needs future exploration, it might require additional research and meetings.)	
Step 5	Identify one to three practical next steps the team is willing to take when re-engaging the learners instructionally. Identify tools that the team needs to develop.	
Step 6	Identify indicators for success. How will the team know if the strategies worked? What additional assessment will it use to measure students' learning that resulted from the new strategies?	

Visit **go.SolutionTree.com/assessment** for a free reproducible version of this figure.

Action Research

Another inquiry-based process, *action research*, serves as a companion to collective inquiry. After teams have gathered their research findings, they isolate a strategy or practice they wish to employ so they can study the impact of that strategy or practice with their own local results to determine whether it really is a best practice for them. Action research allows teams to apply their collective findings and team decisions regarding the instructional strategies they will use to re-engage their learners in productive and supportive instruction. Action research is a focused process that engages teams themselves in investigating the application of best practice so their local results inform next practices. Learning teams design and conduct the process. Throughout the process, teams gather data to analyze and improve their practice.

Ideally, their question is also linked to the best-practice research they discovered during the collective inquiry phase. Ultimately, a team's action research question should stem from their own interest in determining what practices or strategies will work best in their classrooms as they work to close achievement gaps. For example, if a team's inquiry into the best-practice research suggested that heterogeneous grouping could work for intervention purposes, then the team would frame an action research question to determine if that were true in their own context. Their question might be, How could we use collaborative learning processes in heterogeneous grouping to advance the learning for all of our students? With the question in place, they would then go about trying and testing a few key strategies (as recommended in their research) for collaborative learning in heterogeneous settings, gathering their own evidence of effectiveness along the way.

Quality action research questions cannot be answered with a simple *yes* or *no* response. Such answers are not helpful for transfer to other settings or informed practices in the long run. For example, if the answer to the question, Does the use of manipulatives increase engagement in mathematics? is *yes*, how does that change instructional practice for the better? There are both poor and effective ways to use manipulatives, and simply responding with a *yes* offers no guiding clarification or insight into the *how*. Better questions in this example might be, What are the benefits to using math manipulatives well and how can those benefits inform our mathematical practices? or How can we use math manipulatives to increase student engagement and comprehension? In general, action research questions, such as the following examples, have answers that pertain to *how, the why,* or *the what.*

- "Why might engaging learners in a daily dose of close reading with text that is slightly beyond their ready comprehension increase vocabulary and comprehension skills?"

- "What kinds of feedback could we use regarding learners' reading skills to support slow or struggling readers in maintaining a sense of hope and building a base of efficacy?"

- "What targeted and supportive feedback can we provide that will help learners reduce the discrepancy between where they are in their learning and where they need to be?"

- "How will offering feedback—and not grades, until students achieve a specific proficiency level—impact student achievement in writing?"

- "How will employing mathematics talks engage learners in becoming metacognitive about their mathematical understanding?"

- "How can we engage all learners in answering classroom questions and participating in classroom discussions?"

- "How will engaging learners in collaborative scoring, defense of their responses, and self- and peer editing increase learners' capacity to make strong instructional decisions?"

- "Why might the process of involving students in assessing, tracking, and setting goals for their own learning impact their achievement and their motivation positively?"

- "What assessment tools and processes can we use to help learners track their personal progress toward mastery so that we increase student motivation?"

Classroom-based action research invites teachers to apply outside research to their classroom investigations as they try new strategies. The results inform their own understanding. Moreover, in a PLC, significant findings are always shared at the building level, so all collaborative teams can benefit from the work of each team.

It is important that teacher teams involve administrators in the plans and solicit their approval and support for the efforts. Depending on the changes they want to implement, teams may need to seek parent approval as well. Teams should discuss their plans with the administration and involve them in the decision-making process regarding parent approval.

See the reproducible "Action Research Planning Tool (pages 213–215) for a resource to support team planning in this area. Even if the action research indicates that the chosen strategies did not generate the positive results the team sought, the team can still find celebration in that discovery. Even a negative finding can more accurately inform a team's next steps.

Effectiveness Tracking

Too often, a team discovers or refines supportive instructional strategies, but its findings remain confined to the team itself. A PLC always comprises many learning teams, and when learning teams make significant discoveries, it is critical to the PLC's success that teams share and document those strategies. Teams across all grade levels and disciplines deal with different but often related concerns when it comes to closing learning gaps. Healthy organizations find ways to share their learning systemwide.

With the 21st century's technological options, schools can fairly easily create databases that track the effectiveness of each team's instructional interventions. Such documentation will help teams identify and share next practices. In Watertown-Mayer Elementary School in Watertown, Minnesota, reading intervention specialist Marnie Pauly began documenting the effectiveness of every team's reading intervention efforts (personal communication, August 2016). Her unpublished database, similar to the template in figure 7.6 (page 210), helped every team in the K–5 building document the effectiveness of its re-engagement strategies for reading. With each contribution to the database, teams grew stronger in their capacity to teach reading. The database gave them ready access to locally researched next practices, which guided their quick decision making in emerging circumstances. It allowed teams to track what types of mistakes students made for each specific learning target. Note that the number of rows the template provides for documenting types of errors should not limit a team's reporting. While the template includes three such rows, this may not be sufficient for all teams. The document is fluid, and teams can add or subtract rows for documenting types of errors as needed.

Tracking the effectiveness of re-engagement efforts creates a true PLC experience. Documenting results can embolden teams to become explorers in the field of education. They become innovative. They become diligent about attending to details and demanding results. They become precise and responsive in their instructional decision making.

Assessing Learning After Re-Engagement Responses

Teams miss a critical opportunity to learn from their professional experience when they neglect to reassess their students following a re-engagement experience for the learners who needed extra time, support, and especially explicit interventions. Too often, teams might re-engage students who initially demonstrated gaps without reassessing at all. When that happens, teams cannot know if their instructional choices did, in fact, close the identified gaps. Teams can follow several guidelines to support their reassessment work after re-engagement.

- Assess only the areas requiring reassessment. Do not make the learner take the entire assessment again.

- Assess the entire learning target. Do not use replacement items in a full section (for example, if a section has six questions, and the learner missed four, the learner must complete the entire section of questions—all six).

- Use equitable but different questions, prompts, or tasks. Recalling answers that were shared previously provides false positives on whether or not learning happened.

Grade level or department: _____

Team members involved:

_____

_____

_____

Dates of investigation: _____

Resources required: _____

Context of study (audience, subject or topic, circumstances, conditions, and so on):

Learning target:	Type of error:	Instructional response:	Assessment to use:	Effective strategy:	Data to verify effectiveness:
				Ineffective strategy:	Alternate response:
		Instructional response:	Assessment to use:	Effective strategy:	Data to verify effectiveness:
				Ineffective strategy:	Alternate response:
	Type of error:	Instructional response:	Assessment to use:	Effective strategy:	Data to verify effectiveness:
				Ineffective strategy:	Alternate response:
		Instructional response:	Assessment to use:	Effective strategy:	Data to verify effectiveness:
				Ineffective strategy:	Alternate response:
	Type of error:	Instructional response:	Assessment to use:	Effective strategy:	Data to verify effectiveness:
				Ineffective strategy:	Alternate response:
		Instructional response:	Assessment to use:	Effective strategy:	Data to verify effectiveness:
				Ineffective strategy:	Alternate response:

Source: © 2015 by Marnie Pauly. Adapted with permission.

Figure 7.6: Database template for documenting the effectiveness of instructional responses.

*Visit **go.SolutionTree.com/assessment** for a free reproducible version of this figure.*

- Maintain the same level of rigor.

- Maintain the same number of questions, prompts, or tasks.

- Maintain the same criteria for quality.

- Make sure you make the assessment experience positive and not punitive.

- Record the most recent scores as replacements to the original scores (not as averages).

- If the second round of assessment generates a lower score, do not incorporate it or average it with the initial score. Instead, work to isolate the variables that caused the drop in achievement, and reassess with yet another version of the assessment.

Conclusion

Re-engagement is a critical part of the collaborative assessment process. Without it, teams are gathering data for the sake of having data but neglecting to address how they will respond when students don't understand or can't do something or when students know or can already do something. When schools say all students will learn at high levels, they commit to re-engage as many students who need the support as often as the support could possibly be needed.

Team Reflections

Take a few moments to reflect on the following questions.

- How will we respond when learners don't learn?

- How will we extend or enrich learning for learners who have met or exceeded the learning target?

- How will we work together to ensure *all* students learn at high levels?

- What role does student feedback play in our decision-making process? What role could it play? What would we have to do to always be cognizant of student involvement in the process?

Annotated Research Notes Template

Topic:		
Citation:		
Key findings:	Links to current practice:	Remaining questions or concerns:
Specific application ideas:	Recommended changes in current practice:	Next steps:

Action Research Planning Tool

Please fill in the following information to support your team planning.

Team Member's Name	Team Member's Role

Context

Where, when, with whom, and why (for what purpose) will you conduct the action research? Please provide a one-paragraph description of the research study's purpose, subjects, participants, methods and procedures, and desired results or findings.

Action Research Question to Answer

What do you hope to accomplish or learn as a result of this effort?

Your Action Research Question to Explore

Data, Artifacts, and Evidence for Answering the Action Research Question

Classroom Strategies and Actions What strategies will you need to employ or what tools will you need to design in order to answer your question?	Indicators of Success What will indicate success for *each* strategy or tool that you decide to use?	Tools for Monitoring Impact What tools (for example, surveys, rubrics, or achievement data) will you need to use to monitor your progress along the way, support your decision making, and report your final conclusions?
1.	1.	
	2.	
	3.	
2.	1.	
	2.	
	3.	
3.	1.	
	2.	
	3.	
4.	1.	
	2.	
	3.	

Resources

What resources will support your efforts at the classroom level or with the action research process?

The Handbook for Collaborative Common Assessments © 2019 Solution Tree Press • SolutionTree.com
Visit **go.SolutionTree.com/assessment** to download this free reproducible.

Audience

With whom will you share your findings?

Findings

Write up your action research findings in a manner that addresses all of the following. Prepare to share the data with multiple audiences. Record your findings in a manner and place that informs the school's future decisions.

- Share your action research question.

- Share the strategies you employed to answer your question.

- Share the tools you used to gather evidence of whether your strategies worked.

- Share the data—your aggregated findings.

- Share the results—any resulting protocols, schedules, templates, policies, and so on that you employed as your framed your answer to your question.

- Share your new insights and possible next steps you would take if you continued action research at the leadership level.

Epilogue

At times, the process of designing and employing collaborative common assessments might feel daunting. The simple story that follows is meant only as an illustration of how the process can organically evolve, how it can cross multiple disciplines, and how it can embed the assessment of critical competencies as schools strive to prepare learners for a global community. This story features a fictional school. It is set at the sixth-grade level, but the ideas herein easily apply to all other grade levels with minor tweaks in the processes and concepts. May this story spark ideas and generate options worth considering as you take the work of collaborative common assessments more deeply into your own setting.

Establishing a Plan

The sixth-grade team at Ames Middle School had experienced success with common assessments in the past and knew that it needed to use the collaborative common assessment process in order to successfully implement Common Core State Standards. The team members decided to begin with ELA Speaking and Listening standards (NGA & CCSSO, 2010a) for a variety of reasons.

- The standards outlined the productive group work expectations that are critical to college and career readiness as well as the 21st century skills.

- The standards provided the critical bridge between the reading and writing standards.

- The standards were interdisciplinary, so the team could share the work across the entire grade level.

- The standards would provide a meaningful base for their learners to track their progress over the course of the entire year.

- By engaging its learners in rich dialogue and conversation over time and across content, the sixth-grade team's instruction could easily activate some of the most powerful formative assessment strategies that assessment expert Dylan Wiliam (2011, 2018) outlines.

  - Engineering effective classroom discussions, activities, and learning tasks that elicit evidence of learning

- Activating learners as instructional resources to one another
- Activating learners as self-regulators

The team members' choice to use common assessments with the Speaking and Listening standards excited them. It seemed like a win-win-win—win 1, it provided the most reasonable way to integrate standards; win 2, it provided the most plausible way to engage the entire team in using collaborative common assessments; and win 3, they could engage in action research on best practice in formative assessment along the way. The greatest win, however, was that it engaged their students in learning experiences that they needed in order to thrive in the collaborative world beyond sixth grade.

Framing the Work

To begin, the team unpacked the sixth-grade Common Core Speaking and Listening standards. The very first line read, "Engage effectively in a range of collaborative discussions (one-on-one, in groups, and teacher-led) with diverse partners on *grade 6 topics, texts, and issues*, building on others' ideas and expressing their own clearly" (SL.6.1; NGA & CCSSO, 2010a). The team members immediately noticed that they could only assess the standard fully and accurately if they used multiple performance assessments spread out over time. Because the standard was so big, they also would need a clear assessment road map. So they identified their summative assessments in a manner that would help them assess the learners in the various required settings. Figure E.1 reflects the agreements the team made for its CSA plan.

The identified summative assessments would become part of the learners' final portfolios. Speaking and listening represented important skills in all disciplines, and all disciplines agreed to design and use the same rubrics as they engaged their learners in critical conversations. After all, quality speaking and listening skills were the same from one conversation or one discipline to the next.

Before writing any of the actual assessments, the team felt a critical next step involved creating consistent, student-friendly learning targets. The team members worked to pare down the standard to a few manageable targets for their learners. They identified the following student-friendly learning targets.

- I can engage in an effective collaborative discussion with a group or another person who may be very different from me.

- I can prepare for a discussion so that I can readily cite textual evidence or specific information that will generate a thoughtful and logical exchange of ideas.

- I can review or paraphrase what others said before I talk and add to their ideas.

- I can express my ideas clearly, making sure I contribute to the conversation.

Specific Constructs of the Standard to Address in the Assessment Design	Form of Summative Assessment	Course and Content	Timeline
• Large group • Formal discussion rules • Drawing on preparation • Delineating an argument	Socratic seminar	Language arts; unit on author's purpose and narrator's point of view (literary analysis)	November
• Small group • Formal discussion rules • Controversial topics • Drawing on preparation	Juried forums	Social studies; unit on laws, citizenship, and authority (debate)	January
• Small group • Informal discussion rules • Competing perspectives • Drawing on preparation	Pinwheel dialogues	Science; unit on the ethics of researching and producing HeLa cells (three diverse perspectives)	March
• One-to-one • No formal rules, but conversational etiquette always required	Case study with problem-solving partners	Mathematics; unit on statistics (use of random samplings to draw inferences about a population, draw informal comparative inferences about two populations, and construct viable arguments and critique the reasoning of others)	May

Figure E.1: Ames Middle School sixth-grade team's CSA plan.

- I can pose and respond to questions that probe more deeply into a topic or the reasoning employed during the discussion.

- I can make sure everyone participates and hears and considers all ideas.

- I can respond appropriately when someone shares an idea that I don't like or I disagree with (which may or may not occur in a conversation).

- I can resolve contradictions when possible or conflicts when needed.

In order to make this work, the team also needed clear schoolwide criteria and quality measurement tools that could last the entire year and span multiple assessments. It worked on writing rubrics and scales that would measure proficiency for all work related to the Speaking and Listening standards. Also, from this set of targets, the team generated student-tracking and goal-setting sheets, including the following student progress-tracking sheet (figure E.2, pages 220–221). The team members asked the sixth-grade learners to track their progress regarding the shared learning targets over the course of all their assessments. This way, they could monitor their improvement.

Student Tracking

Use the following rubric to track your progress over time.

Criteria: Evidence-Based Responses	
• Specific citations • Data • Links to previous research and articles	1: I need help to figure out what data or evidence would support the argument or discussion at hand.
	2: I attempt to support a conversation by using the right data or evidence in the moment, but the conversation has to stop while I find things to share. Sometimes, the things I share seem to send the conversation in a new direction.
	3: I can support a conversation with the appropriate data or evidence in the moment. I can reference multiple sources and can seamlessly use the information to help the conversation move forward. I can include the citations needed to back up my contributions.
	4: In addition to all of level 3, I can draw inferences and connect the data and evidence from multiple sources explored over time (previous learning). I can extend the conversation to examples that link to the world beyond our classroom walls.

Learning Trajectory

Record your progress data, and shade in the boxes for your corresponding scores on each assessment to create a bar graph of your learning trajectory over time.

4							
3							
2							
1							
Score	1	1	2	2	3	2	3
Date	1/10/14	1/20/14	1/25/14	2/1/14	2/15/14	2/28/14	3/15/14
Name of assessment	Partner dialogue	Small-group discussion	Juried forum	Class discussion	Partner dialogue	Hot seat	Team project

What am I good at when it comes to providing evidence-based responses?

I can find a sufficient amount of evidence from the readings to support my contributions to a conversation, and I often reference where I got the information.

What can I improve when giving evidence-based responses?

Sometimes my provided evidence includes an author's opinion or thoughts. I need to get better at sticking to facts, and I could do a better job of giving better references (like page numbers or dates) rather than just giving the author's name.

What goal do I have for myself when using evidence to support my position in a conversation?

My goal is the same as what I am trying to improve. In future conversations at least 50 percent of my references will include the page number and date of my source (with the author's name), and all of my references will be based in facts instead of opinions.

What evidence will I monitor to know that I am meeting my goal?

I will write some practice responses and highlight the references in one color and the facts I provide in another color, and count them up to make sure I have met my goals. I can record my conversation and translate it into writing to use the highlighting process so I can see how I do in the next conversation.

Figure E.2: Sample student progress-tracking sheet.

The sixth-grade team wanted to do action research to monitor the students' engagement levels and overall success rates when the students tracked their own progress over time. The team members agreed to use the progress-tracking sheets consistently and to make the sheets part of their data meetings as the year progressed.

The team decided it needed a solid formative base for all its learners. Team members wanted to involve the learners in co-creating the materials, and the teachers knew both teacher and student alike would have to practice observing conversations and scoring them during the formative phases in order to get to inter-rater reliability. The grade-level team began creating its formative pathway, and each individual department within the grade level made agreements on when and how it would embed the pathway into their various content areas. In other words, students were going to be observing, scoring, and participating in discussions in every major course. By the end of the year, students should truly be able to engage in evidence-based conversations. The team set up its pathway to move from simple observation into more structured opportunities for students to participate. The entire process was meant to help students clearly understand the Speaking and Listening standards and the criteria against which they would be measured as they engaged in the conversations.

- Observe a series of videos or fishbowl discussions, varying which students are on the inner circle having the conversation and which students are on the outer ring observing the conversation. As an entire class, isolate the criteria that make some discussions rich and interesting following each fishbowl experience. (Every department observes department-specific discussions. It is recommended that teachers use these fishbowl discussions to explore instructional content that continues to deepen the learning required in the unit of study.)

- Co-create a rubric for discussion. (The language arts team leads this process.)

- Compare discussion rubrics from other classes, and work to create a single rubric for the entire department and ultimately the entire grade level. (The language arts team led the process and shared the final rubric with the other departments for use, but the other departments used the same rubric in their classrooms as they watched more videos to ensure everyone—teachers and students alike—scored conversations with consistency.)

- Regularly practice scoring with the new rubric to get to inter-rater reliability (watching videos of student conversations or class discussions, in-class discussions, fishbowl conversations, formal class activities like Socratic seminars, and so on). Provide justification and evidence to back scores.

- Provide practice sessions with different rule sets for the different types of dialogues or discussions.

- Align the reflection forms and tracking sheets to the rubrics for student self-monitoring and goal setting. (Every department engages learners in using the same forms over time and across courses.)

- Create opportunities for students to give written responses that demonstrate challenging ideas, questioning, and responding to questions in a manner that elicits further engagement.

- Engage in listening exercises that require students to generate direct quotes and paraphrases in written form.

- Critique reasoning over time in a manner that will require students to take a stance and argue against opposing perspectives.

While team members agreed that the language arts team would lead the majority of the formative groundwork for rubric development, the other departments would participate in formative components along the way, like exposing students to discussions and practicing with their rubric scoring, in order to set up the learners for success in their various courses. They also agreed that the last three items of their list of formative assessments (having students give written responses to challenging ideas, engaging in listening exercises, and critiquing reasoning) would serve as some of their CFAs. All departments could participate in the same CFAs, but through their own content area, as long as they maintained the same criteria for quality and they practiced scoring and conducting error analysis across the various content areas. They wanted to isolate, for example, whether content posed more issues than process or if consistent process errors crossed all disciplines when it came to critiquing reasoning.

The team anticipated that it had a lot of work to do with each learning target, but early on, it discovered that sixth-grade learners were struggling with the learning target that asked them to pose and respond to questions that probed more deeply into a topic or the reasoning people employed during the discussion. Sixth graders found probing reasoning harder than probing the topic, as it meant that the learners first had to engage in deep levels of reasoning and willingly challenge each other's thinking. The team decided that it had issues of both skill and will on the table. The language arts team and the social studies team agreed that they would continue to address students' will by engaging them in active debates and teaching them how to respectfully challenge each other's thinking. The science and mathematics teachers agreed to tackle students' skill by digging into reasoning processes. Once they made this discovery, the science and mathematics teachers agreed to take a more formal approach to teaching reasoning.

The grade-level team identified common reasoning verbs, critical-thinking processes, and common reasoning fallacies. The teachers selected one key verb at a time, made sure they all agreed on its the definition, examined examples of the reasoning practices in action, and considered possible question stems that would launch critical thinking. At that point, the team got busy writing common reasoning rubrics that all teachers could use with their individual content. All teachers agreed to engage their learners in identifying reasoning within their content, writing reasoning statements, and finding fallacies within poor examples of reasoning. The team agreed to practice writing reasoning-based questions together before instruction began.

As that happened, science and mathematics teachers got started with the work in the classroom. The science teachers used the Next Generation Science Standards and scientific practices (NGSS Lead States, 2013) to guide their work while the mathematics teachers used the Common Core State Standards for mathematics and the Standards for Mathematical Practice (NGA & CCSSO, 2010b). They began by teaching formal terminology regarding reasoning within their content areas. They engaged learners in reading some examples of reasoning and seeing if they could identify the type of reasoning involved. Then they asked the learners to write their own reasoning statements tied to the unit of learning at hand, making sure the learners could identify the reasoning strategies they used. From there, the teachers exposed the learners to common reasoning fallacies within each type of reasoning and asked learners to identify the types of fallacies found in prepared, flawed reasoning statements. Once they felt the learners understood reasoning processes and the common fallacies in the flawed reasoning samples they had designed and provided, they moved the work to student-generated reasoning. Students created and wrote their own problem solutions tied to the unit of learning on the board and then added their reasoning statements to their work. Then the class analyzed each argument in the following ways.

- Students named the type of reasoning the argument used.

- Students identified any fallacies or explained how they knew the argument didn't include a fallacy if they didn't find one.

- Students recreated the statement—if needed—to eliminate flaws.

As a class, students kept track of the fallacies they found on poster paper and then tried to challenge each other's answers with persistence and clarity of language. As a final step, the teachers engaged their learners in finding ways to publicly challenge flawed reasoning without harming the individual responsible for the reasoning.

Gathering Data

Along the way, the science and mathematics teachers used exit tickets to monitor student progress. Each department agreed to heavily emphasize a shared reasoning process in a single week, and at the end of the week, they asked learners to solve a single discipline-specific problem that related to their current unit of study. On an exit ticket, the learners had to explain the thinking behind their solution and then identify the reasoning pattern they used. Both science and mathematics teachers took their exit tickets to the same room at the end of the day, where they had a standing meeting to sort the exit tickets. The science teachers worked at one table and the mathematics teachers worked at another as they sorted their exit tickets into groups of right and wrong answers and then subdivided their wrong answers by the types of mistakes the learners made. When both departments finished this, they stepped back to compare their results from one side of the room to the other. They considered whether the learners made the same types of errors in both disciplines and which errors the teachers saw most often.

For another exit ticket, the mathematics and science teachers worked on analysis. They created a shared definition of *analysis* and then wrote a student-friendly learning target on the concept of analysis that each teacher could embrace or employ in his or her classroom. After some debate, the teams identified the following target: *I can analyze. This means I can conduct a detailed examination of the elements (smaller component parts) or structure of something in order to make a decision, solve a problem, or create a new idea regarding how effective the element or structure currently is.* The mathematics team engaged learners in analysis through the Common Core mathematics standard, "Analyze the relationship between the dependent and independent variables using graphs and tables, and relate these to the equation" (6.EE.C.9; NGA & CCSSO, 2010b). The science team engaged learners in analysis through the Common Core technical reading standard, "Cite specific textual evidence to support analysis of science and technical texts" (RST.6-8.1; NGA & CCSSO, 2010a).

The teams provided direct instruction as well as multiple examples of how to do the work of analysis. As a CFA, each team gave its learners an analysis-based question as an exit-ticket task. Each team had to collaboratively ensure that it asked a high-quality analysis question, and then the teams checked each other's work to ensure they agreed on the content and process of analysis. Then they had all their students complete exit tickets in the last seven minutes of class. At the end of the day, the teachers gathered to sort the exit tickets and classify common errors. They tallied their results and organized their findings, as figure E.3 (pages 226–227) shows. Because the science and mathematics teams isolated the errors, they were able to plan targeted interventions.

Whenever the team members analyzed data and collaborated to problem solve in targeted ways, they discovered they could close significant gaps in understanding within ten minutes if they deeply understood the types of errors students made. They also discovered that if they used error-analysis processes with their learners (for example, students sorted exit tickets without names on them and isolated types of errors), they could engage learners in both spotting errors and challenging faulty reasoning, which was the essence of their entire effort.

Shared Mistakes and Errors	Science 151 students 4 participating classrooms		Mathematics 167 students 5 participating classrooms	
	Total Items Missed and Students' Initials	Classrooms	Total Missed and Initials	Classrooms
The student made reading errors (misread the directions, skipped key words, or misunderstood the question).	5: JN, BV, RE, HY, WD	A, B, C	6: GH, VI, CV, AN, HX, LI	E, H
The student identified the wrong components to analyze (meaningless information or evidence).	5: KL, MN, SA, FR, CV	A, C, D	8: NB, MI, YT, OP, LO, RE, RW, NN	F, H, I
The student identified the right components to analyze but based the conclusion on insufficient or inaccurate evidence *or* misinterpreted accurate evidence.	9: KK, TR, JU, AN, NB, PQ, GJ, KJ, QD	A, B, C, D	12: CD, BR, AW, LO, HU, BV, KM, SD, WE, AV, PK, TH	E, F, G, I

The student based the conclusion on weak reasoning (for example, the student had sufficient or accurate evidence but based the conclusion on faulty logic, like overgeneralizing or inverting causes and effects).	15: KJ, OP, BR, CD, BG, LO, TG, BT, AG, WN, JT, LI, EF, BY, FS	A, B, C, D	22: BY, KL, BT, BG, HN, MR, CK, VR, FC, LO, FS, DO, RW, FT, DS, NI, TY, DE, JU, RT, SQ, YU	E, F, G, H, I

	Totals:
	 • 151 exit tickets from 4 classrooms
	 • 117 accurate answers
	 • 34 inaccurate answers
	    • 5 mistakes
	    • 29 errors
	 Most popular error: Faulty reasoning
			Totals:
			 • 167 exit tickets from 5 classrooms
			 • 119 accurate answers
			 • 48 inaccurate answers
			    • 6 mistakes
			    • 42 errors
			 Most popular error: Faulty reasoning	

	Science classroom teachers: • Johnston, A and B • Mackly, C • O'lgart, D		Mathematics classroom teachers: • Ambray, E • Benton, F, G • Pederson, H • Vance, I	
	14 learners struggling in both mathematics and science: BV, RE, CV, OP, BR, CD, BG, LO, RE, LI, BY, JU, AN, NB			

Figure E.3: Ames Middle School science and mathematics teams' exit-ticket findings.

Along the way, the science and mathematics teams constantly kept their colleagues from the other departments informed of their assessment findings on teaching reasoning, their identified struggling learners, and their resulting instructional decisions. Other departments used the mathematics and science teachers' findings to launch parallel investigations into reasoning processes. They did this to see if they could maintain the support that learners needed in order to have rich conversations and challenge each other's thinking.

The entire grade level worked collaboratively throughout the year. Each team tackled an important part (or parts) of the standard, and the entire grade level continued to try to pull the full standard together through its various summative assessments.

By the end of the year, the entire sixth-grade team felt as if it had contributed to something meaningful. The team had multiple points of data for each learner across multiple disciplines. It could use these to verify each student's proficiency levels with the Speaking and Listening standards. More important, the team felt confident it had increased the level of rigor on its assessments. But most important, the team saw gains in academic achievement, which was exciting given the more rigorous assessments. Each teacher affirmed his or her classroom now had more engaging discussions, learners activated each other as resources, and the students finally worked harder than the teachers.

While engaging in the collaborative common assessment work, the team also had engaging conversations and, like their students, had developed high levels of trust and camaraderie. Team members believed they had experienced profound learning regarding their teaching practices, and they enjoyed the challenge.

But it was clear that their work was not done and that PLC work would forever be a journey with room to improve. The foundation they'd built with the Speaking and Listening standards was only the beginning, and they could continue to build on that foundation as they added new skills like technical reading to their ongoing improvement efforts. To continue its work, the team decided to create a handbook wherein it could add, modify, and maintain a set of protocols and templates to navigate complex PLC work in efficient and effective ways. It was exciting to consider the future learning opportunities that awaited. The team left the school year with genuine enthusiasm and high hopes.

References and Resources

Ainsworth, L. (2003a). *Power standards: Identifying the standards that matter the most.* Englewood, CO: Advanced Learning Press.

Ainsworth, L. (2003b). *"Unwrapping" the standards: A simple process to make standards manageable.* Boston: Houghton Mifflin Harcourt.

Ainsworth, L. (2013). *Prioritizing the Common Core: Identifying specific standards to emphasize the most.* Englewood, CO: Advanced Learning Press.

Ainsworth, L. (2015). *Common formative assessments 2.0: How teacher teams intentionally align standards, instruction, and assessment.* Thousand Oaks, CA: Corwin Press.

Ainsworth, L., & Viegut, D. (2006). *Common formative assessments: How to connect standards-based instruction and assessment.* Thousand Oaks, CA: Corwin Press.

Almond, P., Winter, P., Cameto, R., Russell, M., Sato, E., Clarke-Midura, J., et al. (2010). *Technology-enabled and universally designed assessment: Considering access in measuring the achievement of students with disabilities—A foundation for research.* Dover, NH: Measured Progress.

Anderson, L. W., & Krathwohl, D. (Eds.). (2001). *A taxonomy for learning, teaching, and assessing: A revision of Bloom's taxonomy of educational objectives* (Complete ed.). New York: Longman.

Bailey, K., & Jakicic, C. (2012). *Common formative assessment: A toolkit for Professional Learning Communities at Work.* Bloomington, IN: Solution Tree Press.

Bambrick-Santoyo, P. (2010). *Driven by data: A practical guide to improve instruction.* San Francisco: Jossey-Bass.

Bandura, A. (1977). Self-efficacy: Toward a unifying theory of behavioral change. *Psychological Review, 84*(2), 191–215.

Bandura, A. (1997). *Self-efficacy: The exercise of control.* New York: Freeman.

Black, P., Harrison, C., Lee, C., Marshall, B., & Wiliam, D. (2004). Working inside the black box: Assessment for learning in the classroom. *Phi Delta Kappan, 86*(1), 8–21.

Black, P., & Wiliam, D. (1998). Inside the black box: Raising standards through classroom assessment. *Phi Delta Kappan, 80*(2), 139–148.

Blanchard, K. (2007). *Leading at a higher level: Blanchard on leadership and creating high performing organizations.* Upper Saddle River, NJ: Prentice Hall.

Bloom, B. S. (Ed.). (1956). *Taxonomy of educational objectives, book I: Cognitive domain.* New York: McKay.

Brinson, D., & Steiner, L. (2007, October). *Building collective efficacy: How leaders inspire teachers to achieve* (Issue Brief). Washington, DC: Center for Comprehensive School Reform and Improvement.

Buffum, A., Mattos, M., & Weber, C. (2012). *Simplifying response to intervention: Four essential guiding principles.* Bloomington, IN: Solution Tree Press.

Calkins, L., Ehrenworth, M., & Lehman, C. (2012). *Pathways to the Common Core: Accelerating achievement.* Portsmouth, NH: Heinemann.

Centre for Excellence in Universal Design. (n.d.). *The 7 principles.* Accessed at http://universaldesign.ie /What-is-Universal-Design/The-7-Principles on June 1, 2016.

Chadwick, R. J. (2012). *Finding new ground: Beyond conflict to consensus.* Terrebonne, OR: One Tree.

Chappuis, J. (2009). *Seven strategies of assessment for learning.* Portland, OR: Pearson Assessment Training Institute.

Chappuis, J. (2014). *Seven strategies of assessment for learning* (2nd ed.). Portland, OR: Pearson Assessment Training Institute.

Chappuis, J., Stiggins, R., Chappuis, S., & Arter, J. (2012). *Classroom assessment for student learning: Doing it right—doing it well* (2nd ed.). Upper Saddle River, NJ: Pearson Education.

Chappuis, S., Chappuis, J., & Stiggins, R. (2009). Supporting teacher learning teams. *Educational Leadership, 66*(5), 56–60.

Chenoweth, K. (2008). *"It's being done": Academic success in unexpected schools.* Cambridge, MA: Harvard Education Press.

Chenoweth, K. (2009a). *How it's being done: Urgent lessons from unexpected schools.* Cambridge, MA: Harvard Education Press.

Chenoweth, K. (2009b). It can be done, it's being done, and here's how. *Phi Delta Kappan, 91*(1), 38–43.

Chenoweth, K., & Theokas, C. (2011). *Getting it done: Leading academic success in unexpected schools.* Cambridge, MA: Harvard Education Press.

Clarke, S. (2001). *Unlocking formative assessment: Practical strategies for enhancing pupils' learning in the primary classroom.* London: Hodder Education.

Clarke, S. (2005). *Formative assessment in action: Weaving the elements together.* London: Hodder Education.

Clarke, S. (2008). *Active learning through formative assessment.* London: Hodder Education.

Conzemius, A. E., & O'Neill, J. (2014). *The handbook for SMART school teams: Revitalizing best practices for collaboration* (2nd ed.). Bloomington, IN: Solution Tree Press.

Corcoran, S. P. (2010, September). *Can teachers be evaluated by their students' test scores? Should they be? The use of value-added measures of teacher effectiveness in policy and practice* (Education Policy for Action Series). Providence, RI: Annenberg Institute for School Reform at Brown University.

Daggett, W. R. (2008). *Achieving academic excellence through rigor and relevance.* Rexford, NY: International Center for Leadership in Education. Accessed at www.leadered.com/pdf /Achieving_Academic_Excellence_2014.pdf on April 7, 2011.

Davies, A. (2007). *Making classroom assessment work* (3rd ed.). Courtenay, British Columbia, Canada: Connections.

D'Mello, S., Lehman, B., Pekrun, R., & Graesser, A. (2014). Confusion can be beneficial for learning. *Learning and Instruction, 29*(1), 153–170.

Dolan, R. P., & Hall, T. E. (2001). Universal design for learning: Implications for large-scale assessment. *IDA Perspectives, 27*(4), 22–25.

DuFour, R. (n.d.). *Formative assessments create a change in instructional strategies* [Video file]. Accessed at www.globalpd.com/search/content/ODQ= on March 11, 2019.

DuFour, R. (2008, December 9). *Clarifying collective inquiry* [Blog post]. Accessed at www .allthingsplc.info/blog/view/40/clarifying-collective-inquiry on January 6, 2010.

DuFour, R., DuFour, R., & Eaker, R. (2008). *Revisiting Professional Learning Communities at Work: New insights for improving schools.* Bloomington, IN: Solution Tree Press.

DuFour, R., DuFour, R., Eaker, R., & Many, T. (2006). *Learning by doing: A handbook for Professional Learning Communities at Work.* Bloomington, IN: Solution Tree Press.

DuFour, R., DuFour, R., Eaker, R., & Many, T. (2010). *Learning by doing: A handbook for Professional Learning Communities at Work* (2nd ed.). Bloomington, IN: Solution Tree Press.

DuFour, R., DuFour, R., Eaker, R., Many, T., & Mattos, M. (2016). *Learning by doing: A handbook for Professional Learning Communities at Work* (3rd ed.). Bloomington, IN: Solution Tree Press.

DuFour, R., & Fullan, M. (2013). *Cultures built to last: Systemic PLCs at Work.* Bloomington, IN: Solution Tree Press.

DuFour, R., & Marzano, R. J. (2011). *Leaders of learning: How district, school, and classroom leaders improve student achievement.* Bloomington, IN: Solution Tree Press.

DuFour, R., & Mattos, M. (2013). How do principals really improve schools? *Educational Leadership, 70*(7), 34–40.

Early, D. M., Rogge, R. D., & Deci, E. L. (2014). Engagement, alignment, and rigor as vital signs of high-quality instruction: A classroom visit protocol for instructional improvement and research. *High School Journal, 97*(4), 219–239.

Education Trust. (2015, September). *Checking in: Do classroom assignments reflect today's higher standards?* (Equity in Motion Series). Washington, DC: Author.

Education Trust. (2018, April). *Checking in: Are math assignments measuring up?* (Equity in Motion Series). Washington, DC: Author.

Elmore, R. F. (2003). *Knowing the right thing to do: School improvement and performance-based accountability.* Washington, DC: National Governors Association Center for Best Practices.

Elmore, R. F. (2004). *School reform from the inside out: Policy, practice, and performance.* Cambridge, MA: Harvard Education Press.

Erkens, C. (2016). *Collaborative common assessments: Teamwork. Instruction. Results.* Bloomington, IN: Solution Tree Press.

Erkens, C. (2017, July 26). *Data moments* [Blog post]. Accessed at www.allthingsplc.info/blog/view /351/data-moments on September 18, 2018.

Erkens, C., Schimmer, T., & Vagle, N. D. (2017). *Essential assessment: Six tenets for bringing hope, efficacy, and achievement to the classroom.* Bloomington, IN: Solution Tree Press.

Erkens, C., Schimmer, T., & Vagle, N. D. (2018). *Instructional agility: Responding to assessment with real-time decisions.* Bloomington, IN: Solution Tree Press.

Erkens, C., Schimmer, T., & Vagle, N. D. (2019). *Growing tomorrow's citizens in today's classrooms: Assessing seven critical competencies.* Bloomington, IN: Solution Tree Press.

Erkens, C., & Twadell, E. (2012). *Leading by design: An action framework for PLC at Work leaders.* Bloomington, IN: Solution Tree Press.

Fisher, D., & Frey, N. (2007). *Checking for understanding: Formative assessment techniques for your classroom.* Alexandria, VA: Association for Supervision and Curriculum Development.

Fisher, D., & Frey, N. (2010). *Guided instruction: How to develop confident and successful learners.* Alexandria, VA: Association for Supervision and Curriculum Development.

Fisher, D., & Frey, N. (2011). *The purposeful classroom: How to structure lessons with learning goals in mind.* Alexandria, VA: Association for Supervision and Curriculum Development.

Fisher, D., & Frey, N. (2012). Making time for feedback. *Educational Leadership, 70*(1), 42–46.

Fisher, D., & Frey, N. (2015). *Unstoppable learning: Seven essential elements to unleash student potential.* Bloomington, IN: Solution Tree Press.

Fisher, D., Frey, N., & Hattie, J. (2016). *Visible learning for literacy, grades K–12: Implementing the practices that work best to accelerate student learning.* Thousand Oaks, CA: Corwin Press.

Frey, N., Fisher, D., & Everlove, S. (2009). *Productive group work: How to engage students, build teamwork, and promote understanding.* Alexandria, VA: Association for Supervision and Curriculum Development.

Fullan, M. (2008). *The six secrets of change: What the best leaders do to help their organizations survive and thrive.* San Francisco: Jossey-Bass.

Fullan, M. (2011). *The moral imperative realized.* Thousand Oaks, CA: Corwin Press.

Fullan, M., Bertani, A., & Quinn, J. (2004). New lessons for districtwide reform. *Educational Leadership, 61*(7), 42–46.

Gallimore, R., Ermeling, B. A., Saunders, W. M., & Goldenberg, C. (2009). Moving the learning of teaching closer to practice: Teacher education implications of school-based inquiry teams. *Elementary School Journal, 109*(5), 537–551.

Gawande, A. (2004, December 6). The bell curve: What happens when patients find out how good their doctors really are? *New Yorker.* Accessed at www.newyorker.com/magazine/2004/12/06/the-bell-curve on June 28, 2014.

Gawande, A. (2010). *The checklist manifesto: How to get things right.* New York: Metropolitan Books.

Goddard, R. D., Hoy, W. K., & Hoy, A. W. (2000). Collective teacher efficacy: Its meaning, measure, and impact on student achievement. *American Educational Research Journal, 37*(2), 479–507.

Goddard, R. D., & Skrla, L. (2006). The influence of school social composition on teachers' collective efficacy beliefs. *Educational Administration Quarterly, 42*(2), 216–235.

Guo, Y., Connor, C. M., Yang, Y., Roehrig, A. D., & Morrison, F. J. (2012). The effects of teacher qualification, teacher self-efficacy, and classroom practices on fifth graders' literacy outcomes. *Elementary School Journal, 113*(1), 3–24.

Hargreaves, A., & Fullan, M. (2012). *Professional capital: Transforming teaching in every school.* New York: Teachers College Press.

Hargreaves, E. (2007). The validity of collaborative assessment for learning. *Assessment in Education: Principles, Policy and Practice, 14*(2), 185–199.

Hattie, J. (2009). *Visible learning: A synthesis of over 800 meta-analyses relating to achievement.* New York: Routledge.

Hattie, J. (2012). *Visible learning for teachers: Maximizing impact on learning.* New York: Routledge.

Hattie, J., & Timperley, H. (2007). The power of feedback. *Review of Educational Research, 77*(1), 81–112.

Heritage, M. (2010). *Formative assessment: Making it happen in the classroom.* Thousand Oaks, CA: Corwin Press.

Heritage, M. (2013). Gathering evidence of student understanding. In J. H. McMillan (Ed.), *SAGE handbook of research on classroom assessment* (pp. 179–196). Thousand Oaks, CA: SAGE.

Hess, K. K., Carlock, D., Jones, B., & Walkup, J. R. (2009, June). *What exactly do "fewer, clearer, and higher standards" really look like in the classroom? Using a cognitive rigor matrix to analyze curriculum, plan lessons, and implement assessments.* Presented at the Council of Chief State School Officers National Conference, Detroit, MI. Accessed at www.nciea.org/publications/cognitiverigorpaper_KH12.pdf on August 25, 2015.

Hockett, J. A., & Doubet, K. J. (2014). Turning on the lights: What pre-assessments can do. *Educational Leadership, 71*(4), 50–54.

Hoy, W. K., Sweetland, S. R., & Smith, P. A. (2002). Toward an organizational model of achievement in high schools: The significance of collective efficacy. *Educational Administration Quarterly*, *38*(1), 77–93.

Jacobs, H. H. (1997). *Mapping the big picture: Integrating curriculum and assessment K–12*. Alexandria, VA: Association for Supervision and Curriculum Development.

Kendall, J. (2011). *Understanding Common Core State Standards*. Alexandria, VA: Association for Supervision and Curriculum Development.

Kramer, S. V. (2015). Choosing prevention before intervention. In A. Buffum & M. Mattos (Eds.), *It's about time: Planning interventions and extensions in elementary school* (pp. 15–29). Bloomington, IN: Solution Tree Press.

Langewiesche, W. (2014, October). The human factor. *Vanity Fair*. Accessed at www.vanityfair.com /news/business/2014/10/air-france-flight-447-crash on June 30, 2015.

Lencioni, P. (2005). *Overcoming the five dysfunctions of a team: A field guide for leaders, managers, and facilitators*. San Francisco: Jossey-Bass.

Levin, B. (2008). *How to change 5000 schools: A practical and positive approach for leading change at every level*. Cambridge, MA: Harvard Education Press.

Love, N. (Ed.). (2009). *Using data to improve learning for all: A collaborative inquiry approach*. Thousand Oaks, CA: Corwin Press.

Love, N., Stiles, K. E., Mundry, S., & DiRanna, K. (2008). *The data coach's guide to improving learning for all students: Unleashing the power of collaborative inquiry*. Thousand Oaks, CA: Corwin Press.

Marshall, K. (2008). Interim assessments: A user's guide. *Phi Delta Kappan*, *90*(1), 64–68.

Marzano, R. J. (2003). *What works in schools: Translating research into action*. Alexandria, VA: Association for Supervision and Curriculum Development.

Marzano, R. J. (2009). *Designing and teaching learning goals and objectives*. Bloomington, IN: Marzano Research.

Marzano, R. J. (2013, May 23). *Proficiency scales for the Common Core* [Webinar presentation materials]. Accessed at https://mkt.solution-tree.com/MRL_2013_35MEU_Proficiency ScalesfortheCommonCoreWebinarRecordingRegPage on September 18, 2018.

Marzano, R. J., & Kendall, J. S. (2007). *The new taxonomy of educational objectives* (2nd ed.). Thousand Oaks, CA: Corwin Press.

Marzano, R. J., Yanoski, D. C., Hoegh, J. K., & Simms, J. A. (2013). *Using Common Core standards to enhance classroom instruction and assessment*. Bloomington, IN: Marzano Research.

Mattingly, K. (2016, June 8). *A teacher's journey to assessment literacy*. Keynote address presented at the Assessment for Learning Conference, Denton, TX.

Mattos, M., DuFour, R., DuFour, R., Eaker, R., & Many, T. (2016). *Concise answers to frequently asked questions about Professional Learning Communities at Work.* Bloomington, IN: Solution Tree Press.

McMillan, J. H. (2013). Why we need research on classroom assessment. In J. H. McMillan (Ed.), *SAGE handbook of research on classroom assessment* (pp. 3–16). Thousand Oaks, CA: SAGE.

McTighe, J., & Ferrara, S. (2000). *Assessing learning in the classroom.* Washington, DC: National Education Association.

Meisels, S. J., Atkins-Burnett, S., Xue, Y., Nicholson, J., Bickel, D. D., & Son, S.-H. (2003). Creating a system of accountability: The impact of instructional assessment on elementary children's achievement test scores. *Educational Policy Analysis Archives, 11*(9). Accessed at http://epaa.asu .edu/ojs/article/view/237/363 on August 25, 2015.

Moore, S. (2016). *One without the other: Stories of unity through diversity and inclusion.* Winnipeg, Manitoba, Canada: Portage & Main Press.

Moser, J. S., Schroder, H. S., Heeter, C., Moran, T. P., & Lee, Y.-H. (2011). Mind your errors: Evidence for a neural mechanism linking growth mind-set to adaptive posterror adjustments. *Psychological Science, 22*(12), 1484–1489.

Moss-Kanter, R. (2006). *Confidence: How winning streaks and losing streaks begin and end.* New York: Crown.

Moss, C. M., & Brookhart, S. M. (2012). *Learning targets: Helping students aim for understanding in today's lesson.* Alexandria, VA: Association for Supervision and Curriculum Development.

Muhammad, A. (2018). *Transforming school culture: How to overcome staff division* (2nd ed.). Bloomington, IN: Solution Tree Press.

Muller, D. A. (2008). *Designing effective multimedia for physics education.* (Unpublished doctoral thesis). School of Physics, University of Sydney, Australia. Accessed at www.physics.usyd.edu.au/super /theses/PhD%28Muller%29.pdf on February 12, 2015.

National Council for the Social Studies. (2013). *The college, career, and civic life (C3) framework for social studies state standards: Guidance for enhancing the rigor of K–12 civics, economics, geography, and history.* Silver Spring, MD: Author. Accessed at www.socialstudies.org/system/files/c3 /C3-Framework-for-Social-Studies.pdf on August 25, 2015.

National Council of Teachers of English. (2008). *21st century literacies.* Accessed at www.ncte.org /governance/literacies on July 1, 2014.

National Education Association. (n.d.). *Preparing 21st century students for a global society: An educator's guide to the "four Cs."* Accessed at www.nea.org/assets/docs/A-Guide-to-Four-Cs.pdf on March 14, 2014.

National Governors Association Center for Best Practices & Council of Chief State School Officers. (2010a). *Common Core State Standards for English language arts and literacy in history/social studies, science, and technical subjects*. Washington, DC: Authors. Accessed at www.corestandards .org/assets/CCSSI_ELA%20Standards.pdf on November 4, 2015.

National Governors Association Center for Best Practices & Council of Chief State School Officers. (2010b). *Common Core State Standards for mathematics*. Washington, DC: Authors. Accessed at www.corestandards.org/assets/CCSSI_Math%20Standards.pdf on November 4, 2015.

National Research Council of the National Academies. (2014). *Training students to extract value from big data: Summary of a workshop*. Washington, DC: National Academies Press.

Newmann, F. M., Carmichael, D. L., & King, M. B. (2016). *Authentic intellectual work: Improving teaching for rigorous learning*. Thousand Oaks, CA: Corwin Press.

NGSS Lead States. (2013). *Next Generation Science Standards: For states, by states*. Washington, DC: National Academies Press.

Novak, K., & Rodriguez, K. (2018, February 1). *UDL progression rubric (based on CAST UDL guidelines)*. Accessed at http://castpublishing.org/novak-rodriguez-udl-progression-rubric on September 18, 2018.

Odden, A. R., & Archibald, S. J. (2009). *Doubling student performance . . . and finding the resources to do it*. Thousand Oaks, CA: Corwin Press.

Ogle, R. (2007). *Smart world: Breakthrough creativity and the new science of ideas*. Boston: Harvard Business School Press.

Organisation for Economic Co-operation and Development. (2011). *Strong performers and successful reformers in education: Lessons from PISA for the United States*. Paris: Author.

Patterson, K., Grenny, J., Maxfield, D., McMillan, R., & Switzler, A. (2008). *Influencer: The power to change anything*. New York: McGraw-Hill.

Pink, D. H. (2005). *A whole new mind: Moving from the information age to the conceptual age*. New York: Riverhead Books.

Pink, D. H. (2010). *Drive: The surprising truth about what motivates us*. New York: Riverhead Books.

Popham, W. J. (2012a). Appropriate and inappropriate tests for evaluating schools [Pamphlet 1]. In *Mastering assessment: A self-service system for educators* (2nd ed.). Boston: Pearson Education.

Popham, W. J. (2012b). Assessment bias: How to banish it [Pamphlet 4]. In *Mastering assessment: A self-service system for educators* (2nd ed.). Boston: Pearson Education.

Popham, W. J. (2012c). Interpreting the results of large-scale assessments [Pamphlet 9]. In *Mastering assessment: A self-service system for educators* (2nd ed.). Boston: Pearson Education.

Popham, W. J. (2012d). Reliability: What is it and is it necessary? [Pamphlet 11]. In *Mastering assessment: A self-service system for educators* (2nd ed.). Boston: Pearson Education.

Protheroe, N. (2008). Teacher efficacy: What is it and does it matter? [Research report]. *Principal*, *87*(5), 42–45.

Reeves, D. (2002). *The leader's guide to standards: A blueprint for educational equity and excellence.* San Francisco: Jossey-Bass.

Reeves, D. (2005). *Accountability in action: A blueprint for learning organizations* (2nd ed.). Englewood, CO: Advanced Learning Press.

Reeves, D. (2006). *The learning leader: How to focus school improvement for better results.* Alexandria, VA: Association for Supervision and Curriculum Development.

Reeves, D. (Ed.). (2007). *Ahead of the curve: The power of assessment to transform teaching and learning.* Bloomington, IN: Solution Tree Press.

Resnick, L. B., & Berger, L. (2010). *An American examination system.* Austin, TX: Center for K–12 Assessment and Performance Management. Accessed at www.k12center.org/rsc/pdf /ResnickBergerSystemModel.pdf on May 30, 2014.

Ripley, A. (2013). *The smartest kids in the world: And how they got that way.* New York: Simon & Schuster.

Rodriguez, E. R., Bellanca, J., & Esparza, D. R. (2017). *What is it about me you can't teach? Culturally responsive instruction in deeper learning classrooms* (3rd ed.). Thousand Oaks, CA: Corwin Press.

Rodriguez, M. C. (2004). The role of classroom assessment in student performance on TIMSS. *Applied Measurement in Education, 17*(1), 1–24.

Rodriguez, M. C., & Haladyna, T. M. (2013). Writing selected-response items for classroom assessment. In J. H. McMillan (Ed.), *SAGE handbook of research on classroom assessment* (pp. 293–311). Thousand Oaks, CA: SAGE.

Ross, J. A., & Gray, P. (2006). Transformational leadership and teacher commitment to organizational values: The mediating effects of collective teacher efficacy. *School Effectiveness and School Improvement, 17*(2), 179–199.

Ruiz-Primo, M. A., & Li, M. (2011, April). *Looking into the teachers' feedback practices: How teachers interpret students' work.* Paper presented at the annual meeting of the American Educational Research Association, New Orleans, LA.

Ruiz-Primo, M. A., & Li, M. (2013). Examining formative feedback in the classroom context: New research perspectives. In J. H. McMillan (Ed.), *SAGE handbook of research on classroom assessment* (pp. 215–232). Thousand Oaks, CA: SAGE.

Schmoker, M. (2011). *Focus: Elevating the essentials to radically improve student learning.* Alexandria, VA: Association for Supervision and Curriculum Development.

Scobie-Jennings, E. (n.d.). *"Josh could do better": Bringing out the best in underachieving gifted and talented students.* Accessed at www.academia.edu/4714396/Josh_could_do_better_Bringing _out_the_best_in_Underachieving_Gifted_and_Talented_Students on February 12, 2015.

Sergiovanni, T. J. (1992). *Moral leadership: Getting to the heart of school improvement*. San Francisco: Jossey-Bass.

Shaughnessy, M. F. (2004). An interview with Anita Woolfolk: The educational psychology of teacher efficacy. *Educational Psychology Review, 16*(2), 153–176.

Social Sciences and Humanities Research Council of Canada. (2016, April 4). *Shelley Moore: Transforming inclusive education* [Video file]. Accessed at https://www.youtube.com/watch ?v=RYtUlU8MjlY on September 18, 2018.

Stiggins, R. (2008, April). *Assessment manifesto: A call for the development of balanced assessment systems*. Portland, OR: ETS Assessment Training Institute.

Stiggins, R., & Chappuis, J. (2005). Using student-involved classroom assessment to close achievement gaps. *Theory Into Practice, 44*(1), 11–18.

Stiggins, R., & Herrick, M. (2007). *A status report on teacher preparation in classroom assessment*. Unpublished manuscript.

Strong, R. W., Silver, H. F., & Perini, M. J. (2001). *Teaching what matters most: Standards and strategies for raising student achievement*. Alexandria, VA: Association for Supervision and Curriculum Development.

Supovitz, J. A., & Christman, J. B. (2003, November). *Developing communities of instructional practice: Lessons from Cincinnati and Philadelphia* (CPRE Policy Brief No. RB-39). Philadelphia: Consortium for Policy Research in Education.

Tacheny, S., & Plattner, L. (2005) Giving 'data' its own assessment. *Education Week, 24*(36), 37–38.

Talbert, J. E. (2010). Professional learning communities at the crossroads: How systems hinder or engender change. In A. Hargreaves, A. Lieberman, M. Fullan, & D. Hopkins (Eds.), *Second international handbook of educational change* (Vol. 23, pp. 555–571). London: Springer.

TEDx Talks. (2016, March 11). *Shelley Moore: Under the table—The importance of presuming competence* [Video file]. Accessed at https://youtube.com/watch?v=AGptAXTV7m0 on September 18, 2018.

Thompson, S. J., Johnstone, C. J., & Thurlow, M. L. (2002, June). *Universal design applied to large scale assessments* (NCEO Synthesis Report No. 44). Minneapolis, MN: National Center on Educational Outcomes. Accessed at http://education.umn.edu/NCEO/OnlinePubs/Synthesis44 .html on February 12, 2015.

Timperley, H. (2009). *Using assessment data for improving teaching practice*. Accessed at http://research .acer.edu.au/cgi/viewcontent.cgi?article=1036&context=research_conference on April 3, 2012.

Tomlinson, C. A. (2014). One to grow on: Let's not dilute mastery. *Educational Leadership, 71*(4), 88–89.

Tomlinson, C. A., & Moon, T. R. (2013). Differentiation and classroom assessment. In J. H. McMillan (Ed.), *SAGE handbook of research on classroom assessment* (pp. 415–430). Thousand Oaks, CA: SAGE.

Torrance, H., & Pryor, J. (2001). Developing formative assessment in the classroom: Using action research to explore and modify theory. *British Educational Research Journal, 27*(5), 615–631.

Umphrey, J. (2008). Producing learning: A conversation with Robert Marzano. *Principal Leadership, 8*(5), 16–20.

Vagle, N. D. (2015). *Design in five: Essential phases to create engaging assessment practice.* Bloomington, IN: Solution Tree Press.

Wagner, T. (2008). Rigor redefined. *Educational Leadership, 66*(2), 20–25.

Webb, N. L. (1997, April). *Criteria for alignment of expectations and assessments in mathematics and science education* (Research Monograph No. 6). Washington, DC: Council of Chief State School Officers.

Webb, N. L. (2002). *Depth-of-knowledge levels for four content areas.* Unpublished manuscript. Accessed at www.hed.state.nm.us/uploads/files/ABE/Policies/depth_of_knowledge_guide_for _all_subject_areas.pdf on August 30, 2014.

Webb, N. L., Alt, M., Ely, R., & Vesperman, B. (2005). *Web alignment tool (WAT) training manual.* Madison, WI: Wisconsin Center for Education Research.

Wellman, B., & Lipton, L. (2017). *Data-driven dialogue: A facilitator's guide to collaborative inquiry* (2nd ed.). Charlotte, NC: MiraVia.

Wiggins, G. (1989). A true test: Toward more authentic and equitable assessment. *Phi Delta Kappan, 70*(9), 703–713.

Wiggins, G., & McTighe, J. (2005). *Understanding by design* (2nd ed.). Alexandria, VA: Association for Supervision and Curriculum Development.

Wiggins, G., & McTighe, J. (2007). *Schooling by design: Mission, action, and achievement.* Alexandria, VA: Association for Supervision and Curriculum Development.

Wiliam, D. (1998, July). *The validity of teachers' assessments.* Paper presented to Working Group 6 of the 22nd annual conference of the International Group for the Psychology of Mathematics Education, Stellenbosch, South Africa.

Wiliam, D. (2001). Reliability, validity, and all that jazz. *Education 3–13: International Journal of Primary, Elementary and Early Years Education, 29*(3), 17–21.

Wiliam, D. (2009, May 7). *The reliability of educational assessments.* Presentation slides from the Ofqual Annual Lecture, Coventry, West Midlands, England. Accessed at www.dylanwiliam.org/Dylan _Wiliams_website/Presentations_files/Ofqual talk.ppt on August 25, 2015.

Wiliam, D. (2011). *Embedded formative assessment.* Bloomington, IN: Solution Tree Press.

Wiliam, D. (2013). Feedback and instructional correctives. In J. H. McMillan (Ed.), *SAGE handbook of research on classroom assessment* (pp. 197–214). Thousand Oaks, CA: SAGE.

Wiliam, D. (2018). *Embedded formative assessment* (2nd ed.). Bloomington, IN: Solution Tree Press.

Wiliam, D., & Thompson, M. (2007). Integrating assessment with learning: What will it take to make it work? In C. A. Dwyer (Ed.), *The future of assessment: Shaping teaching and learning* (pp. 53–84). Mahwah, NJ: Erlbaum.

Wright, R. J. (2008). *Educational assessment: Tests and measurements in the age of accountability.* Thousand Oaks, CA: SAGE.

Xu, Y. (2013). Classroom assessment in special education. In J. H. McMillan (Ed.), *SAGE handbook of research on classroom assessment* (pp. 431–447). Thousand Oaks, CA: SAGE.

Index